LOOKING FOR LEGENDS

Scott *(right)* is a multisport athlete, equestrian, coach, mentor, and explorer, all while being a mother of four, grandmother of eight and great-grandmother of fifteen. She has traveled to more than fifty countries, been to places high and low, and knows how to go along in order to get along.

Tarantino *(left)* is an entrepreneur and private investor. His extensive library allows them to travel even when they stay at home.

LOOKING FOR LEGENDS

LET US TAKE YOU SOMEWHERE YOU'VE
NEVER BEEN BEFORE, AND INTRODUCE
YOU TO OUR FRIENDS

SCOTT AND TARANTINO

Cartography and Drawings
ERIN GREB

Cover and Interior Design
JOHN LOTTE

WHOLE WIDE WORLD PUBLISHING

We thank our quotation, photo, and illustration contributors. We greatly enjoyed looking for you and have tried to credit you as you wished. Where we couldn't find you or have made a mistake in our credits, we ask for your forgiveness and good faith, and we stand willing to credit and compensate you, as we have with our other contributors.

Published by Whole Wide World Publishing

Copyright ©2024 by Looking for Legends, LLC

All rights reserved

No part of this book may be reproduced, distributed, stored in a retrieval system, or transmitted in any form by any means, electronic, mechanical, photocopy, recording, or otherwise without prior express written consent.

For inquiries, please contact info@lookingforlegends.com

Hardcover ISBN: 979-8-9894018-2-6
Paperback ISBN: 979-8-9894018-1-9
eBook ISBN: 979-8-9894018-0-2

First edition

This book is dedicated to you, Dear Reader,
whether you're an armchair traveler, an occasional tourist,
a seasoned globetrotter, a daring adventurer,
or an intrepid explorer. There is something here for each and
every one of you . . . but you have to *look* for it.

PLACES TO GO

PEOPLE TO SEE

TABLE OF CONTENTS

Contents by Topography *x*

Prologue *1*

In the Beginning: Princeton, New Jersey *3*

Wadi Rum, Jordan *17*

San Antonio de Areco, Argentina *30*

Luxor, Egypt *40*

Ilulissat, Greenland *57*

Badaling, China *69*

Zermatt, Switzerland *80*

Riobamba, Ecuador *90*

El Chaltén, Patagonia *101*

Abiquiu, New Mexico *111*

Takanawa, Japan *124*

Villnöss, South Tyrol *135*

Al-Ain, United Arab Emirates *147*

Lhasa, Tibet *159*

Bygdøy Peninsula, Norway *173*

Isla Negra, Chile *188*

St. Petersburg, Russia *205*

Stavros Beach, Crete *223*

Kaladhungi, India *231*

Marrakesh, Morocco *249*

Bangkok, Thailand *263*

Kathmandu, Nepal *278*

Manaus, Brazil *292*

At the End: Tsodilo Hills, Botswana *312*

Epilogue *324*

Acknowledgments *327*

Appendices

    I: Knud Rasmussen's Thule Expeditions *331*

    II: Edward Whymper's Climbs Along the Avenue of Volcanoes *332*

    III: The Forty-Seven Ronin *334*

    IV: First Ascents of the 8,000 Meter Mountains *335*

    V: First Ascents of the Seven Summits *338*

    VI: Jim Corbett Hunts the Man-Eaters of Kumaon *340*

    VII: Successful Ascents of Mount Everest *344*

Notes *347*

Bibliography *389*

Photo and Illustration Credits *413*

CONTENTS BY TOPOGRAPHY

MOUNTAINS

Zermatt, Switzerland *80*

Riobamba, Ecuador *90*

El Chaltén, Patagonia *101*

Villnöss, South Tyrol *135*

Lhasa, Tibet *159*

Kathmandu, Nepal *278*

LITERARY HAUNTS AND RAIN FORESTS

In the Beginning: Princeton, New Jersey *3*

San Antonio de Areco, Argentina *30*

Isla Negra, Chile *188*

St. Petersburg, Russia *205*

Stavros Beach, Crete *223*

Manaus, Brazil *292*

POLAR AND ASIAN

Ilulissat, Greenland *57*

Badaling, China *69*

Takanawa, Japan *124*

Bygdøy Peninsula, Norway *173*

Kaladhungi, India *231*

Bangkok, Thailand *263*

DESERTS

Wadi Rum, Jordan *17*

Luxor, Egypt *40*

Abiquiu, New Mexico *111*

Al-Ain, United Arab Emirates *147*

Marrakesh, Morocco *249*

At the End: Tsodilo Hills, Botswana *312*

Which would you rather have,
dreams or memories?

PROLOGUE

AN INTRODUCTION TO OUR INTRODUCTIONS

Travel is a dream. But before you know it, you're there and back. And then it's just a memory.

What's next?

For us, it was simple: plan another trip. Books to read. Maps to study. Places to go. People to see.

Travel is an escape. When we're gone, no one *here* knows where we are or what we're doing. When we're gone, no one *there* knows who we are or what we've done. And even when it isn't safe to go, we do, wandering through our library, where no one can find us.

Foremost, travel is a search. In the beginning, it was for places, the further away and the further out of the way, the better. The maps tell it all: North America, South America, Europe, Asia, and Africa. Mountains, deserts, literary haunts, and rain forests. From polar ice to steamy tropics.

We've been around.

Wherever we went, however, we found more than places. We found people, people who captured the spirit of their place. They should have been worldwide, household names, but, outside of their settings, they were pretty much unknown or forgotten. And, if most of them were dead, so what? They were still very much alive for us.

In time, we realized we weren't looking for places any more. We were looking for people.

We were *Looking for Legends*.

Here's who we found: A backpacker, a desert fighter and a husband-and-wife pair of rock climbers, a gaucho/tango dancer, a linguist, a dogsled musher, and a marathon runner and fellow traveler. Two mountain and volcano climbers, two self-styled "dirt bags," a gentleman rancher, the leader of forty-seven loyal men, the king of the mountains, a desert explorer and a sheikh, and an escaped prisoner of war. Three men in a boat, a dangerous poet, a defiant witness, a madman and a saint, and a tiger hunter/conservationist. A pasha and a painter, a silk merchant/spy, a record-keeper, a botanist, and, last but not least, a mystic.

We have reached the point in our lives where *"Who do you want to be?"* has been replaced by *"Who do you wish you had been?"* If anyone other than ourselves, it's they.

———

Don't be in a hurry reading this book. After all, it's only taken us twenty-five years to write. Savor it, as we did, in both the traveling and the writing.

Try one chapter at a time. Start with the first and end with the last, but in between, read them in any order you like.

Ponder the maps. Stare at the photos. Think about the quotes. And, if you want more, check out the appendices, notes, and bibliography. There's some pretty good stuff there.

So, without further ado, let us take you somewhere you've never been before, and introduce you to our friends.

IN THE BEGINNING: PRINCETON, NEW JERSEY

> May had come at last to Princeton.
>
> —RICHARD HALLIBURTON, *THE ROYAL ROAD TO ROMANCE*

Princeton University (EQ ROY/ALAMY)[1]

*A*s an opening line, it's not bad.[2] The month of May was Reading Period, a time after classes had ended but before exams began, when those who had studied could play and those who had played better study.

May also meant that June and graduation were just around the corner.

Is there ever a better time for dreams?

Richard Halliburton, Class of 1921, sure had them:

> I wanted freedom, freedom to indulge in
> whatever caprice struck my fancy, freedom
> to search in the farthermost corners of the earth
> for the beautiful, the joyous, and the romantic.[3]

He got just that. Upon graduation, he set out to travel, spending almost two years with a knapsack on his back.

What better inspiration? What better inspiration to read books, go places, meet people, and write stories — our story of their stories.

Halliburton didn't have any money — his parents did, but he wanted to make his own way. He crossed the oceans working on cargo ships or oil tankers. If he couldn't get work, he stowed away, sleeping in the hold. On land, he made a game of bumming rides and avoiding train conductors.

He was young, he was foolish, he was way too enthusiastic, but he could write . . . and soon his reporting earned him just enough money to keep going.

His stories reflected his character: charming and optimistic, with a dash of bad behavior. He met a shy, demure young lady who turned out to be a star of the Folies Bergère. On a Christmas Eve, he sneaked into the Alhambra, one of Islam's most iconic buildings. He squeezed through a locked gate and climbed the Rock of Gibraltar at night, only to get arrested the next day for taking photographs. He talked his way out of jail.

He climbed the Great Pyramid in Giza and spent the night on top, looking at the stars. He went skinny-dipping in the Nile and was swept downstream from his clothes.

He visited a missionary in the jungle. He went on a tiger hunt. He hid from the guards and stayed overnight at the Taj Mahal, even "swimming" in its one-foot-deep reflecting pool.

Halliburton at the Taj Mahal
(RICHARD HALIBURTON / PRINCETON UNIVERSITY)

He hitchhiked his way through the Vale of Kashmir, rode ponies up into the Himalayas, and tramped to Leh, the hidden capital of Ladakh. There, he found polyandry, a society where the women had many husbands and the men did all the work. There he found religion, where the streets were filled with pilgrims whirling prayer wheels and chanting *"om mani padme hum, om mani padme hum."*

He returned to India through the Khyber Pass riding in a military mail truck and avoided arrest on the train to Calcutta by hiding in the coal car. He stumbled into the local American Express office and found he had new blood: a check for one of his articles.

He booked a boat to Burma, marched through a Malaysian monsoon, and waded up leech-infested waters to reach the Trans-Peninsula Railway.

He took the train, as he said, through "Bangatore, Bangatang, Bang Peunon, and Bang Bang," all the way to Bangkok. He wandered alone through the endless corridors of the Temple of Angkor Wat, said to be the largest religious monument in the world.

He beachcombed in Bali. He made the first solo winter ascent of Japan's Mount Fuji. And finally, *finally*, he came home.

He had gone all around the world.

When Halliburton put these stories together, they became a best-seller, *The Royal Road to Romance* (1923), with its memorable, above-quoted first line.

Speaking of romance, we met at Princeton. Scott was a mother of four and a three-sport coach at a local private girls school. The rules for basketball were changing and she needed an assistant. Tarantino was one of only eighty-two high school basketball captains in the Class of 1969. He volunteered. And when he graduated, he told her, "I hope I can find someone just like you." Thirteen years later, he did.

———

Halliburton wanted an encore.

Why not follow the greatest traveler of all and retrace the Odyssey? That's it! He would "sail beyond the sunset . . . until . . . (he) died." [4]

He had no idea just how prophetic those words would be.

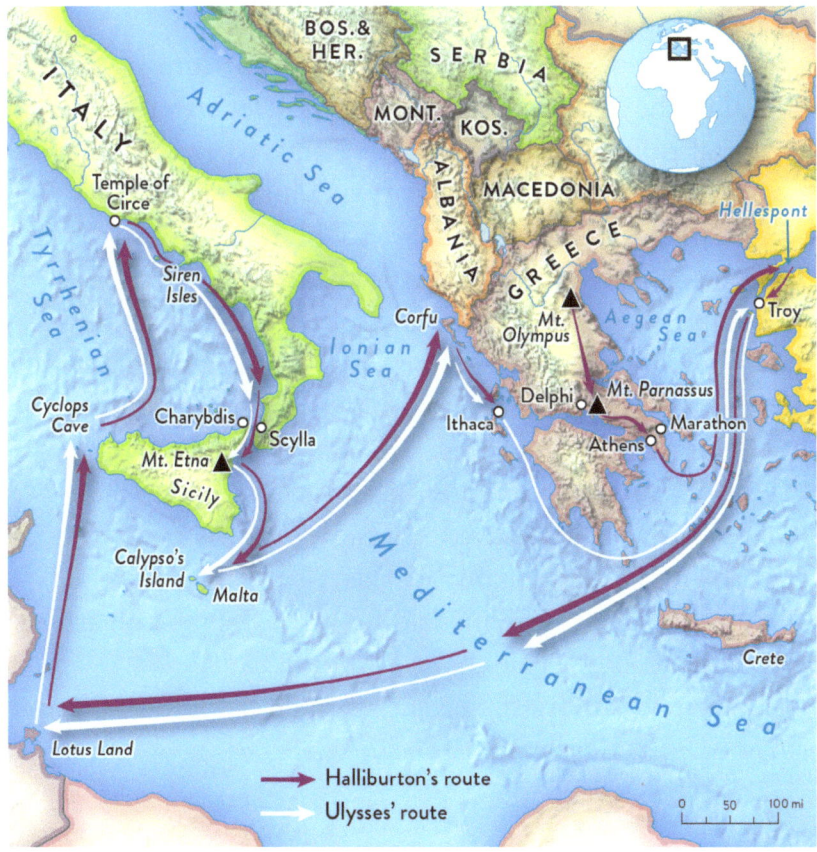

HALLIBURTON FOLLOWING ULYSSES

Halliburton began by climbing Mount Olympus, the Throne of the Gods. From there, he brought a laurel wreath to the Oracle at Delphi and, to ensure his success, stood on Mount Parnassus to behold the sun bursting from the sea.

Next, a stop in Athens, where he climbed the cracks and crevices of the Acropolis to see the moon rise over the Parthenon and spent a night in quiet conversation with its marble mavens.

Then, as final preparation, he ran the marathon and swam the Hellespont.

Ulysses left Ithaca and spent ten years besieging Troy (until his wooden horse finally won the day) and then another ten returning home.

As shown on the map, Halliburton put him to shame, repeating the trip in only six months. Departing from the immortal ruins, he went to Lotus Land, where Ulysses had fought off the forgetfulness of its fruits and flowers. He traced him past the Cyclops Cave to the Temple of Circe, and then sailed down the coast of Italy through the Siren Isles.

Halliburton dove into the Strait of Messina between the jagged, deadly Rocks of Scylla and the sucking, roaring Whirlpool of Charybdis. He climbed Mount Etna to see the Sun God rise in the morning.

He rode the current to an island near Malta, where the goddess Calypso had saved Ulysses from a storm, only to imprison him. And finally, just as Ulysses had escaped to Corfu and then home to his faithful wife, Halliburton arrived in Ithaca.

The trip was more than a success, and he immortalized it as *The Glorious Adventure* (1927).

Princeton, also, was an adventure. And even though Tarantino studied too much, walked on the wild side way too little, tried to believe what his teachers taught him, and ended up throwing away all his textbooks, he did learn to think for himself.

As for Halliburton, he'd seen the Old World. What was left? The New One, of course, and with it came the title of his next book: *New Worlds to Conquer* (1929).[5]

He journeyed a thousand miles by land into the heart of the Yucatan, climbed the great Mayan temple in Chichén Itzá (at midnight of course), and followed the quarter-mile Sacred Way to the Well of Death.

Halliburton Jumps into the Well of Death (RICHARD HALLIBURTON, PRINCETON UNIVERSITY)

There, at dawn, the eternal moment of sacrifice, he plunged seventy feet into the deep, dark, black pit. He survived. But after climbing up the moss-covered walls, he had to jump back down to pick up the boots he had left behind.

He swam the Panama Canal, demanding to pay, like all ships, according to his "tonnage." The toll: thirty-six cents. It took him nine days and three million strokes. Somehow, he survived the tropical sun, alligators, water snakes, and barracudas, to say nothing of the vile, polluted water, to complete the fifty-mile passage from the Atlantic to the Pacific.

Next stop: the Peruvian Andes, where he followed a sixty-mile-long gorge, and hacked his way through the jungle, overcoming roots and choking vines, to "discover" Machu Picchu. He found a city perched on a pinnacle of rock, and was greeted by a double rainbow.

Before returning home, Halliburton visited Devil's Island, the notorious prison colony in French Guiana, the worst place in the world reserved for the worst criminals in the world, where no one escaped alive and countless vultures waddled around, unmolested, just waiting for the next attempt. Of course, he smuggled himself in as a prisoner for a night—who wouldn't?

How do you top this?

Simple. Get in a plane and fly around the world. And name the plane after the most magical of all transports: *The Flying Carpet* (1932).[6] It wasn't a bad book title either.

In Africa, he flew over the Atlas Mountains and crossed the Sahara. He overcame blazing sun, leagues and leagues of nothingness, and the occasional sandstorm.

His destination: Timbuktu. Upon arrival, the city disappeared, blotted out by a dark cloud of storks, wheeling and flapping, bewildered, agitated, scared to death by the biggest bird of them all: his. And for every stork, there were one hundred bats.

He flew back up over the continent to Sidi bel Abbès in Algeria, the home of the French Foreign Legion. He noted the international character of the Legionnaires—only 10 percent of them were "French." All of them, however, were looking for that one last chance . . . or maybe they weren't.

The Flying Carpet (Pilot Moye Stevens, Jr on left; Halliburton on right)
(RHODES COLLEGE DIGITAL ARCHIVES)

What would you expect Halliburton to do? He joined them, for a five-day, 150-mile march through the desert. The Legion had a routine: At 3 a.m., start. March fifty minutes, rest ten, march fifty minutes, rest ten. At 8 a.m., one-half hour for lunch. At noon, stop, set up tents, and sleep. At twilight, let the wine flow: *pinard, pinard, pinard.*

> Fortunately, there is always enough pinard.
> Food may give out; pinard, never.[7]

He set off again. In Venice, he swam the Grand Canal. In Istanbul, he slept inside the Aya Sofia Mosque and climbed its minaret with the *muezzin* for the morning call to prayer. Then, on to Baghdad, a city that very much appreciated a flying carpet. There, he took the prince on a plane ride straight out of the *Arabian Nights.*

This is how we were introduced to travel. If Halliburton could dream it, he could do it. And even if he only did half of what he says he did, it still was pretty incredible.

Halliburton flew to India, following the tracks of Alexander the Great. He tried to fly around Mount Everest, noting that someday, someone would climb it. Why? As George Mallory said: "Because it's there."[8]

He flew to Borneo where he took the Dayak tribal chief for a plane ride and received twelve shrunken heads as thanks. Waving goodbye, he set off for Manila, only to throw the heads overboard, one by one, because they smelled so bad. In Manila, he loaded the plane on the grand ship *SS President McKinley* and sailed home.

We could see the exhilaration, but we could also feel the exhaustion. It was the 1930s, the Great Depression. There was no television, no Internet, only Richard Halliburton, and he was the most popular travel writer in the world.

It was a blessing. It was also a curse.

Soon, Halliburton was again on the move. He put on his *Seven League Boots* (1935) and got a new commission:

> ... to go anywhere in the world I wished and write about whatever pleased me. My only orders were to move fast, visit strange places ... try to meet whomever I thought interesting and important — and to start at once.[9]

He visited Sans Souci, the ruined nineteenth-century palace built by an illiterate ex-dishwasher who became the self-crowned King of Haiti.

He interviewed the bed-stricken assassin of Czar Nicholas II and his Russian Royal Family. He got the confession and all the details.

He dropped in on the monks of Mount Athos (where women were not allowed) and became a monk himself. But only for a week.

He walked among the lepers in the island colony of Spinalonga.

He paid his tribute to kings, from the six-foot, nine-inch Ibn Saud of Saudi Arabia to the five-foot, two-inch Haile Selassie of Ethiopia.

Seven League Boots (RHODES COLLEGE DIGITAL ARCHIVES)

He became the first person in more than two thousand years (after Hannibal) to ride an elephant over the Alps, summiting at St. Bernard's Pass, 8,124 feet above sea level.

———

Richard Halliburton, as you can see, has trapped us in his own private Reading Period and won't let us go. Our only escape: we graduated.

———

Halliburton didn't know it, but he had just one trip left. He would sail beyond the sunset. And die.

It was an opportunity too good to refuse. San Francisco was to host the 1939 World's Fair. It needed an exciting kickoff event. The idea: Richard Halliburton, world-famous celebrity traveler, would go to China, buy or build a large, colorful Chinese junk, sail it back across the Pacific to San Francisco, and arrive just in time to open the fair. It would celebrate the connection between Asia and San Francisco. It would celebrate the opening of the city's Golden Gate Bridge. It would celebrate the World's Fair. Always game for a new adventure, Halliburton said yes.

Build a boat he did, the *Sea Dragon*.[10]

The Sea Dragon (PUBLIC DOMAIN)

It was good enough for a trial run, it was good enough for a departure, it was good enough to avoid the pirates, but it was not good enough to cross the sea. Hit by a typhoon, going down, Halliburton kept his naughty-boy sense of humor to the end. His boat's last radio message:

> Southerly gales, rain squalls, lee rail under water,
> wet bunks, hardtack, bully beef,
> having wonderful time,
> wish you were here instead of me.[11]

We died with him that day, but we were still alive. And we were determined that we, too, would travel the world.

And why not? If we could dream it, we could do it.

WADI RUM, JORDAN

> We wheeled into the Avenue of Rum,
>   Still gorgeous in sunset color . . .
>   It was . . . magically haunted . . .
>   Vast and echoing and godlike.
>
> —T. E. LAWRENCE, *SEVEN PILLARS OF WISDOM*

THE MIDDLE EAST

Tucked into the southwest corner of Jordan, Wadi Rum is right in the middle of the Middle East.

WADI RUM, JORDAN | 18

The Seven Pillars of Wisdom (AHMAD ATWAH/ALAMY)

Portrait of T. E. Lawrence by James McBey, 1918
(NPL – DEA PICTURE LIBRARY, G. NIMATALLAH, BRIDGEMEN IMAGES)

A desert valley sitting between two sandstone and granite mountain ranges, it is aptly named. *Wadi* means valley and *Rum* means mountains, so it is, literally, a valley of mountains.[1] It encompasses not only the Valley of Rum but also the rest of the neighborhood, extending north, east, west, and south over a 150 square-mile area.

There were two reasons we went there. The first was Lawrence of Arabia: Lawrence the man, Lawrence the book, Lawrence the movie. Without a doubt, we were looking for Lawrence.

The locals were pleased to oblige. From the visitor's center, we stared directly at a rock formation called "the Seven Pillars of Wisdom."

No, Lawrence's book was not named after the formation, the formation was named after the book.[2]

Our tour included visits to "Lawrence's Spring," located a short distance from Rum village, and "Lawrence's House," pretty much just ruins. (Be patient, there will be another map.) And if we wanted to buy something in the village of Rum, we had two choices: the "Lawrence of Arabia Super Market" or the "Super Market Seven Pillars of Wisdom." Were the merchants shameless or were they laughing at us? Probably a little of both. We bought a pair of woolen place mats decorated with camels, and we still have them on our dining room table.

What was it about T. E. Lawrence that so captured our hearts and drew us there? Yes, he was a British Army officer who helped lead the Arab Revolt during World War I. Yes, his guerrilla attacks were creative and his victories dramatic. Yes, the public relations were terrific, making him a hero.

But these were not enough. Perhaps it was his *introspection:*

> All men dream, but not equally. Those who dream by night in the dusty recesses of their minds wake in the day to find that it was vanity. But the dreamers of the day are dangerous men, for they may act their dream with open eyes, to make it possible. This I did.[3]

More likely, though, it was his *integrity*. He refused a knighthood, sought obscurity, and punished himself for not living up to his ideals (for being part of the great betrayal of the Arabs). As he confessed:

> The Cabinet raised the Arabs to fight for us by definite promises of self-government afterwards. Arabs believe in persons, not institutions. They saw in me a free agent of the British Government, and demanded from me an endorsement of its written promises.
>
> So, I had to join the conspiracy, and, for what my word was worth, assured the men of their reward . . .
>
> It was evident from the beginning that if we won the war these promises would be dead paper, and had I been an honest adviser of the Arabs I would have advised them to go home and not risk their lives fighting for such stuff.[4]

Lawrence's book, *Seven Pillars of Wisdom,* had its own adventures. Working from his wartime notes, Lawrence completed a 250,000-word first draft in December 1919. Unfortunately, he lost it while changing trains at the Reading Railroad Station, just outside London. In response, he wrote a 400,000-word second draft entirely from memory. And he completed it in just three months.

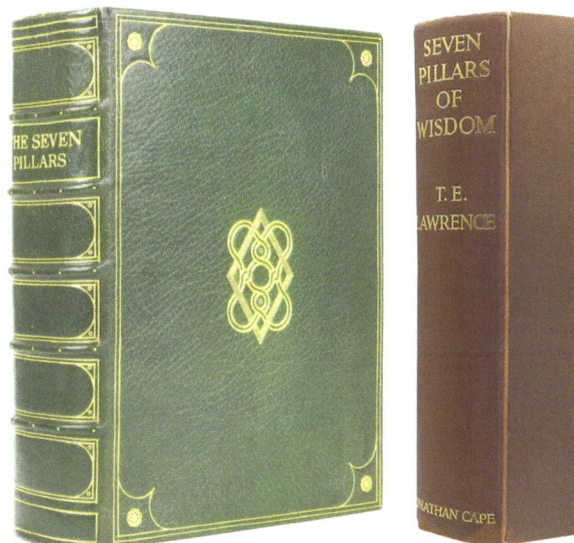
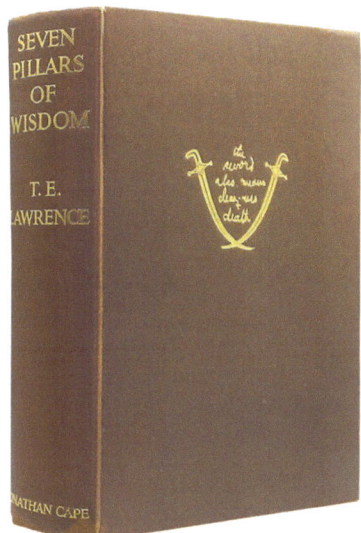

left: Subscribers Edition (JONKERS RARE BOOKS)
right: First Trade Edition (MERRILL WHITBURN, PRIDE AND PREJUDICE BOOKS)

He then spent two years polishing and condensing it. In early 1922, he printed the 335,000-word "Oxford Edition." Using the Oxford Times presses, he published eight copies, to be reviewed by fellow members of his Expeditionary Force and selected literary critics. In 2001, when one of these copies last sold at auction, it went for almost $1,000,000.[5]

At the urgings of his friends, Lawrence prepared a lavish, limited edition for private subscribers. He trimmed the book to 250,000 words, found illustrators and arranged for fine, handcrafted leather bindings. In 1926, this "Subscribers Edition" had a print run of about 200 copies. To encourage his subscribers, Lawrence promised, among other things, that there would be no library or review copies and no republication of the book's *complete* text during his lifetime. Nearly a century later, copies of this edition command up to $100,000.[6]

However, the book's production cost Lawrence three times what he received from its sale. His solution? He prepared an abridgement, *Revolt in the Desert* (1927). While somewhat of an embarrassment with his subscribers, it was such a financial success that it not only paid off his bank debt, it also provoked so much interest in the Subscribers Edition that its price at auction rose to almost twenty times the subscription cost. Who could then complain? [7]

Lawrence died in a motorcycle accident in May 1935. Lo and behold, just ten weeks later, a complete "First Trade Edition" was published in London for general circulation. Today, copies of this in good condition sell for as much as $10,000.

Both the Subscribers Edition and the First Trade Edition can be found at rare book dealers and on the Internet.

Seven Pillars of Wisdom was subsequently published in the United States (1936). It, too, can be found in the marketplace. A "First American Trade Edition," as it is called, can be had, if you're lucky, for only $1,000.

Later reprints, marked up, in bad condition, without dust jackets (call them "Reading Copies") go for as little as $10.

One book, five prices. Take your pick.

And, by the way, there's nothing wrong with a reading copy—isn't that what books are for?

Finally, there was the movie, *Lawrence of Arabia* (1963). For most of us, this was our introduction to the man. The movie was glorious and iconic. Peter O'Toole exploded on the screen as Lawrence. Alec Guinness was a wise and deftly ironic Prince Faisal. And who can forget Anthony Quinn, as the great Howeitat leader Auda Abu Tayi, exclaiming, "Come with me to Wadi Rum!!!" [8]

Wadi Rum (YOUSEF, DISCOVERY TERHAAL AND KE/ADVENTURE TRAVEL) [9]

Lawrence described how you might feel when you arrived:

> Our little caravan grew self-conscious, and fell dead quiet, afraid and ashamed to flaunt its smallness in the presence of the stupendous hills.[10]

And so, the second reason we went was Wadi Rum, itself.

The hills that intimidated Lawrence have become a rock climber's heaven, offering a surprising wealth of treks and climbs. Up until the 1980s, however, this was all just desert. The only residents were native Bedouin who climbed when hunting or collecting plants and herbs. To help each other, they had marked the hills with "Bedouin Steps" (rickety piles of stones, used to pass overhangs), "Bedouin Ladders" (branches jammed into cracks), and "Bedouin Cairns" (road signs directing a climber where or where not to go).[11] Still, no one ever thought of climbing simply as recreation.

WADI RUM, JORDAN | 24

This all changed because of the husband-and-wife rock-climbing team of Tony Howard and Di Taylor. We were only looking for Lawrence, but, as it turned out, we found a whole lot more. We found Tony and Di.

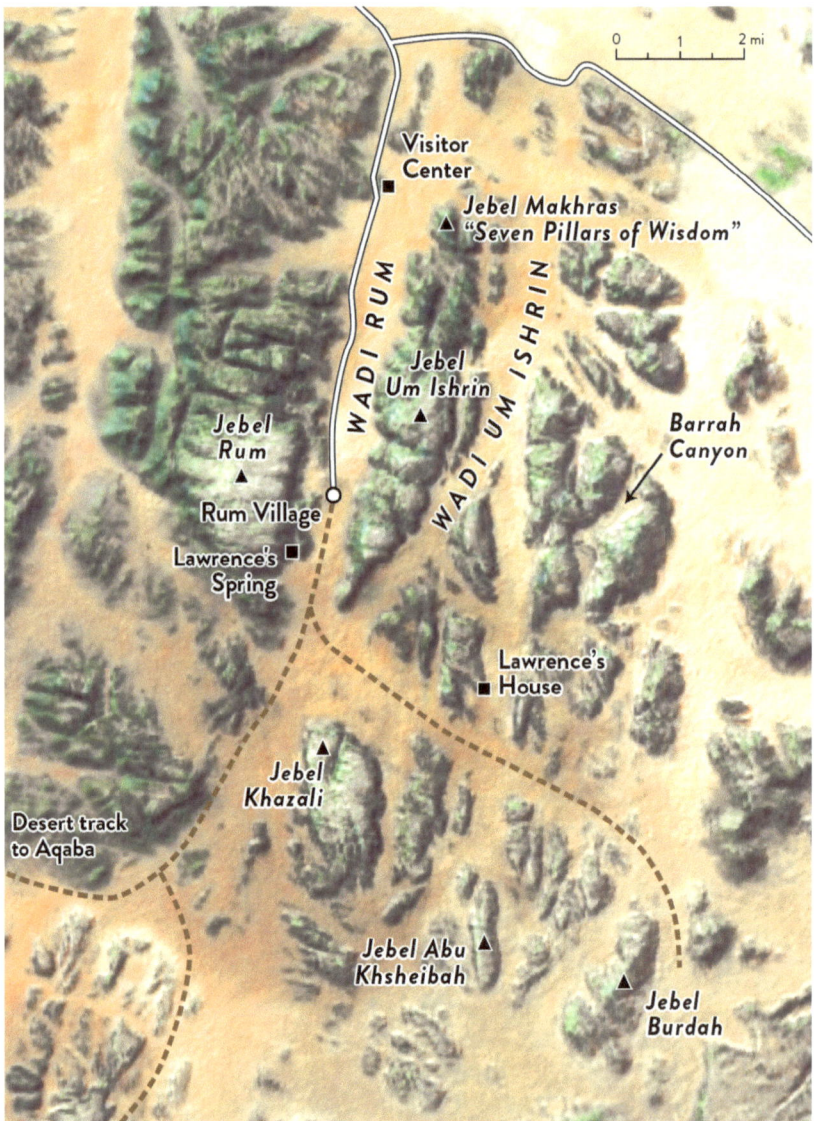

WADI RUM

In 1984, they *(shown below with HM Queen Noor of Jordan)* received permission from Jordan's Tourism Ministry to explore Wadi Rum as a possible location for adventure tourism: rock climbing and mountaineering.

Tony Howard and Di Taylor with, at right, HM Queen Noor of Jordan
(COURTESY OF TONY HOWARD)

Tony and Di and their compatriots quickly decided that the desert, its wadis, *siqs* (narrow canyons) and *jebels* (mountains) offered a wilderness experience not to be found anywhere else in the world. And just as quickly, they determined that the local Bedouin, with their warm hospitality and roguish humor, made fantastic hosts and guides.

The climbers worked to do what climbers do: develop routes and name them. Word got out. Climbers from France, Switzerland, Austria, Italy, Spain, and Germany all made contributions. Every day a new climb, every day a new name.

WADI RUM, JORDAN | 26

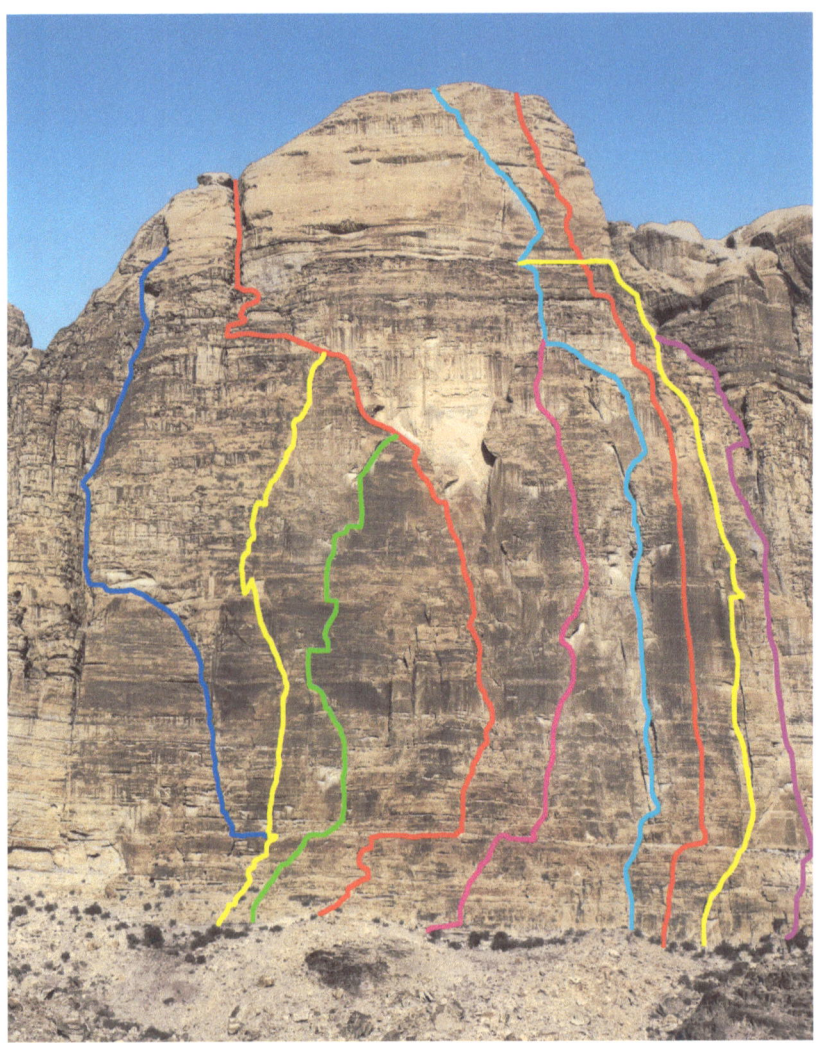

East Face of Jebel Rum (WALTER NESER, WWW.AFRICANVULTURES.ORG)

Were they obsessive? Were they territorial? Were they crazy? Yes, yes, and yes. Just look at this one section of the east face of Jebel Rum.

Nine different routes to the top, with nine different names: from left to right, IBM (Inshallah, Bokra, Mumkin — God Willing, Tomorrow, Possibly), Towering Inferno, Revienta o

Burila, The Inshallah Factor, Raid mit Dem Camel, The Red Sea, Sultan Al Mujahidin, Atallah, and Aquarius. Go ahead, try one.

Over a thirty-year period, Tony and Di have documented almost 400 treks and climbs in Wadi Rum. These include over one hundred around and on Jebel Rum and over one hundred around and on Jebel Um Ishrin, the two mountain ranges that flank Wadi Rum *(see the map)*.

They have also documented over eighty treks and climbs in and around Barrah Canyon and over sixty climbs on Khazali, Burdah, and the Domes of Abu Khsheibah. Their guide books, including *Treks and Climbs in Wadi Rum, Jordan* (1987), list them all by name, first climbers, grade of difficulty, and date of first ascent.

Do they have favorites? Of course. They would start with a traverse of Jordan's most famous mountain, Jebel Rum, using "Sheikh Hamdan's West-to-East Route" on the ascent. This was the first recorded climb anywhere in the area: In 1952, two English women were led to the top by Hamdan Amad, "who climbed with bare feet as surely as a mountain goat."[12]

They would descend using "Hammad's Route" on the east face (Hammad was the son of Sheikh Hamdan and became Tony and Di's close friend).

Together, the up-and-down is a classic combination of Bedouin hunting routes and beautiful scenery, with just a little danger thrown in for fun.

Then, they would take the "Thamudic Route," along which one finds two-thousand-year-old inscriptions. It's one of the oldest known rock climbs in the world.

Next, they would vote for the "Haj." Located in a very remote area just off the desert track to Aqaba, it is a stunning black pyramidal wall with a great series of cracks and chimneys on the way to the top. It finishes with the hardest moves over an increasingly difficult slab, leaving the outcome always in doubt.

Finally, Tony and Di would choose (you guessed it) "The Pillar of Wisdom," which they and good friend Wilf Colonna first climbed and named. It starts just above Lawrence's Spring in Wadi Shellali and ends with precarious holds over one thousand feet above the desert.[13]

We wonder how something like this got started. Tony and Di (still truckin' after all these years) attribute their inspiration to the movie.[14]

Indeed, like a great pickup line in a bar, how can anyone resist: "Come with me . . . to Wadi Rum!!!"

Di Taylor and Tony Howard (COURTESY OF TONY HOWARD)

STILL TRUCKIN', INDEED

Supported by Her Majesty Queen Noor, Tony and Di began exploring beyond Wadi Rum. By the year 2000, they realized that all their Jordanian walks, treks, and climbs were pieces of a jigsaw puzzle that could become a country-length trail. Together with Jordanian friends, and after years of hard work, the four hundred-mile Jordan Trail was completed in 2016. Since its inauguration the following year, the 52 villages along its route have all benefited.

But that wasn't enough. Tony and Di have also assisted in developing the Wadi Rum Trail, a seventy-mile, ten-day circuit that combines hiking, rock climbing, and abseiling. It is led and managed by Bedouin Tribesmen from the local community who know the best of the region's landscapes and heritage *(See www.wadirumtrail.org)*.

It is a sister project of Egypt's Sinai Trail and Red Sea Mountain Trail created by their friend Ben Hoffler.

All these trails connect old trade, travel, shepherd, hunting, and Hajj routes, forming an intercontinental system *(See www.bedouintrail.org)*.

That's right, the newest trails enable us to travel the oldest way: on foot.

SAN ANTONIO DE ARECO, ARGENTINA

"I am a nobody. I am a gaucho, and I want to be free."

—RICARDO GÜIRALDES, *DON SEGUNDO SOMBRA*

La Portena Writing Room (HEMIS/ALAMY)

We walked up the stairs and entered an almost empty writing room. There they were. Bound in red leather. Shelved in a five-foot-tall custom-made oak bookcase, the room's only piece of furniture.

We had stopped at La Portena, an *estancia* located just outside San Antonio de Areco, a small country town two hours northwest of Buenos Aires.[1] We were on our way to the *Dia de la Tradición*, the National Gaucho Festival, held every November in San Antonio since 1937. But we were looking for something else.

ROUTE TO SAN ANTONIO DE ARECO

And there they were — twenty-nine volumes, some water-damaged and ruined, some unopened and pristine. They were all that was left of the personal effects of novelist and poet Ricardo Güiraldes. They were the *eleventh edition* of *The Encyclopedia Britannica*.

The eleventh edition? Why the eleventh edition?

As its advertising confidently said, it was the sum of all knowledge: all that was new with new views of all that was old, the costliest literary venture in history. And "it explained everything that was explainable." [2]

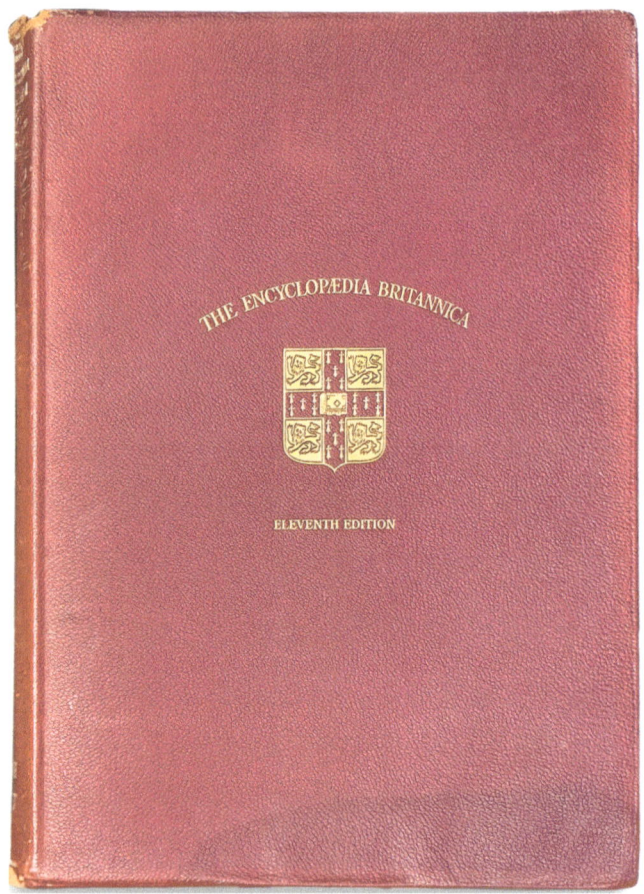

The Encyclopedia Britannica: Eleventh Edition (AUTHOR PHOTO)

The eleventh was the first edition of an encyclopedia to release all its volumes together as a complete set. The eleventh was the first edition of an encyclopedia with a separate index volume. The eleventh was the first edition of an encyclopedia to include biographies of living people. And the eleventh was the first edition of an encyclopedia to sell one million sets.

A British-American joint project, the eleventh edition was dedicated to His Majesty King George V and U.S. President William Howard Taft. It was published in 1910/1911 by

Cambridge University (over the objections of some of its snobbish dons but in exchange for a royalty of 5 percent of sales) and, as you can see, proudly featured the university's seal on its red leather cover.³ It promised self-improvement, limitless progress, and a glowing future, all available to the common man. If only he would buy it.

The eleventh edition featured contributions from all the great minds of the day, in all the fields of arts and science: geography, pure and applied science, history and social studies, literature, and fine arts. It was scholarly yet readable, even with forty thousand articles and forty-four million words. It presented more women contributors than ever before. It was the last great encyclopedia. More than one hundred years later, it is still acknowledged as the best edition of *The Encyclopedia Britannica* ever written.

We were surprised, that, somehow, the eleventh edition had made its way to a writing room at the edge of the Argentine pampas. We should have known better. This wasn't an ordinary writing room. This was the writing room of the man who introduced his country's heart and soul to the rest of the world.

Gaucho and tango. Tango and gaucho. Close your eyes and, in just two words, you can see Argentina.

What did the eleventh edition say about them? Nothing. Not an entry, not a mention in the "Argentina" section, not even a line in the Index. Its silence was eloquent testimony that the eleventh *almost* explained everything that was explainable.

What makes for a life? What makes us happy at the end, thinking that we have mattered, that we have made a difference, that we will be remembered for something? Something more than family, something more than loved ones. Something for everyone. We would take gaucho, we would take tango. Ricardo Güiraldes left us both.

In the beginning, of course, was the land. No owners, no fences, no fancy estancias. Just the land, and the land went on forever. Here, a man riding horseback was the master of his fate. He was a nomad, a wanderer, so what? If he were hungry, he found a cow and killed it. If his horse faltered, he captured and trained another. Private property had not yet been invented, so how could he be a thief? He was a gaucho.

But civilization — and barbed wire — caught up with him. By the 1870s, the Argentine Pampa had been subdivided, and the gaucho had become a ranch hand, a peon, drifting from place to place, looking for whatever work he could find.

However, just as the gaucho was dying, he was being reborn, as a symbol and as a myth. He may have been poor, but he had few needs, and he was free. Free.[4]

It was Ricardo Güiraldes who breathed new life into the gaucho and turned him into *Don Segundo Sombra* (1926), the classic, grade-school-required-reading, coming-of-age novel in which a boy learns of life.[5]

The boy was an orphan, or at least he thought he was. Placed with two elderly women who were supposedly his "aunts," he was lonely and unhappy. As a result, he did what every child in his position longs to do: he ran away from home. *Don Segundo Sombra* was the boy's story and Don Segundo was the boy's hero.

Don Segundo taught the boy to be a man — even better, to be a gaucho. He didn't just teach him to ride a horse. He taught him to lasso, to rope and hobble, to break a horse, to ride in a rodeo, and to make reins, halters, leads, and saddle trimmings. He taught him to slaughter a cow, shear a sheep, and cure hoof disease and worms. He taught him to sleep out in the rain with only a poncho for protection, to endure the summer heat, and to survive the winter cold. He taught him how and when to use a knife. He taught him not to complain.

And when the boy learned that he was *not* an impoverished orphan after all, but a son who had just inherited his father's ranch and riches, it was an *unhappy* ending, for it meant that *he* could no longer *be* . . . a gaucho.

Don Segundo Sombra, 1926 Edition Dust Wrapper (PUBLIC DOMAIN)

SAN ANTONIO DE ARECO, ARGENTINA | 36

Don Segundo with Ricardo Güiraldes (PUBLIC DOMAIN)

Don Segundo Sombra was an elegy to an imaginary hero, but it was also a tribute to a real man, Segundo Ramírez, who had helped raise Güiraldes as a child.

The book was such an overwhelming success that Ramírez was no longer Ramírez, he became Sombra, even to his relatives. When he died, he was laid to rest in the San Antonio cemetery, right next to his creator. And San Antonio de Areco? It became the Gaucho Capital of Argentina.

Ricardo Güiraldes, sitting in this writing room, had produced a masterpiece. But he could do more than write. He could dance.

Tango. Is it a vertical expression of a horizontal desire?[6] A sad thought that is danced?[7] Or a dance of love and death?

Born on the south side of Buenos Aires in the late 1880s, the tango was what men did with each other as they waited in line at the brothels. It was considered vulgar: no respectable woman would ever dance the tango, and all the disrespectable women were busy.[8]

It was a great time to be alive in Argentina. Refrigeration had just been invented, making it possible to ship meat costing less than a penny to Europe where it sold for far more than a pound. Immigrants were flowing in, most of them men from Italy and Spain. Most of them remained in Buenos Aires to work in the export businesses. And most of them were single and lonely.[9]

They were joined in line by the well-heeled sons of the *estancieros* and other families with aristocratic surnames. These dedicated frequenters of the brothels took the new dance to heart. Buenos Aires's high society, however, refused to accept this "reptile" from the slums.[10]

Meanwhile, few people in Paris had ever heard of the tango. It wouldn't take long. By 1900, the sons of the estancieros began showing up, either to represent their family businesses or to begin their Grand Tours. They loved everything about Paris, particularly the nightlife. They spent wildly. Thanks to the meat business, they were among the richest people in the world. And the city embraced them, soon devising its ultimate compliment: *"riche comme un Argentin"* (rich like an Argentine).[11]

And the most influential force in fashionable Paris was a writer and poet named . . . Ricardo Güiraldes.

It Takes Two. (BUENOS TOURS / PALACIO TANGO)

Ricardo Güiraldes (PUBLIC DOMAIN)

Rich, glamorous, elegant, cosmopolitan, he was the handsome seducer, the charming romantic, the archetypal ladies' man. His poem "Tango" set the mood:

> Red spot that coagulates into black.
> Fatal tango, arrogant and coarse.
> Notes lazily dragged, on a twangy keyboard.
> Tango, honest and sad.
> Threatening tango.
> A dance of love and death.[12]

In 1912, at a heralded salon, Güiraldes was asked to do something that best represented his country. In response, he took the hand of another guest and, to her surprise and the room's amazement, led her through an entire tango. Güiraldes had introduced the dance to Paris.[13]

A craze was born: "Tangomania." There were tea dance tangos, champagne tangos, charity tangos, dinner tangos, and, of course, nightclub tangos. Paris could not get enough. Neither could the world.[14]

In time, the "reptile" circled back to Buenos Aires, where the very same people who had spurned it as indecent behavior welcomed it as a new, exotic import.

―――――

Gaucho and tango. Tango and gaucho. What makes for a life? We would take gaucho; we would take tango. Ricardo Güiraldes left us both.

LUXOR, EGYPT

Je tiens l'affaire,
je tiens l'affaire.

—JEAN-FRANÇOIS CHAMPOLLION

The Rosetta Stone (HEMIS/ALAMY)

*I*t measures three feet, eight inches tall by two feet, six inches wide, and eleven inches thick. It weighs 1,679 pounds. Long thought to be a block of black basalt, it is, instead, a fine-to-medium-grained quartz-bearing rock containing feldspar, mica, and amphibole.

It is a fragment inscribed in 196 BCE with a decree — the Decree of Memphis — praising the young King Ptolemy V as a god. What remains are fourteen lines of Egyptian Hieroglyph, thirty-two lines of a script now known as Demotic, and fifty-three lines of Greek. It is the most popular single object in the British Museum. It is the most famous rock in the world.[1]

It is the Rosetta Stone.

It was named after Rosetta, a small port on the Mediterranean Sea, where it had been used in the construction of a wall. Excavated and saved in July 1799, it remained a building block, but in the process of deciphering hieroglyphs and opening up three thousand years of Egyptian history.

However, in 1799, the man born to translate hieroglyphs, Jean-François Champollion, was only nine years old. We had never heard of him before we went to Luxor, so we certainly weren't looking for him. Nevertheless, we found him, and we found him everywhere we looked.

Napoleon is remembered for many things, many defeats really. There was the war with Russia in 1812, where he was defeated by winter. There was Waterloo in 1815, where he was defeated by Wellington. Without a doubt, though, his most successful defeat was in Egypt.

ANCIENT EGYPT

Landing in Alexandria on the July 3, 1798, he swept across the country in a mere eighteen days and overwhelmed the ruling Mamluks at the celebrated Battle of the Pyramids.

He had a great sense of history and a flair for the dramatic:

> My soldiers, remember that forty centuries are looking down at you from the height of these Pyramids and will applaud your victory.[2]

The following day he entered Cairo as a conqueror.

His triumph did not last long. Just ten days later, on August 3, 1798, the British fleet surprised the French at

Alexandria and destroyed fifteen of their seventeen ships at the Battle of the Nile. Napoleon was marooned. His supplies were cut off. While the French would hold out until 1800 negotiating surrender terms, Napoleon had, in essence, won and lost Egypt in a month.[3]

But out of defeat came discovery: Napoleon's engineers found the Rosetta Stone. French scholars immediately went to work. By translating the Greek, they understood that the stone's text was recorded in three different languages:

> ... the decree should be written on a stela of hard stone in sacred writing (i.e. hieroglyphs), document writing (i.e. demotic) and Greek writing ...[4]

They thought that, with work, the stone could be used to decipher the hieroglyphs.

Imagine their disappointment when, instead, the Rosetta Stone became a bargaining chip in Napoleon's surrender negotiations. An initial treaty with the British would have allowed it to remain in French custody. Had that happened, it would now sit in the Louvre. However, this treaty was rescinded by the British government, which insisted upon unconditional surrender and wanted all significant archeological finds, including the stone. Efforts to save it, such as hiding it under a French general's bed, were for naught. The stone reached the British Museum in 1802, where it still resides, more than two centuries later.[5]

Even though the French had lost possession of the stone, they kept copies of its text. These had been obtained by "rubbings," taken from the stone's surface. These rubbings were distributed to scholars all over the world for study.

Jean-François Champollion had an incredible gift for languages. By the age of sixteen, he had mastered a dozen: Latin, Greek, Hebrew, Arabic, Syriac, Chaldean, Chinese, Persian, Ethiopic, Sanskrit, Amharic, and Avestan.[6] Still, for him, this was just preparation. His dream was to translate the hieroglyphs.

Born in Figeac, a small village in southwest France, he was the second son of an itinerant bookseller. His older brother, Jacques-Joseph, was also his godfather and biggest supporter. Jacques-Joseph looked after Jean-François all his life. And after he died, Jacques-Joseph spent thirty-five years completing his younger brother's work.[7]

Portrait of Jean-François Champollion by Léon Cugniet, 1831 (ZURI SWIMMER/ALAMY)

Champollion was not working alone. Others paved the way. Silvestre de Sacy achieved a breakthrough by identifying the name Ptolemy. Thomas Young confirmed this discovery and correctly assigned five alphabetic letters to hieroglyphs. Giovanni Belzoni, a one-time circus strongman, helped by uncovering two sources of hieroglyphs that would be used in the translation process: an obelisk on the island of Philae near Aswan and the Great Temple of Abu Simbel, which he literally dug out of the sand.[8]

What is a hieroglyph?

The word comes from the Greek: *hieros* means "sacred," and *glyphien* means "to carve." Quite literally, then, a hieroglyph is a "sacred carving." But what is it? A picture, an idea, a word, a letter? And do you read it from left to right, or right to left? Just look at this block from the Temple of Horus at Edfu.

A Hieroglyph from the Temple of Horus (MIKE P. SHEPHERD / ALAMY)

How was it translated?

By trial and error.

In the United States there is a popular television game show, *Wheel of Fortune*. Contestants are given a clue regarding a hidden phrase. In turn, everyone guesses a letter. If the letter appears in the phrase, they get to guess again. A contestant wins by being the first person to solve the phrase correctly. That, essentially, is how to translate any language.

Only it wasn't phrases that led to the breakthrough; it was names. But how could one guess that hieroglyphs spelled a name? By consulting the Rosetta Stone. The same hieroglyphs appear six times on the stone, each time circled for emphasis. Since the decree inscribed on the stone honored Ptolemy, it was a reasonable guess that the hieroglyphs inside the circle spelled out his name. If true, seven letters had been found.

The French called these circles *cartouches*, because they were shaped like gun cartridges (*cartouche* is the French word for "cartridge"). The circles signified eternity and, when they surrounded a name, they evidenced the god-like quality of the person involved and acted as an amulet, providing protection.[9]

Look back at at the block, the figures are encircled. They must be a name.

There was, however, a lot more on the Rosetta Stone than six circled names. Thus, the original question remained: Were the hieroglyphs pictures, ideas, words, letters, or all of the above?

In December 1821, Champollion decided to do a numerical analysis of the stone. He counted 1,419 hieroglyphs compared to 486 Greek words. His conclusion: the hieroglyphs could not be words; they had to be parts of words (i.e., letters).

LUXOR, EGYPT | 47

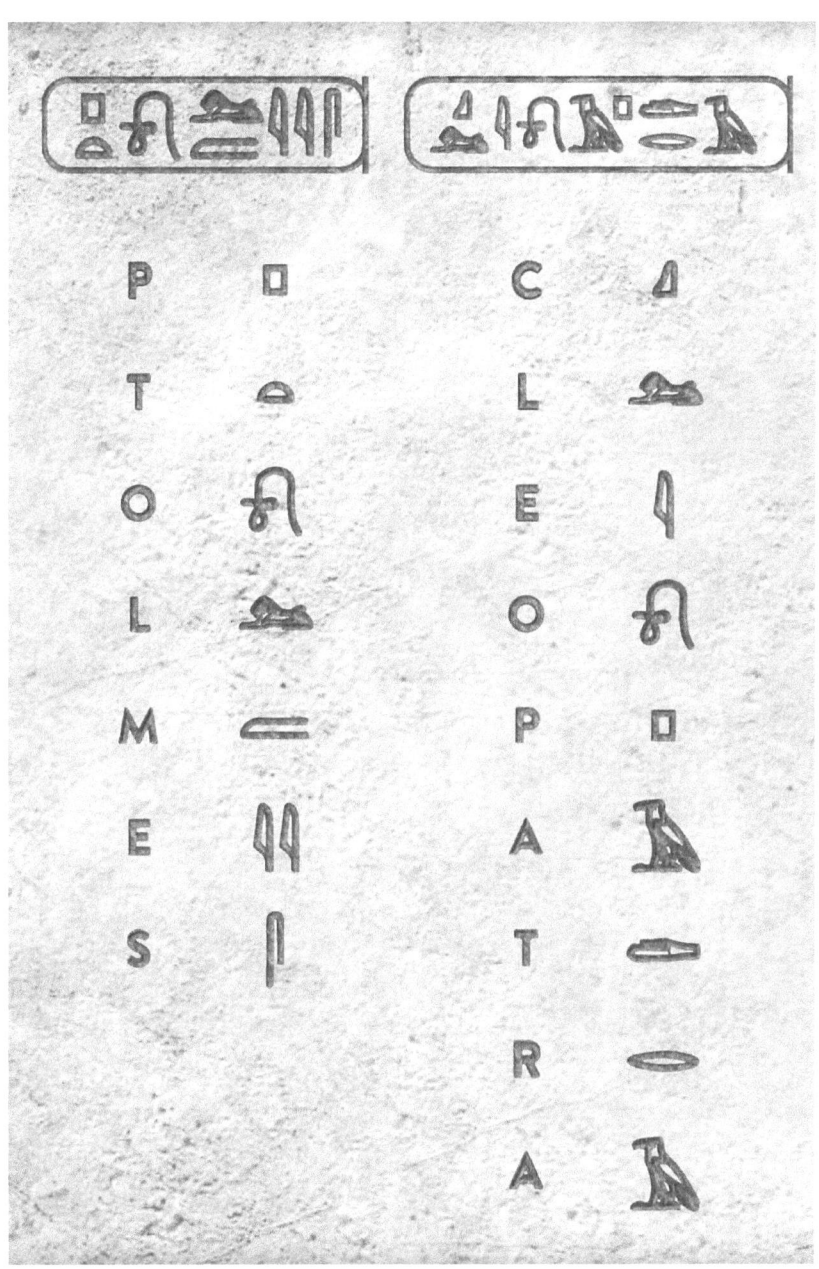

PTOLMES AND CLEOPATRA

He then tried to identify groups of hieroglyphs to determine if they "spelled out" a word. He identified 180 groups, which, again, did not match up to the 486. His conclusion this time: the hieroglyphs *could be both* letters and words.[10]

What Champollion needed was more material to study, more names to expand his alphabet. In January 1822, he received a copy of the inscription on the obelisk that Belzoni had obtained from Philae. It bore two names encircled in cartouches. One was "PTOLMES." Given that the base was inscribed with Greek text honoring Ptolemy and Cleopatra, he deduced that the name in the second circle was "CLEOPATRA."[11] With the two names, he had ten letters.

And now we know that hieroglyphs can be read from both the left and the right, depending upon which direction the animals face. Just compare the "Cleopatra" on the prior page with the "Cleopatra" on the block from the Temple of Horus.

Back to Champollion. On September 14, 1822, he received copies of hieroglyphs from the Temple of Abu Simbel. He saw two encircled names that he had never seen before.

One had as its first sign a picture of the sun. From Egyptian Coptic, another language he had learned, he knew the word for sun was "RA." He also knew that the last two signs meant "S," which would have given him "RA . . . SS." If the remaining, middle sign were an "M," he would have "RAMSES," a name used by many Pharaohs, including the greatest of them all, Ramses II.

Champollion applied the same process to the other cartouche. He knew that the bird depicted was an ibis, recorded as the symbol of the god Thoth. Having determined that the middle sign was an "M", he deduced that the name was "TUTHMOSIS," another well-known Pharaoh.

RAMSES AND TUTHMOSIS

At last, Champollion had broken the code. Overjoyed, he flew down the stairs, burst out of the house, and ran up the street to his brother's office, screaming, "*Je tiens l'affaire, je tiens l'affaire!*" or, "I've done it, I've done it!" Exhausted, he collapsed, and was bedridden for five days.[12]

Shortly thereafter, on September 27, 1822, Champollion presented his findings to the French Academy of Inscriptions and Literature and published them in his famous "Letter to Monsieur Dacier." It included a table of alphabetic hieroglyphs and a list of deciphered Greek, Roman, and Egyptian names. After years and years of hard work, he was an overnight success.

He followed with two other publications: the *Panthéon Égyptien*, a series of illustrated guides to the gods and goddesses of Egypt, and *Précis du système hiéroglyphic des anciens Égyptiens*, or *A Summary of the Hieroglyphic System of the Ancient Egyptians*.

He continued to work, studying more and more original material, writing with pride and joy:

> All my results are based on the monuments . . .
> no longer is a single one silent for me . . .[13]

His alphabet had become the key to understanding hieroglyphs.

Finally it was time for Champollion to visit the source. In 1828, he made his first and only trip to Egypt, leading the French-Tuscan Expedition. He went to Memphis, where he recorded the remains of a colossal statue of Ramses II. At Saqqara, he found evidence of the ancient Egyptian calendar, with twelve hours in a day, twelve hours in a night, and three seasons in a year: the Flood Season, Spring, and Harvest.[14]

His excitement was relentless. Everything, *everything* was opening to him. He was the first person since the fourth century to understand what he was seeing. He was the *only* person in the world who could understand. How could he sleep?

He was unlocking the secrets of the ages:

> Our alphabet is good: it has been applied with equal success first of all to the Egyptian monuments of the time of the Romans and the Greeks, and afterwards, which becomes of much greater interest, to the inscriptions of all the temples, palaces, and tombs of the pharaonic times.[15]

At last, Champollion reached Luxor where, almost two hundred years later, we made his acquaintance.

Luxor has had many names. It has been called "Waset" by the ancients, "Thebes" by the Greeks, and "Al-Uqsur" ("The Castles") by the Arabs. Say it three times: Al-Uqsur, L-Uqsur, Luxor.

We stayed at the Old Winter Palace Hotel, in a spacious room with a balcony that overlooked the Nile. We had a view past the hot air balloons to Meretseger, the mountain that protects the tombs of the Pharaohs.

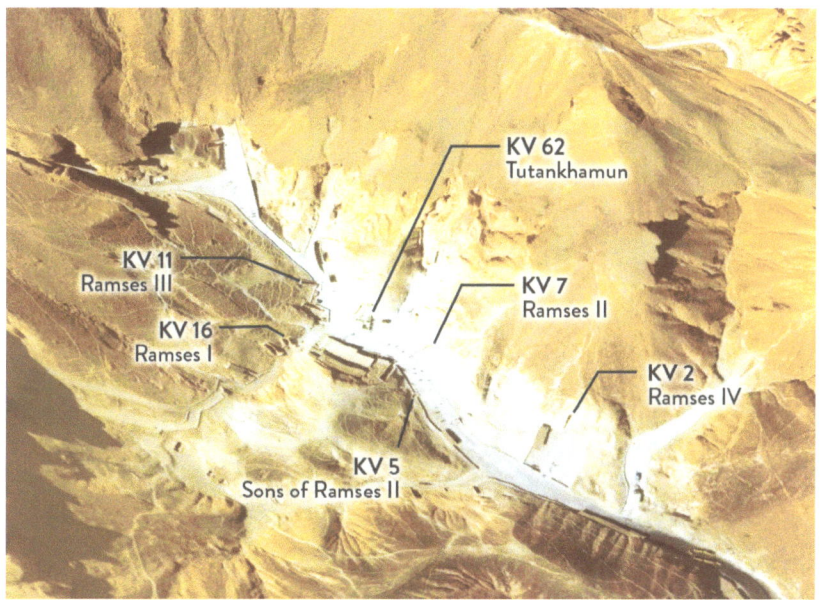

VALLEY OF THE KINGS

Off we went.

Our first stop was to the valley that contained these tombs. The Arabs call it "Biban el-Muluk," the "Great Necropolis of Millions of Years of Pharaoh," but in the West, it is commonly referred to as "The Valley of the Kings." And who, you might ask, gave it that name? Champollion.

To date, sixty-three tombs have been found in the valley, and they are numbered according to the order in which they were discovered. Each tourist ticket admits you to only three tombs, and a separate ticket is required for KV62, the tomb of Tutankhamun.

So many tombs, so little time. We wandered around, unsure of ourselves. We stumbled into KV2, the tomb of Ramses IV. Only later did we realize that Champollion, nine companions, and two pets (a gazelle and a cat) had lived there for several weeks during his 1828 Expedition. Pretty tight quarters.

LUXOR, EGYPT | 52

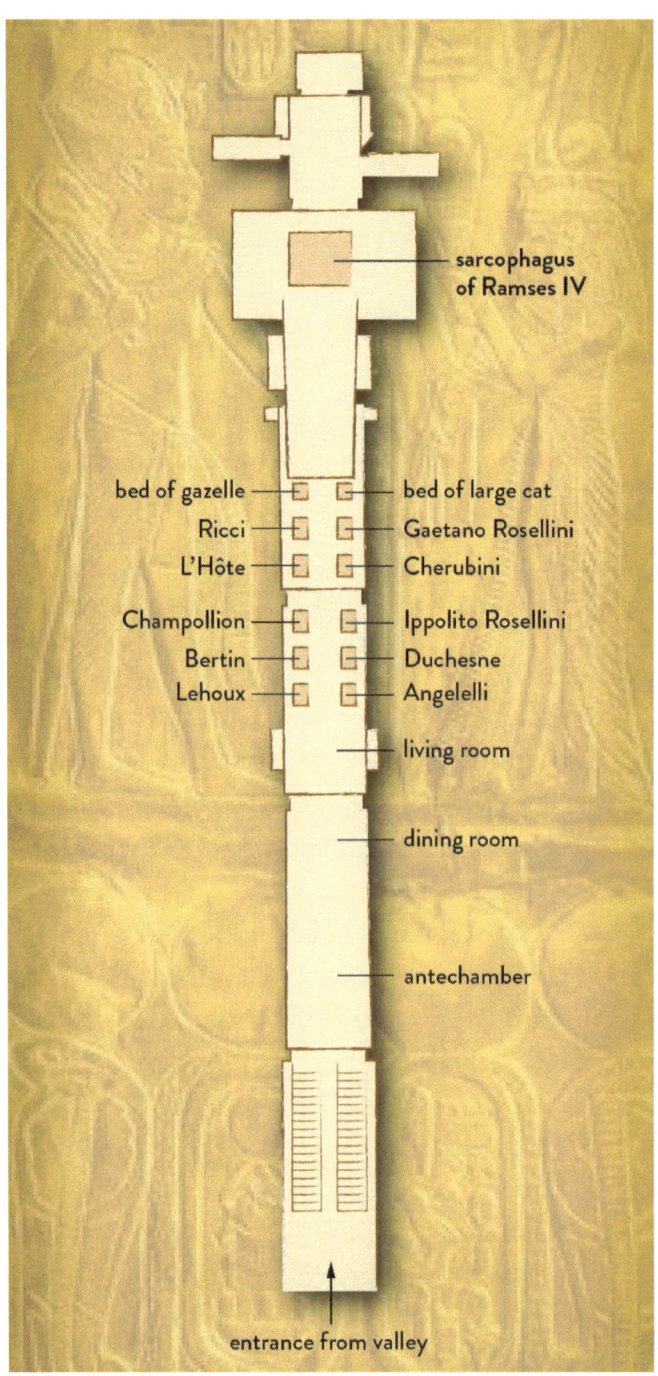

KV2: TOMB OF RAMSES IV

Moving on, we visited the Ramesseum, the great mortuary temple of Ramses II himself. Champollion didn't name this one. He didn't have to. He read the hieroglyphs. They told him whose temple it was.

The Greeks had called Ramses II "Ozymandias" after his official name, Usermaatre Setepenre Ramessu Meryamen. Ruined by an earthquake, his temple inspired Shelley's famous poem with its haunting final refrain:

> "My name is Ozymandias, King of Kings,
> Look on my works, ye Mighty, and despair!"
> Nothing beside remains. Round the decay
> Of that colossal wreck, boundless and bare
> The lone and level sands stretch far away.[16]

The Ramesseum (DIEGO FIORE / ALAMY)

The Temple of Luxor (ALFREDO GARCIA SAZ / ALAMY)

Champollion's presence at Luxor is so pervasive that it even touches the missing obelisk at the Temple of Luxor in the center of town.

Where is it? Where did it go?

It's in Paris, erected in the center of the Place de la Concorde in October 1836. It's the oldest monument in the city.

Who do you think suggested to the King of France that:

> "... if the government wants an *obelisk* in Paris, it is a matter of national honour to have one of those at Luxor (that on the right when entering), a monolith of the greatest beauty and seventy feet in height ... of an exquisite workmanship and astonishingly preserved." [17]

Need we answer? Champollion really was everywhere we looked, even when what we were looking at wasn't there.

STILL NOT THERE

Please look again at the base of the remaining obelisk. Animals decorate it. They are baboons, standing in a row, raising their hands to the sun, offering a full-frontal view.

The obelisk taken to Paris had an identical base, but it was considered too racy for French society in the 1830s. Accordingly, it was removed and, as you can see below, replaced. The engravings on the new base praised the French king and showed how the obelisk was lowered in Egypt and then raised in Paris.

The Luxor Obelisk in Place de la Concorde (ANDIA / ALAMY)

Here Comes the Sun. (ALAIN GUILLEUX / ALAMY)

As for the removed base, it wasn't destroyed; it was stored in the Louvre. Almost two hundred years later, the Louvre created a regional museum in Lens, a small city in northern France. It sent the formerly censored 5.3-ton base to this museum where it — and its baboons — are proudly on display in the "Galerie du Temps" (Gallery of Time).

ILULISSAT, GREENLAND

Give me winter, give me dogs, you can have the rest.

—KNUD RASMUSSEN

The Red House (EDWARDJE/DREAMSTIME)

The red house sits in the middle of a field in a small town. It looks across a road, over a church, and onto a bay filled with icebergs. The town is Ilulissat, which, not surprisingly, means "icebergs" in the Greenlandic language. It is the country's most popular tourist destination, sitting on Disko Bay, just above the Arctic Circle, at the edge of the northern hemisphere's largest and most active glacier.

Don't Ride Into the Sun. (IMAGEBROKER/ALAMY)

Ilulissat has 4,000 people and 5,000 dogs. It's not a quiet town, especially during the summer when we visited. The dogs have nothing to do but eat, sleep, and complain about the twenty-four-hour sunlight. Yes, they bark a lot.

Up here, dogs are truly a man's best friend. They aren't pets, they're partners. It takes training — for both man and dogs — to create the right balance, speed, and coordination needed for a working dogsled. Please note, however: if you ever take a dogsled ride, don't ride into the sun.

Up here, the relationship between a man and his dogs is as close as a marriage, with one exception: if the trip gets really rough (temperatures go to forty degrees below zero plus the wind chill), if the hunting is poor, if the food is gone, and if it looks like all may be lost, a man can always eat his dogs.[1]

FLYING TO GREENLAND

A direct flight from New York City to Ilulissat, if available, would take about four hours. We flew commercial, so it was twenty-four hours and six flights: JFK to Reykjavik, to Kulusuk, to Nuuk, to Sisimiut, to Kangerlussuaq and then, at last, in a *cargo plane*, to Ilulissat. It may have been longer and more inconvenient, but these flights certainly gave us a feel for how far away we were going, or so we thought.

We were fogged in for hours at Kulusuk. Worried that we would miss our connections, we asked about them at the check-in counter. The attendant told us to relax, that the airline would hold the planes for us. When we asked why, she said, "because you're the only passengers."

What we should have worried about was missing dinner. We were staying at the Hvide Falk, the oldest hotel in town. On Thursday nights, it offers a Greenlandic buffet featuring polar bear, seal, reindeer, muskox, and caribou.

We had timed our visit accordingly. Even with the flight delays, we made it to the hotel by 6 p.m., just as the buffet was opening. By 6:10 p.m., we had finished checking in and were ready to eat.

"Do you have reservations?" the clerk asked.

"No," we replied. "Why would we need them in a place this remote?"

"Well, you can't eat without them, we're all sold out. And even if you had reservations, you're too late, all the food's gone."

"In ten minutes?" we asked.

We looked. He was right. Maybe we weren't that far away after all.

———

Don't Jump, Don't Fall. (BRUCE YUANYUE BI / GETTY IMAGES)

The main attraction in town is the glacier. It sits at the end of a fjord that empties into Disko Bay. On average, it produces enough ice each day to provide water to New York City for a year. And when it calves an iceberg, watch out: it produces a tidal wave thirty feet tall, easily capable of sweeping us away if we were standing too close to the shore.

We took a hike to the hills outside of town and watched the icebergs march slowly by. The hills were high enough to protect us, but we had to be careful not to fall into Kaellingekloften, otherwise known as "Suicide Gorge."

Life here is tough, marginal, and always at risk. When locals become old, infirm, or otherwise unable to contribute to their community, they walk up to the gorge and jump off.

Ice is why we went to Greenland. It covers 81 percent of the country, making the country's name one of the great misnomers in the world. In one local dictionary, there are twenty-three words for "ice," each with a separate and distinct meaning.

Okay, let's do it:

> kaniq, qirihuq, qirititat, nilak, nilaktaqtuq, hiku, hikuaq, hikuaqtuaq, ilu, hikuiqihuq, hikurhuit, hikuqihuq, hikuliaq, manirak, hikup hinaa, qainnguq, manillat, kassut, iluliaq, ilulissirhuq, auktuq, quihaq, hirmiijaut

As for translations, here are a few:

> rime frost, freshwater ice, sea ice, thin ice, ice on the inside of the tent, pack ice, new ice, a smooth expanse of ice, the ice edge, solid ice attached to the shore, hummocky ice, pressure ridges, pieces of floating ice, icebergs in the water, melting ice [2]

The one local word we did not find, however, was the word for "disappearing ice." Disko Bay used to freeze over during the winter so people could dogsled from Ilulissat across the bay to Disko Island. Not anymore. And the glacier, itself, is retreating rapidly because of global warming. If you want to see the ice before it's gone, you better hurry.[3]

Ilulissat has a second attraction, the red house. Now the town's museum, it is where, in 1879, Knud Rasmussen, Greenland's greatest explorer, and just the person we were looking for, was born. Knud spent the first twelve years of his life here. His father, the local pastor, was Danish and his mother was a Greenland native, so he learned to speak both languages.[4]

At seven, Knud drove his first dogsled while helping an injured hunter back to town. After that, he was given his own dogs and sled. At twelve, Knud was sent to Denmark to study. An indifferent student, he barely got by.

In 1902, twenty-three-year-old Knud got a break, joining an expedition back in his native Greenland. Between June 1902 and September 1904, Knud took part in what is known as the "Danish Literary Expedition." It was the first scientific study of the polar Inuit living on the upper northwest coast of Greenland in an area that has become known, thanks to him, as *Thule*.

———

Thule has always been a mythical destination, the "northernmost place" in the world. Since at least the fourth century BCE, explorers have searched for it, wondering where it might be. Pytheas the Greek thought it was the Shetland Islands. For others, it has been, variously, Iceland, Norway, Svalbard, and, of course, the North Pole itself.[5]

Knud had long dreamed of visiting this place and meeting its residents:

> When I was a child, I used often to hear an old Greenlandic woman tell how, far away north, at the end of the world, there lived a people who dressed in bearskins and ate raw flesh . . . Even before I knew what traveling meant, I determined that one day I would go and find them.[6]

Who were they? The Greenlandic word *Eskimo* means "eaters of raw meat." Now thought to be slightly insulting, it has been replaced by *Inuit*, which means "people." That word, however, is not good enough for some. They insist on being called *Inughuit*, which means "the great people." Let's keep it simple and use Inuit.

What *do* the Inuit eat? Whatever can be found: muskox, hares, birds, reindeer, seal, walrus. And yes, regardless of what we call them, they do, indeed, eat their meat raw.

Their special dish is *kiviaq*. It is made by stuffing un-plucked, un-cleaned, dead auks (small black and white birds) into seal skins and burying them under stones where they are bathed in the melting seal fat. After a time, decomposed and fermented, the birds are served up as a delicacy.[7]

Little wonder that, when first offered Western food, the Inuit found it inedible.

Traveling by dogsled, Knud and the Danish Literary Expedition collected the first information on the Inuit. They heard stories of creation, of the soul, of life, of death. They heard tales of murder and retribution, of animals and spirits. They recorded everything:

> These fables . . . were written down during the Polar Night. They are told in the houses . . . when the Inuit, after great banquets of raw, frozen meat late in the evening, are digesting their food and are heavy and tired. Then it is the task of the storyteller to talk his hearers to sleep. The best storytellers boast of never having told any story to the end.[8]

Kiviaq — Yum. (SEABIRD/ALAMY)

Knud Rasmussen (PUBLIC DOMAIN)

Upon his return to Denmark, Knud published his findings. *The New People* (1908) portrayed the previously unknown lives of the Inuit with admiration, sympathy, and respect.[9]

The book opened a lot of eyes. At the time, Westerners did not yet see the Inuit as people. One incident illustrates the point. In the early twentieth century — and even today — there was a controversy over who first reached the North Pole. Was it Dr. Frederick A. Cook or Admiral Robert E. Peary? In the United States the debate was nationwide, fueled by all sorts of official and unofficial investigations. Yet no one ever called on either explorer's support staff — the Inuit who guided them — to serve as witnesses one way or the other.[10]

Knud was also the first Western explorer to bring the Inuit into his activities as equal partners rather than as "natives," the reluctant, local, hired hands. They trusted and loved him, calling him *Kunuunnguaq* (Our Knud).

This relationship enabled Knud to establish a trading post on North Star Bay in northwest Greenland. He picked a spot that was a natural crossroad, the only practicable passage between Greenland, Ellesmere Island, and Arctic Canada. Knowing his history, he named the trading post "Thule."[11]

Knud's trading post was an independent business, backed by neither church nor state. In exchange for fox skins, he sold knives, tools, guns, matches, and food — the essentials. With his profits, he financed his expeditions. Beginning in 1912, he conducted seven of them, calling them the "Thule Expeditions." They are summarized in Appendix I.

Two of these stood out.

The Second Thule Expedition (1916–18) set out to map a previously unknown area on Greenland's north coast and to cross the country's ice cap. It planned to succeed where other, more richly equipped explorers had failed. Instead of weighing down his sleds with supplies, Knud chose to travel like a native:

> We must . . . break entirely with the general practice of expeditions and completely rely on the hunt.[12]

He planned to eat muskox and seal, which could be hunted along the way. But the hunting was not good. In order to survive, they, indeed, ate their dogs.

Upon his return, Knud learned that, while he had been struggling in "primitive" Greenland, his more "civilized" counterparts in the European world had all been killing each other. World War I, a four-year struggle, saw forty million casualties, including at least ten million military and ten million civilian deaths.[13]

ROUTE OF THE FIFTH THULE EXPEDITION 1921-1924

The Fifth Thule Expedition (June 1921–October 1924) was the most ambitious: Knud set out to find the origins of the Inuit race. His plan was simple, but daunting. Beginning in Greenland, he proceeded by dogsled across the top of Arctic Canada, interviewing natives as he found them, listening to their folktales, and noting their histories. He traveled for three and one-half years, and covered twenty thousand miles. That's over a thousand and one nights . . . and days, with no shower, no toilet, no toothbrush. No thank you.

Knud didn't stop until he reached Siberia, becoming the first person to cross the Northwest Passage by dogsled. His resulting book, *Across Arctic America* (1927), an abridgement of thirty notebooks, is a classic. He had found that the natives of Greenland and Alaska, and those in Canada along the way, shared the same language, customs, and folktales. He had retraced an ancient migration route known only to the Inuit for thousands of years. In effect, he had discovered an invisible country stretching across the top of the world.[14]

We could never be like Knud. We've experienced a "white out" on a dogsled, when the snow and sleet prevented us from knowing where we were. We might have the courage, the confidence, and the faith to believe for fifteen minutes that:

> It's impossible to be lost, that would mean we were nowhere.[15]

Could we keep it up for three and one-half years? Not a chance. Then again, had we lived during World War I, our answer probably would have been different. We would have taken winter and dogs and told "civilization" it could have the rest.

BADALING, CHINA

*We ate with the Wall,
slept with the Wall, thought Wall.*

—WILLIAM EDGAR GEIL, *THE GREAT WALL OF CHINA*, 1909

William Lindesay Running *(COURTESY OF WILLIAM LINDESAY)*

*If you see a long wall, an old wall, and you're a runner,
then you want to run along it.*

—WILLIAM LINDESAY, *ALONE ON THE GREAT WALL*, 1989

BADALING, CHINA | 70

*A*n English schoolboy saw a map of China and wished he could run along the snake-like structure defending its borders ... and then promptly forgot about it. He grew up to be a marathon runner and, one day, after running alongside Hadrian's Wall in Northern England, also built to keep out barbarians, he remembered that childhood dream.

Two years later, in 1986, Queen Elizabeth and Prince Philip made England's official visit to newly opened China. William Lindsay, marathon runner, followed them, hoping to *run* the Great Wall. Surely, he thought, he would be the first Westerner to travel its length.

LINDSAY'S RUN: STAGE ONE & STAGE TWO 1986-1987

Off he went. He began in the desert, intending to run to the sea. In the summer of 1986, he started at the great western fortress of Jiayuguan. He ran, jogged, got sick, was arrested, police-escorted, and sent to Beijing.

He returned to Jiayuguan in the spring of 1987 to start over. From there, he ran, jogged, walked, and was arrested again—but this time, he ran away.

Then, he ran and jogged some more, hurt himself, and limped into a hospital to recover. When ready, he ran, jogged, and was arrested for the third time, but he escaped into a sandstorm. Finally, he ran and jogged until he was arrested yet again and ordered to leave China. He had gone halfway.

Undeterred, Lindesay acquired a new visa in Hong Kong and returned in the fall of 1987 for stage two. Starting almost from where he left off, he ran, jogged, and limped some more (shin splints this time). He was stopped and interrogated, but escaped. He was arrested again, escaped again, got a new passport, and was arrested again. He climbed onto and ran and jogged on the Great Wall itself. He was arrested one last time, but finally, *finally*, obtained an Alien's Travel Permit and, most importantly, an official guide who escorted him on his last run to Shanhaiguan on the coast of the Yellow Sea.

One thousand five hundred miles, give or take, and it gave Lindesay something to write about. *Alone on the Great Wall*, published in 1989, was enthusiastically received by its English audience. Then, in 1991, after he gave a talk on the radio, a little old lady sent him a book with a polite note, concerned that "perhaps it is too late to be of use."[1]

He opened the book to learn that *he had not been alone*.

Wanli Changcheng. The "ten thousand-*li* long wall." Taken literally, it means the three-thousand-mile wall, since a mile is equal to about three li. And this, notwithstanding that a li is a flexible unit of measure, being shorter going uphill and longer going down, measuring both distance and time.

Wan li also has a poetic meaning: endless, infinite, as if the Great Wall were one continuous creation. In fact, however, "it" is really a "they," for eleven different dynasties developed entirely separate segments that we, over time, have merged into one.[2]

Of the various walls, four stand out: the Qin Great Wall (221–206 BCE), the Han Great Wall (206 BCE–220 CE), the Jin Great Wall (1115–1234 CE), and the Ming Great Wall (1368–1644 CE). All were built to keep out nomadic tribes and included watch towers and military barracks. All but the Ming have suffered from the ravages of time, including sandstorms and looting. The Ming Wall is the one that most people seek for their Great Wall experience. And it is along the Ming Wall that Lindesay ran.

When Lindesay opened the book the lady sent him, he met another William: William Edgar Geil. Geil had spent eighty-two days traveling along the Great Wall in 1908, going from east to west, from the sea to the desert, exactly the same route as Lindesay, only in reverse. Geil, an American evangelist and explorer, was the first Westerner to travel along the Great Wall of China.

Lindesay was struck by Geil's book, *The Great Wall of China* (1909), not because of the words but because of the photos. One in particular caught his attention: "East of the Mule-Horse Pass."

East of Mule-Horse Pass, William Geil Sitting (COURTESY OF WILLIAM LINDESAY)

East of Mule-Horse Pass, William Lindesay Running (COURTESY OF WILLIAM LINDESAY)

Lindsay realized that he had been there himself and had been photographed in almost the exact same place that Geil had sat. He noticed, however, that the tower in the 1908 photo had crumbled by the time he got there in 1987.

"Rephotography" is the act of taking a photograph of the same subject after the passage of time to show what, if anything, has changed between then and now. It shows, if you will, the before and the after.[3]

Lindesay was so taken by the coincidental rephotography at Mule-Horse Pass that he spent the next fifteen years searching for earlier photos of the Great Wall, finding their locations, and then rephotographing the sites.

However, there weren't many to be found because few people with cameras explored the Great Wall prior to the 1940s, and after that, China was closed to outsiders. Time and time again, one William was chasing another as Lindesay kept finding only Geil's photographs. But Geil himself, who had once been as famous in the United States as Lewis and Clark, had disappeared.

In a way, it wasn't Lindesay who found Geil, but Geil who found Lindesay. In 1925, while returning from a trip, Geil died. His wife was so grief-stricken that she locked up his travel materials, his notebooks, his photos, and his souvenirs, and hid them from the public. When she died in 1959, all of these were bought by a rare book collector who, in turn, stored them in his barn. When he died, in 2005, his daughters took them to the local Historical Society. While trying to find out who this Geil fellow was, one of the society's researchers went on the Internet and stumbled upon Lindesay.[4]

William Edgar Geil (COURTESY OF WILLIAM LINDESAY)

As a result, William Lindesay and William Edgar Geil were together at last. In 2008, Lindesay published *The Great Wall Revisited* in honor of the one hundredth anniversary of Geil's exploration. It features page after page of comparison photographs.

Pictures *are* worth a thousand words. Why tell people that things have changed, sometimes for better, sometimes for worse, when you can show them? This is what the two Williams have done.

The Great Wall in Disrepair (COURTESY OF WILLIAM LINDESAY)

The portion of the Great Wall closest to Beijing is at Badaling. By the 1880s, it had fallen into almost complete disrepair.

One hundred years later the country responded to its leader's call: "Love China, Rebuild the Great Wall."[5] By 1986, this very same section of the Great Wall was ready to receive British royalty and U.S. presidents.

They came, and so did everyone else. So many, in fact, that a structure originally built to keep people out has become the country's most popular way to bring them in. Indeed, prior to the COVID-19 pandemic, the Great Wall at Badaling received over five million visitors a year.

And, when it comes to rephotography, nothing beats joining queens and presidents in the "Very Important Person Section" for a once-in-a-lifetime opportunity.[6]

BADALING, CHINA | 77

A Smiling HM Queen Elizabeth and HRH Prince Philip at the Great Wall
(PA IMAGES/ALAMY)

U.S. President Barack Obama Greeted at the Great Wall (REUTERS/ALAMY)

The Lindesay Family at the Great Wall (COURTESY OF WILLIAM LINDESAY)

Look for that exact location when you get there. We did. And don't forget to bring your camera. You never know who you might run into, maybe even Mr. Lindesay and his family.[7]

ENCORE

Well, what did you do during COVID? If you were William Lindesay's sons, James and Thomas, you planned an outdoor adventure. And the adventure you planned was to follow in your father's footsteps: to run the Great Wall.

This they did, starting at Jiayuguan in the west and ending at Shanhaiguan in the east, just like their father. They, too, ran from the desert to the sea. It took them 131 days, averaging 15 miles of running per day.

Yes, they had backup (a crew, vehicles, and supplies) that their father didn't. But when their father ran, China was closed only to foreigners. During COVID, it was closed to everyone, foreigners and Chinese alike.

Don't we all wish we had such sons . . . and daughters.

James and Thomas Running the Great Wall (COURTESY OF WILLIAM LINDESAY)

ZERMATT, SWITZERLAND

One crowded hour of glorious life.

—EDWARD WHYMPER, *SCRAMBLES AMONGST THE ALPS*

The Broken Rope (EMANUEL AMMON / MATTERHORN MUSEUM)

What if the best day in your life became the worst, the day you will always remember became the one you most want to forget, and your greatest triumph became your biggest tragedy?

July 14, 1865.

Exactly 150 years later, we were standing in a museum, staring into a glass-enclosed case. Inside, resting on red velvet, was one of Switzerland's cultural icons: the Broken Rope.

We were looking for Edward Whymper and Jean-Antoine Carrel.

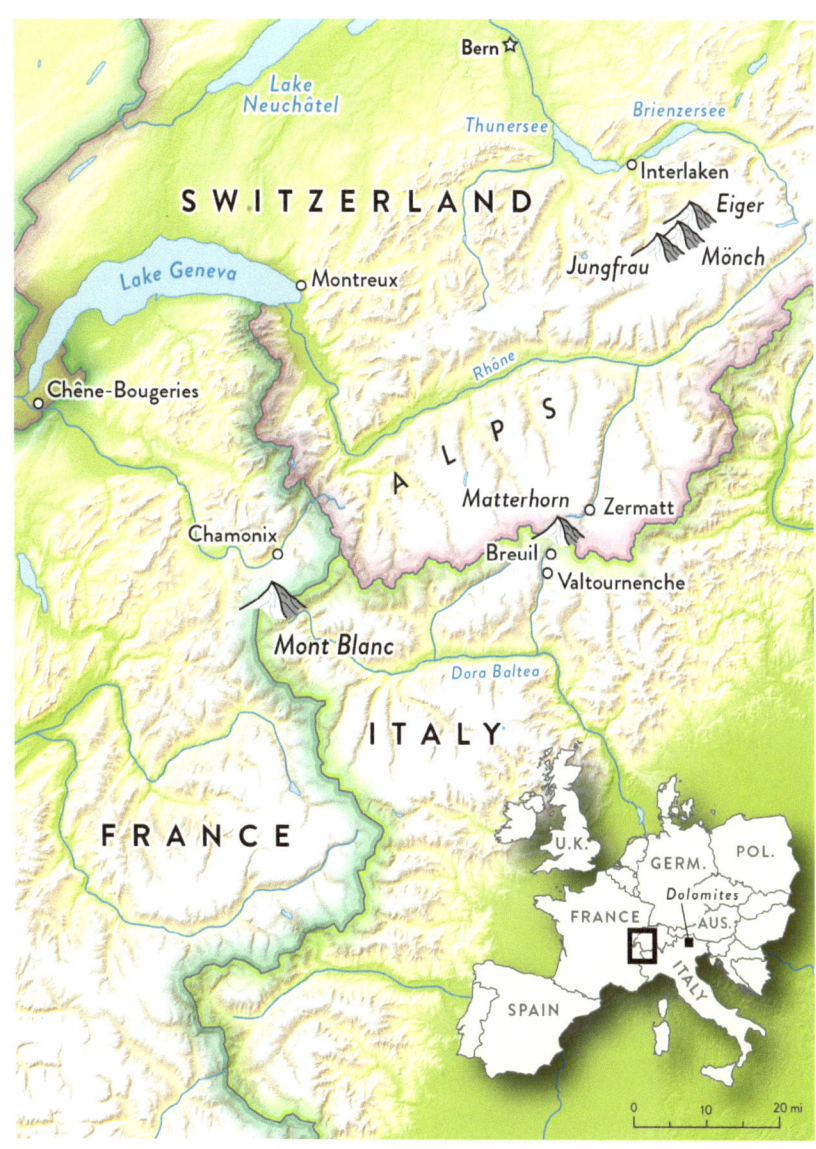

THE ALPS

ZERMATT, SWITZERLAND | 82

The Matterhorn (FUNKYSTOCK — PAUL WILLIAMS / ALAMY)

At the beginning of the nineteenth century, the Alps were regarded as a far-off, distant, unreachable place. Mountains were dangerous and mountain climbing even more so. Still, it caught on, especially with the British, and by mid-century, many of the major Alpine peaks had been climbed.

For the British, the period between 1854 and 1865 was the "Golden Age of Mountaineering." And, in 1864 and 1865, their invasion reached its height. Of forty-three "First Ascents" (the designation for the first successful climb to the top of a mountain or top of a particular climbing route) made in the Alps during those years, thirty-eight were by British climbers.[1]

One mountain, however, remained unconquered and, to most people, unconquerable: the Matterhorn.[2] Straddling the Swiss/Italian border, its proud shape beckoned and repelled those few who might try to climb from either Zermatt on the north or Breuil on the south.

But there were two who braved the mountain, who dreamed it could be climbed, who kept trying to summit: Edward Whymper, an English artist, and Jean-Antoine Carrel, an Italian guide.

Whymper was a talented wood engraver. In 1860, at the age of twenty, he was hired to make sketches of the Alps for a book. In 1861, he made a first ascent and learned that drawing the mountains was not enough; he had to climb them.

Carrel lived at the base of the Matterhorn, in the small Italian village of Valtournenche. Generally acclaimed as the "cock of the valley," he was the finest rock climber that Whymper had ever seen. He was the only native who believed, in spite of all discouragements, that the mountain could be mastered.

left, Edward Whymper (THE PRINT COLLECTOR / ALAMY)
right, Jean-Antoine Carrel (G L ARCHIVE / ALAMY)

By 1865, Whymper and Carrel had each made seven attempts, including three together. They had come to know every rock, every hill, every gully, every landmark on the climb. They had even named them: Glacier du Lion, Great Staircase, Tete du Lion, Col du Lion, Chimney, Great Tower, Crete du Coq (where they carved their initials), Cravate, Shoulder.[3]

With each new name, we could sense them, step by step, getting closer and closer to the top. Both men wanted to be the first. Only one would be. And it came at a terrible price.

In July 1865, Whymper thought he had engaged Carrel to be his guide on a joint attempt at the mountain. However, bad weather delayed their start. Carrel then announced that he could not help Whymper after July 11 because he had a prior engagement with "a family of distinction."

What Carrel did not disclose was that he had little choice. This "family of distinction" included Signor Quintino Sella, an Italian government officer and president of the Italian Alpine Club.[4] The group's unabashed goal was to make the first ascent of the Matterhorn (the mountain they called Monte Cervino), and to make it from the Italian side.

When Whymper found out, he was humiliated, and immediately made his way to Zermatt, with the hope of climbing from the Swiss side. He assembled a team of seven people: three guides and four British climbers, including himself.

Carrel had a head start. On July 6, he made a preliminary inspection of the route. On July 9, he laid up provisions. On July 11, his group departed.

Whymper, however, reasoned that, with so much equipment, Carrel's group would be delayed and, if he traveled light, he still had a chance. He started from Zermatt on July 13.

Everyone carried their share, but Whymper knew what was most important, even in a time of strict competition:

> The wine-bags . . . fell to my lot to carry, and throughout the day, after each drink, I replenished them secretly with water, so that at the next halt they were found fuller than before! This was considered a good omen, and little short of miraculous.[5]

They spent a night halfway up the mountain. Some shared their only tent, some slept outside. All dreamed of the next day's triumph.

The morning of July 14, 1865, broke clear. The climb resumed. The higher that Whymper's group got, the more excited they became. Would they make it to the top? Would they beat the Italians? Finally, the slope eased and Whymper and the head guide ran neck-and-neck to the summit. At 1:40 p.m., the world was at their feet.

But where was Carrel?

Whymper and the guide peered over the edge, half-doubting, half-expecting, and spied the Italian group twelve hundred feet below them. They began yelling, screaming, trying to catch their attention. But there was no response. When they resulted to throwing rocks, the Italians turned and fled.

Whymper was sad. He thought of Carrel, and how much he respected him:

> Still, I would that the leader of that party could have stood with us at that moment, for our victorious shouts conveyed to him the disappointment of the ambition of a lifetime. He was *the* man, of all those who attempted the ascent of the Matterhorn, who most deserved to be the first upon its summit.[6]

ZERMATT, SWITZERLAND | 86

Gustave Doré, *Arrival at the Summit* (MATTHIAS TAUGWALDER/KEYSTONE)

Gustave Doré, *The Fall* (MATTHIAS TAUGWALDER / KEYSTONE)

The mountain was theirs, and theirs alone. The head guide planted a tent pole. He removed his shirt and fashioned it into a flag. They all enjoyed the view.[7]

An hour later, it was time to go. They put their names in a bottle, propped it next to the tent pole, and began their descent.

Coming down a mountain is far more dangerous than going up. Statistically, 80 percent of all deaths happen on the descent. It makes sense. Climbers are celebrating, they are less careful, they are tired, they think they are finished. They have forgotten that when they reached the top, they were only halfway there.

Whymper understood. He arranged the party of seven with the most experienced guide first, the least experienced man second, other guides in between, and himself last. For safety, they all roped themselves together. Down they came. Slowly, slowly.

And then it happened. The number-two man slipped off his feet onto his back. His feet hit the leader and knocked him over. The two began to fall, dragging the number-three and number-four men with them. Whymper and the remaining two guides planted themselves, and prepared for the jerk of the rope.

Instead of holding fast, it broke.

And, one by one, the four men slid down the mountain on their backs, with their arms spread, until they fell over the precipice to the glacier four thousand feet below.

It was the worst mountain climbing disaster in history. It was a sensation. Overnight, Edward Whymper became the most famous mountain climber in the world.[8] Overnight, Zermatt became the most famous mountain climbing destination.[9]

Books were written. Lithographs, paintings, and movies were made.[10] And the rope was saved.

As we looked into the glass case, we could hear Whymper's words:

> Climb if you will, but remember that courage and strength are naught without prudence, and that a momentary negligence may destroy the happiness of a lifetime. Do nothing in haste; look well to each step; and from the beginning think what may be the end.[11]

Whymper was criticized and investigated. You might have thought he was finished.

He wasn't.

Fifteen years later, halfway around the world, he would again be on top, with one special person by his side: Jean-Antoine Carrel.

And we would be right behind them.

Riobamba: ready or not, here we come.

RIOBAMBA, ECUADOR

We know very well what is your object! You wish to discover the TREASURES which are buried in Chimborazo, and, no doubt, there is MUCH treasure buried there; and we hope you will discover it; but we hope when you have discovered it, you will not forget US.

—EDWARD WHYMPER, *TRAVELS AMONGST THE GREAT ANDES OF THE EQUATOR*

The Whymper Refuge (BORISS ANDEAN / WWW.SUMMITPOST.ORG)

Only five hundred feet to go. Only five hundred feet to go. The air was getting thinner. We wanted to stop, but if we could just make it to the refuge, we would be closer to the sun than the top of Mount Everest.

Why were we there? As we told you, we were still looking for Whymper and Carrel.

What is the shape of the Earth? This was one of the most celebrated scientific questions of the eighteenth century. By then, everyone agreed it was round. If it were perfectly round, the distance between each of its 360 degrees of latitude would be the same.

What if it were not? It could be elongated like a standing egg (on left) or it could be flattened like a sitting loaf of bread. The alternatives are shown below.

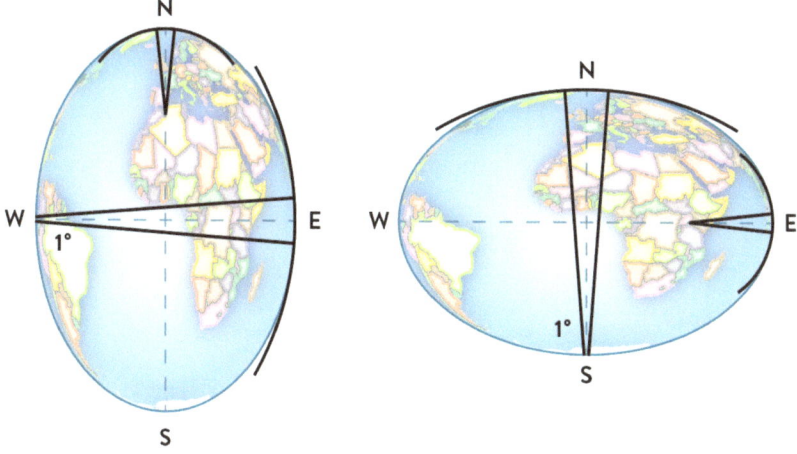

ELONGATED OR FLATTENED?

French scientists supported René Descartes's theory that the Earth was like the egg. If so, a degree of latitude would cover more miles at the equator than at the poles. British mathematician Isaac Newton argued the opposite, that the Earth was like the loaf of bread, its spin causing it to bulge at the middle. As a result, a degree of latitude would cover fewer miles at the equator than at the North or South Pole.

It was a lively, impassioned debate, with very practical military and political consequences. Knowing the number of miles in a degree of latitude would enable governments to more accurately locate their ships at sea.

The French Academy decided that physically measuring the number of miles in a degree of latitude in two different locations and then comparing them was the only way to settle the matter. It sent out two Geodesic Missions to do just that. One went to the Arctic. The other to the equator.

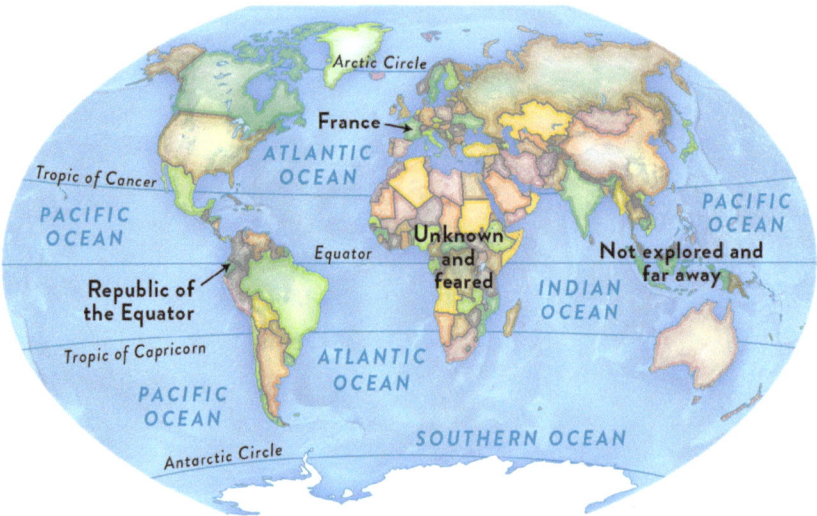

EIGHTEENTH CENTURY WORLD

In the 1730s, the French Academy had few options regarding the equator. Look at the above world map. The equator crosses the middle of Africa, which at that time was unknown and feared territory. It crosses the Asian islands, which were far away and had not been fully explored. And it crosses the northern part of South America, where, at that time, an enemy (Portugal) ruled one colony (Brazil), and a friend

(Spain) governed another (Peru, part of which would become Ecuador). The choice for where to measure was obvious.[1]

Accordingly, in 1736, the French Geodesic Mission embarked on the first major international scientific expedition. Upon arriving in Quito, the scientists set up a baseline northeast of the city. Using long-distance surveys, geometric triangulations, astronomical observations, and mathematical calculations, they determined the length of a single degree of latitude at the equator. It helped prove that the Earth was flatter at the poles and wider in the middle. Newton was right.

Which explains why we were trying to reach the refuge. It is the last resting place before beginning a serious climb of Mount Chimborazo, a volcano just outside Riobamba. Because of the equatorial bulge, Chimborazo's peak goes higher into the atmosphere than the top of Mount Everest. Reaching the refuge would, therefore, give us some "top of the world" bragging rights.

What *is* the tallest mountain in the world? It depends. It depends on your frame of reference. If you are measuring from sea level, it is Mount Everest. If from the base of the mountain (even if under water), it is Mauna Kea in Hawaii. But if you are measuring from the center of the earth, the mountain top farthest away is Chimborazo. It reaches more than a mile further into the atmosphere than Mount Everest. The refuge is less than a mile from its top and is thus "higher" than Everest.

Would it surprise you to learn that this resting place is called the "Whymper Refuge?"

After the 1865 Matterhorn tragedy, Edward Whymper gave up mountain climbing as a sport, but not as a dream. He began to study the effects of high altitude on people. The concept of acute mountain sickness had not yet been medically accepted, and this gave him a scientific excuse to resume doing what he loved.[2]

It took him almost fifteen years, however, to organize another climbing expedition. At first, he planned a trip to the Himalayas but, in 1874, just as he was ready to depart, the political situation in India changed, and he was advised to defer. Then he considered Peru, which everyone believed had the highest peaks outside the Himalayas, but Peru and Bolivia went to war against Chile, and that ended that plan.

Finally, he settled on a newly independent and newly named country, the "Republic of the Equator," more commonly known by its Spanish name, "Ecuador."

Beginning in December 1879, Whymper traveled north from Riobamba to Quito, a distance of only one hundred miles. He made his way through the "Avenue of the Volcanoes," passing through twenty-four of them, three with smoking craters.[3]

He could have picked any guide he wanted, but only one would do: his former competitor, Jean-Antoine Carrel. Carrel brought along his nephew, Louis.

Whymper's first challenge was Chimborazo, Ecuador's tallest volcano and, once again, the highest mountain in the world, if you measure from the center of the earth. His climb on January 4, 1880, was a first ascent, surpassing the 1802 effort of Alexander von Humboldt, the naturalist and explorer who named the Avenue of the Volcanos, and the

1822 attempt by Simón Bolivar, the "liberator" of much of South America. To mark their triumph, Whymper and Carrel planted a flag.

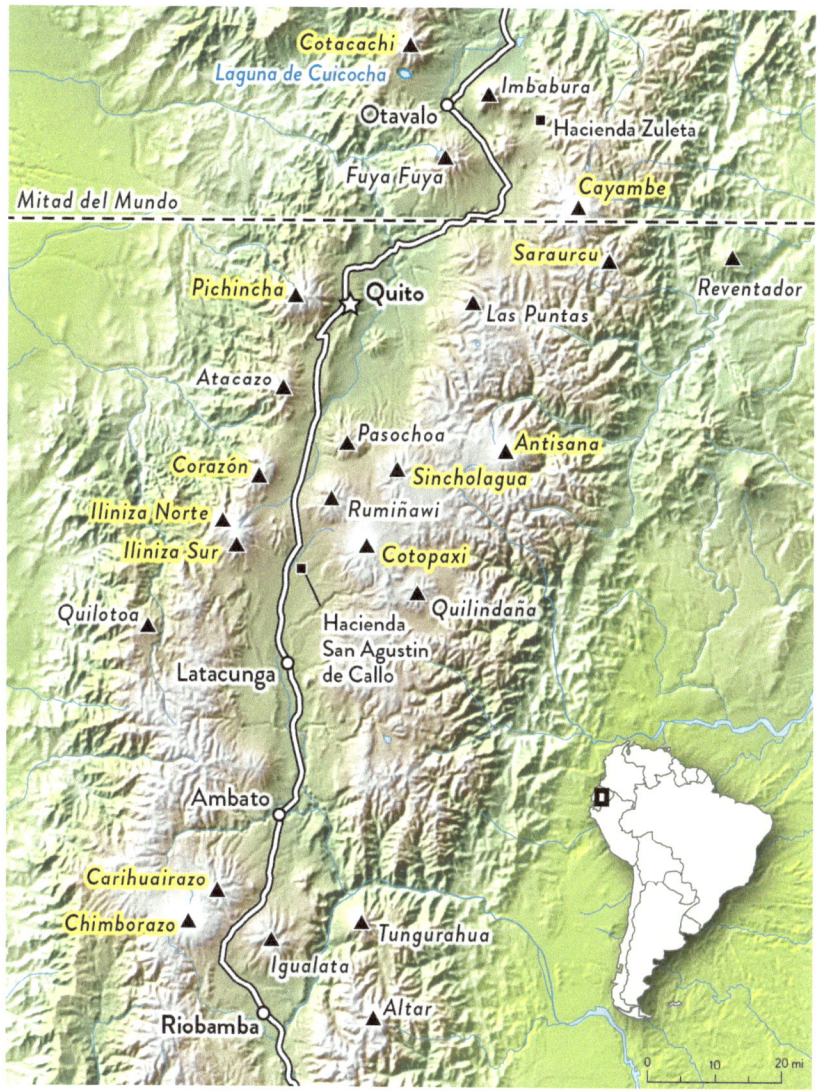

AVENUE OF THE VOLCANOES

The Heart of the Andes by Frederic Edwin Church (METROPOLITAN MUSEUM OF ART)

Chimborazo has a mythical presence. In 1859, American artist Fredric Edwin Church made it his subject in *The Heart of the Andes,* a work that established him as one of the country's foremost landscape painters, and the mountain as one of the world's most elusive destinations.[4]

You can see why.

Chimborazo is on the left, in the back, hiding.

———

Was treasure really buried in the mountain? So the natives said. In 1532, the Spanish conquistador Francisco Pizarro captured the last great Inca king. After negotiations, Pizarro agreed to free him in exchange for a room filled with gold. An Inca general was on the way with the ransom when he learned the king had been killed. In response, the general took the gold to the mountains and hid it. No one thought that foreigners would *ever* come and *not* be looking for it.

From Chimborazo, Whymper continued north, his expedition climbing a total of twelve peaks (highlighted in yellow on the map), including seven other first ascents. Crossing the equator, he went from summer to winter and back again, overnight. His climbs included the country's other highest volcanoes, Cotopaxi (where he spent a night camped out on the rim of the smoking volcano), Cayambe (located directly on the equator) and Antisana (where he hunted condors).[5] For a chronological order of his climbs in the Avenue of the Volcanoes, see Appendix II.

Did Whymper study the effects of high altitude? Of course, but when it came to prescribing a cure, he rather liked Carrel's belief that:

> For all human ills, for every complaint, from dysentery to want of air, there was, in his opinion, but one remedy; and that was Wine . . . Red Wine.[6]

As an appropriate conclusion, Whymper's final climb on the way back to the coast was a second ascent of Chimborazo. This time, he took two native witnesses (Javier Campana and David Beltram) so no one could ever dispute his claim to a first ascent of the mountain. When they reached the top, they found the flag that Whymper and Carrel had planted earlier. At almost the same time, Cotopaxi, located sixty miles away (and where they had just recently stayed overnight) erupted, turning the sun green, the sky black, and covering them in ash.[7]

Covered in Ash, Etching by Edward Whymper (PUBLIC DOMAIN)

Chimborazo is a living monument to Edward Whymper and Jean-Antoine Carrel. If you drive here for a climb, your first stop will be at the Carrel Refuge. After unloading your car, pack yourself up and go. An hour or two later, depending on your hiking speed, your next stop will be the Whymper Refuge.

As you move further along toward the summit, you may use the Whymper Route. You may pass, or stop to climb, the Whymper Needles, two spiky rock outcroppings. And you will have a choice of summits, the tallest one being the Whymper Summit.[8]

We would like to think that we have finally found Whymper and Carrel. But really, they have been here all along, just waiting for us.

Chimborazo and the Avenue of the Volcanoes have two modern-day guardians. One is a man of the land. The other is a man of the air.

Marco Cruz first climbed Mount Chimborazo when he was fourteen years old. Since then, he has scaled it almost one thousand times. He has climbed all the major peaks in Ecuador, the highest mountains in South America, and the most famous ones in the Alps. He was on the first successful Spanish Expedition to Mount Everest. And the last time we looked, he still operates his trekking company and a mountain lodge at Chimborazo Base Camp. Marco Cruz knows the mountain better than anyone else alive.[9]

Besides all that, he is, as you can see, a Keeper of the Flame.

Marco Cruz (COURTESY OF IAN MOUNT)

The True Heart of the Andes (COURTESY OF JORGE JUAN ANHALZER)

Jorge Juan Anhalzer is a man of the air. He gets into his small plane and photographs not only the volcanoes but also the "Avenue." He has made this his life's work, flying closer and closer to the true heart of the Andes.

Cruz and Anhalzer both know the secret; the treasure is not *in* the mountains; the treasure *is* the mountains.

EL CHALTÉN, PATAGONIA

*Fitzroy was a peak to climb,
Cerro Torre one to have climbed.*

— DOUG TOMPKINS

The Road Less Traveled (ROBERTO BENZI / ALAMY)

Before you can climb a mountain, you have to dream about the mountain. But you can only dream about the mountain if you know about the mountain. And that is where books come in.[1]

During the 1930s, a Catholic missionary, Alberto Maria de Agostini, explored Patagonia, taking photographs of the various glaciers and mountains that he found at *el fin del mundo* (the end of the world). He was a good photographer, and his many panoramic foldouts were assembled into a book titled *Andes Patagónicos* (1945).[2]

This book is impossible to find in the United States but, in a small convenience store in El Chaltén, we saw a copy sitting high up on the shelf behind the counter. It was just waiting, the owner said, for the right person to come along.

We weren't the first ones drawn to it. In the 1950s, a French mountain climber named Lionel Terray picked up a copy and was inspired. Having just been part of a group that made the first climb of an eight thousand meter mountain (Annapurna in 1950), he could pretty much do whatever he wanted.

And what he wanted was to climb one of the mountains photographed in the book and shown above on the right: Mount Fitz Roy.

This mountain had been named after Robert Fitz Roy, the British Captain of the *HMS Beagle*, a ship that had explored the waters off the south of Patagonia.[3]

In 1952, Terray and Guido Magnone made the first ascent of Fitz Roy. In his autobiography, *Conquistadors of the Useless* (1963), Terray called it his hardest climb:

> A great ascent is more than the sum of its severe pitches. The remoteness of Fitz Roy from all possibility of help, the almost incessant bad weather, the verglas with which it is plastered, and above all the terrible winds, which make climbing on it mortally dangerous, render its ascent more complex, hazardous, and exhausting than anything to be found in the Alps.[4]

It wasn't until 1965 that Fitz Roy was climbed again, this time by two Argentines. Three years later, one of them traveled to California where he hung out with a pair of rock-climbing, self-styled "dirt bags," Yvon Chouinard *(second from the left)* and Doug Tompkins *(on the left)* and told them of his adventures.

Chouinard and Tompkins were looking for something to do. They gathered their friends, piled their surfboards, skis, and climbing gear into a van, and spent three and one-half months driving 16,500 miles to the bottom of South America. Then they took sixty days, thirty-one of which found them pinned down in ice caves, so they could finally spend thirty hours straight getting to the top of Mount Fitz Roy and back, using a route that had never been taken before.[5]

The "Dirt Bags" and Their Van (PATAGONIA HISTORICAL ARCHIVES)

We can just imagine them talking on their way home: "Now what do we do?"

"Well," Chouinard might have said, "I really like this outdoor stuff. I think I'll create a clothing company using Fitz Roy as our logo and name it after where we just were." That's right, *Patagonia*.

"Not bad," Tompkins might have replied. "I like this outdoor stuff, too. I've already created a clothing company that I named after the hardest side of a mountain to climb."

Yes, the *North Face* is the hardest side to climb . . . in the Northern Hemisphere, where it doesn't get much sun and is cold and unfriendly. But on Fitz Roy, the winds from the Pacific Ocean sweep across the Southern Patagonia Icefield, and its west face is the most dangerous.

Forty years later, in 2008, Chouinard and Tompkins, guided by younger associates who wanted to make their own marks, repeated their trip, this time climbing a smaller mountain. They wrote a book about it and, in honor of Lionel Terray, gave it a familiar name: *180° South: Conquerors of the Useless* (2010).[6]

Useless indeed. When you get to the top of a mountain, you discover that there's nothing there. So, you go climb another one . . . which, as our opening photo shows *(on the left, this time)*, is just a couple of miles away.

Cerro Torre: it's a powerful up-thrust of granite, with a small mushroom-shaped snow cone on top. It's impossible. It's otherworldly. It's a "scream of stone."[7]

In 1959, Italian mountaineer Cesare Maestri claimed to have made its first ascent with his Austrian partner, Toni

Egger. However, coming down, Egger was swept away by an avalanche, and there were no photographs or other evidence to support Maestri's claim. Over time, more and more people came to doubt him, so he went back in 1970 to climb the mountain again.

But Maestri didn't try to re-climb his original route. He took an entirely different one. And he approached Cerro Torre in an entirely different manner: he didn't climb it, he assaulted it. He brought a gasoline-powered air compressor and jack-hammered almost four hundred bolts into the side of the mountain so that he could proceed safely on a rope from bolt to bolt. When he was finished, as a last show of contempt, he left the compressor hanging on the side of the mountain.[8]

The world's climbing community went nuts: "Rape, Pillage, Desecration, Sacrilege." "You Have Murdered the Impossible." "You Did Not Climb by Fair Means."[9]

Left Hanging on Cerro Torre (LINCOLN ELSE / NOVUS SELECT)

Still, the route became the usual way to get to the top. Known, as you might expect, as the "Compressor Route," everyone used it for more than forty years — until 2012.

Then, two North American climbers got to the top without using the bolts and, on the way down, cut most of them off, destroying an historic route.

As for the climbing community? Many of them were set off again; "Taliban on Cerro Torre." [10]

El Chaltén is a small frontier town still not shown on many maps. Founded in 1985 to help Argentina in a border dispute with Chile, it has since become the trekking and climbing capital of the country. Although we don't even qualify as hikers, we did go for a look. We had two choices.

First, we could hike to Laguna de Los Tres. It is long and hard, sixteen miles roundtrip, and takes eight to ten hours. However, there is a lookout only ninety minutes outside of town, Mirador Fitz Roy. On a clear day, it has a good-enough view of Mount Fitz Roy to justify both continuing on and turning back. But if it's raining, find something else to do.[13]

We chose the second, a hike to Campo de Agostini, named after the Catholic missionary photographer. It is the most popular hike from El Chaltén, and although it is fifteen miles roundtrip, it takes only six to seven hours. Again, there is a turnaround spot only ninety minutes from town, Mirador Torre, with a great view of Cerro Torre. If it's clear, why not walk forward to see more? If it's foggy or cloudy, it's time to turn back. But for us, it was raining, and we wondered what we were doing there in the first place.

TWO CLASSIC HIKES FROM EL CHALTÉN

Even though El Chaltén is in the middle of nowhere at the bottom of South America, it's not that far away.

We took an early evening flight from Philadelphia to Miami, an overnight from there to Buenos Aires, switched to the domestic airport, caught an afternoon flight to El Calafate, got a car and, three hours later, arrived at El Chaltén in time for dinner.

What if you live in Seattle? Easy. Catch the noon flight to Dallas, and then the overnight from Dallas to Buenos Aires. You will arrive early the next day, with plenty of time to catch the domestic flight to El Calafate.

If you are coming from London, leave at night. With the time difference, you, too, will arrive in Buenos Aires early the next morning. Then, just keep going.

EL CHALTÉN, PATAGONIA | 108

SOUTHERN PATAGONIA AND TIERRA DEL FUEGO

Last, but not least, what if you start in Beijing? Leave in the afternoon. You will cross the date line and arrive in Dallas the same day you left. Then, continue on with the folks from Seattle.

So, wherever you live, you can, like us, probably get there by tomorrow.

THANK YOU

Let's go back to Chouinard and Tompkins.

These guys started with nothing. And they both created billion-dollar businesses without selling their souls. In fact, their businesses enabled them to fulfill their missions. They were the yin and yang of environmentalism, and best friends all their lives.

Yvon Chouinard (TERRY STRAEHLEY / SHUTTERSTOCK)

Doug Tompkins (MCT / GETTY IMAGES)

Yvon Chouinard spent fifty years building Patagonia. Along the way, the company constantly campaigned against climate change, donated to grass-roots environmental activists, protected undeveloped land, and promoted self-sustaining products. And yes, they sold a lot of them.

In 2022, the Chouinard family didn't sell their three-billion-dollar company, they gave it away . . . to a nonprofit organization that will continue their work. As they have come to say: "The Earth is now our only shareholder."[11]

Doug Tompkins did it differently. He sold his companies, North Face and then Esprit, and with the proceeds bought land, land, and more land, millions and millions of acres in Chilean and Argentine Patagonia. Independently, or with governments and other landowners, he turned the land into fifteen national parks and two marine parks. He officially designated as "protected" more than fourteen million land and twenty million sea acres. He launched over twenty conservation projects, reintroduced thirteen species (and eight jaguar cubs) into their natural, "rewilded" habitats.[12] And, if he ever needed money, Yvon sent it.

We don't know of any two people who have done more to save our planet and encourage others to do the same than Chouinard and Tompkins.

Thank you, gentlemen.

ABIQUIU, NEW MEXICO

Theology? Theology is what you do.

— GHOST RANCH JOURNAL

The Ghost Ranch Sign (B HAMMOND/ALAMY)

From an unsettled Spanish Land Grant, to a cliff-protected hideout for cattle rustlers, to an abandoned, rattlesnake-infested wreck won in a poker game, to a dude ranch for Princeton millionaires, to a source of artistic inspiration, to a weekend getaway for top-secret physicists inventing the atomic bomb, to a hunting ground for two-hundred-million-year-old dinosaurs, to the Presbyterian retreat (and occasional movie set) it is today, the Ghost Ranch, located just an hour and a half outside Santa Fe, has been many things to many people.[1]

Pueblo Indians were the first humans to roam northern New Mexico — home of the Ghost Ranch — beginning thousands of years ago. More recently, Navajo, Apache, and Plains Indians used the area for hunting.

Then, in the 1700s, Conquistadores followed the Rio Grande north and claimed the territory for Spain. In return, the Crown rewarded a military captain with a fifty-thousand-acre land grant, covering what would become the Ghost Ranch, but he never took possession.

Next came the outlaws. In the 1880s, when the West was still wild and the Badlands were just that, two brothers stumbled upon Yeso Canyon. It was perfect for hiding stolen cattle. There was one trail in and out, which was easily guarded by riflemen watching from high on the cliffs on either side. They could see approaching riders coming a mile away, either from their horses' dust or from their profiles against the horizon.

Feeling safe, the brothers built two dwellings for themselves and called the place "Rancho de les Brujos," or "Ranch of the Witches." They used it as the base from which to conduct their raids. One brother even had a wife and child, both of whom were virtual prisoners. Finally, one brother killed the other in a fight over hidden gold. The wife and child escaped, and a returning posse hung the surviving brother from a nearby cottonwood tree.

Yeso Canyon thus became a place to avoid. However, in 1918, a descendant of the brothers filed a homestead claim, only to promptly sell the property to someone, who promptly sold it to someone else, who promptly lost it in a poker game to someone who gave it to his wife, who, after they divorced in 1931, moved in.

To support herself, she turned it into a dude ranch. She changed the name from Ranch of the Witches to "Ghost Ranch." She hung an ox skull on the sign at the entrance. She had good ideas, but she struggled.[2]

———

Arthur Newton Pack. An easterner from Princeton, New Jersey, he went west in 1933 with his wife and three children because one of the children needed a dry climate to improve her health.

Pack had inherited both a fortune and a philosophy. His grandfather had been a lumber millionaire, owning the largest sawmill in the Northwest. His father learned selective cutting and reseeding while visiting the Black Forest in Germany. With his "use/rest/reseed" practices, he led his own profitable crusade to save America's forests.

Pack followed in their footsteps. With his father he founded the American Nature Association and its publication, *Nature Magazine*, which had one hundred thousand subscribers, quite a lot for the 1930s. The Association, along with the National Geographic Society, helped lead the conservation movement in the United States.

In 1933, Pack and his family needed a new place to live. They heard about the Ghost Ranch and came out for a look. One night, one night under the stars; that's all it took. This was what they'd dreamed about. The next day they bought a building site and started construction. Six months later, they moved into a house they called "Rancho de los Burros."[3]

Children on Burros (MCKINLEY/PACK COLLECTION/GHOST RANCH ARCHIVES)

It was named after the animals his three children used for transportation.

Pack had money and, trying to help, loaned some to the Ghost Ranch's owner to keep it afloat. But this was the Great Depression, and she still couldn't afford to maintain the place. So, in 1935, Pack bought the ranch and what would become twenty thousand acres. He woke up the day after his purchase and found himself in the tourist business.

Pack marketed both the Ghost Ranch's natural beauty and his philosophy. It would not become an artificial "dude" ranch with a golf course or tennis courts (although there was a swimming pool). He wanted it to remain a "real" working ranch where one enjoyed nature and wilderness.

His regular guests included his Princeton friends. Among them were the Johnson brothers of BAND-AID fame, a Rockefeller relative, and the airplane pioneer Charles Lindbergh. They reveled in the simple life. The Johnsons invited many people, and had only one condition for invitees: "the first guy who talks about business goes home."[4]

Pack's Ranch guests also included a certain woman whose name would become synonymous with desert painting: Georgia O'Keeffe.

Pedernal (ANN MOORE / ALAMY)

From her first visit in 1934, she, like Pack, simply had to live at the Ranch. Once there, she wanted to be alone, and Pack let her. She was free to see, to feel, and to paint, particularly Mount Pedernal, which was sitting right in her front yard.

She also loved to paint the cliffs out back.

ABIQUIU, NEW MEXICO | 116

The Cliffs Out Back (LIZ COUGHLAN / ALAMY)

My Backyard, 1937, by Georgia O'Keeffe (© 2023 GEORGIA O'KEEFFE MUSEUM / ARTISTS RIGHTS SOCIETY (ARS), NEW YORK)[5]

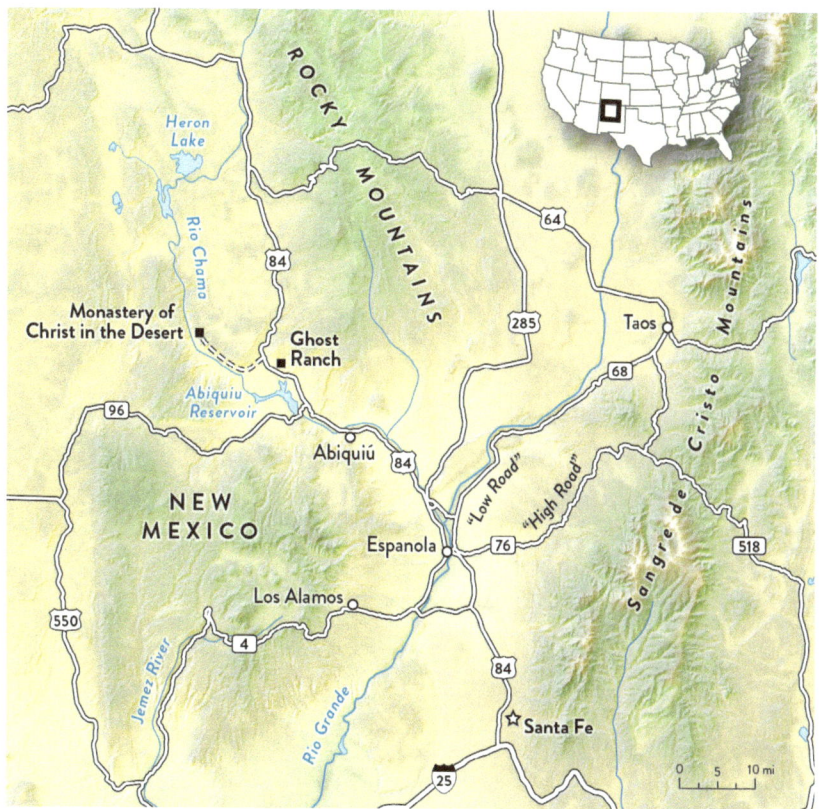

AREA AROUND THE RANCH

Then, in 1940, Pack sold her the Ranch of the Burros and seven surrounding acres, the first house she had ever owned. By the time she moved in, World War II had begun. She had thought that World War I was the War to End All Wars. It wasn't, but maybe a new weapon would be.

When the U.S. Government began to develop the atomic bomb, the Manhattan Project had certain key criteria for its location: isolation, controlled access, little or no local population, adequate water, moderate climate, west of the

Mississippi and at least two hundred miles from an international border or the Pacific Ocean. Put them all together and they spelled "New Mexico." [6]

In October 1942, the government seized the Los Alamos Boys Ranch School and began its two-billion-dollar project. It was hard, lonely, secret work, and neighbors wondered what was going on. Was it a home for pregnant WACs, a nudist colony, or a secret base for submarines?

Los Alamos was only thirty miles from the Ghost Ranch. It didn't take long for the government to come calling. Might its scientists use the ranch for rest and relaxation? Everything would be hush-hush and no guest names could ever be known. Of course, Pack agreed.

The Trinity Detonation, July 16, 1945 (JACK AEBY / PUBLIC DOMAIN)

And so, beginning in the summer of 1943, Robert Oppenheimer and his fellow scientists became regulars at the ranch, spending many a weekend just staring at the cliffs. It wasn't until July 16, 1945, that the product of their research was tested. It worked.

Three weeks later, it worked again at Hiroshima and then one more time at Nagasaki.

A whole new world had begun—the Nuclear Age.

———

However, a visitor who stares at the Ghost Ranch cliffs isn't staring at the future, but at the past.

Geologists measure time vertically, with the oldest era at the bottom and the youngest at the top, just as new rock formations are deposited on top of old ones. Eras are then subdivided into periods and periods into epochs.

At the Ghost Ranch, therefore, while the cliffs look like a painting, they are also a geologic table. They reveal the three periods of the Mesozoic Era, the second-to-last era of the earth's geologic history. From the bottom up, they are the Triassic, Jurassic, and Cretaceous periods.

———

Indeed, you just knew those cliffs were hiding something. After World War II ended, a different type of scientist arrived, hoping to find it. Edwin H. Colbert, a paleontologist from the American Museum of Natural History, was traveling to the Petrified Forest in Arizona. He had obtained a rare government permit to dig there for dinosaur bones. On the way, he and his friends decided to stop off at the Ghost Ranch for a little fossil prospecting. Lo and behold, in late June 1947, they discovered what became "the greatest find ever made in the Triassic of North America."[7]

Working in a quarry not far from the Ghost Ranch's dining hall and swimming pool, Colbert and friends discovered hundreds of Coelophysis skeletons. A dinosaur from the Triassic period, Coelophysis was far older than the gigantic dinosaurs of *Jurassic Park* fame. Colbert found bones from specimens of all different ages, ranging from the newly born, to the fully grown, to the elderly.

Digging there during 1947 and 1948, Colbert's team cut and removed thirteen fossilized blocks, which were transported to the American Museum of Natural History, the Yale Peabody Museum, and other institutions for analysis and reassembly.

As shown here, they were even used as models for a New York City subway station display.

The Fossil in the Subway (THE AMERICAN NATURAL HISTORY MUSEUM)

Colbert had succeeded beyond his wildest dreams. And Pack thought all that digging was fine since it didn't damage the swimming pool.

None of us can be on the stage forever, and it is the wise man who anticipates the end. So, too, with Arthur Pack. He thought of giving the Ghost Ranch to his children — he had five of his own and adopted three more. But he knew that none of them could afford to take over, and he didn't want to burden them.[8]

Pack believed the ranch was a spiritual, magical place. He looked for an organization that shared his vision and would be able to continue it. He thought of giving the property to the YMCA or the Boy Scouts of America but twenty thousand acres — larger than the island of Manhattan — was a lot of responsibility. Finally, in 1955, he chose the Presbyterian Church. It would turn the Ghost Ranch into an education center and retreat, but *not* a luxury resort. Nature and wilderness would remain the central attractions.

Only one person was displeased. As the deal was being signed, in walked Georgia O'Keeffe:

> Arthur, what's this I hear about your giving the Ranch away?! If you were going to do that, why didn't you give it to me?![9]

But she knew better. She knew the ranch would need financial angels to support it and really, what she most wanted was to be alone and paint. Indeed, she remained at the ranch until she died at age 98, lovingly calling it the "Faraway Nearby."

Yes, the Presbyterians still own and operate the Ghost Ranch, right out there on Highway 84. It has also been the set for some notable western movies: *Silverado* (1985), *City Slickers* (1991), *Wyatt Earp* (1994), *Wild Wild West* (1999), *The Lone Ranger* (2013), and most recently, *Hostiles* (2017).

A trip there makes for a very nice, quiet, long weekend.[10] We combined our visit to the ranch with a trip to Santa Fe and Taos. It was a great week.

Arthur Newton Pack. He had money, and he used it well. He rescued a failing dude ranch. He allowed a desert artist to make part of it her home. He welcomed government researchers during wartime. He permitted other scientists to remove invaluable artifacts. In the end, he found a worthy successor to carry on his dream.

Theology *is* what you do.

Arthur Newton Pack with Baby Antelope (MCKINLEY/PACK COLLECTION / GHOST RANCH ARCHIVES)

TAKANAWA, JAPAN

Kaze sasou hana yori mo nao ware wa mata
haru no nagori o ikani toka sen
The wind seems to lure away the cherry blossoms as well,
but I — how shall I deal with what remains of spring?

—ASANO TAKUMINOKAMI NAGANORI, FEUDAL LORD OF AKO

Lord Asano (CPA MEDIA PTE LTD / ALAMY)

What would you do if your lord and master were ordered to take his own life?

In March 1701, Asano Takuminokami Naganori, the feudal lord of Ako in the Japanese province of Harima, was called to serve at the shogun's castle in what is now Tokyo. As a man from the countryside, he was unskilled in court etiquette. Accordingly, Lord Kira Kozukenosuke Yoshinaka, the castle's master of ceremonies, was assigned to teach him the proper protocol.

Lord Kira was arrogant and corrupt. He tried to seduce Lord Asano's wife. He solicited bribes. When he failed at both, he became relentless with his false instructions, making Lord Asano look the fool. Kira's insults were even worse, calling Lord Asano a frog, making him kneel before him and tie his shoelaces, and then tapping him on the chest with his fan.

Finally, on March 14, 1701, Lord Asano couldn't take it anymore. He attacked Kira in the Great Corridor of Pines, a celebrated hallway in the castle. He tried to kill, but only slightly wounded him. Nevertheless, Lord Asano had drawn his sword in the shogun's castle. This was a capital offense.

At that time, there was a judicial principal known as *kenka ryoseibai*: in a quarrel, both parties are equally to blame. Nevertheless, it was only Lord Asano who was punished. He was ordered to commit *seppuku* (suicide), and to do it in an open yard like a commoner rather than in a private room like a lord. Still, his death poem, rendered above, expressed his understated nobility.

All of Lord Asano's lands were forfeited, his *samurai* were dismissed, becoming unemployed, masterless, *ronin*. For many, this one-sided result was quite unfair.[1]

Oishi Kuranosuke Yoshio was the head of Lord Asano's samurai. He met with his men to determine how they should react to their lord's forced suicide and loss of lands. Some argued for peacefully surrendering their castle and dispersing. After all, this was what the shogun had ordered. Some argued for fighting the government forces and then killing themselves as the castle fell. Some argued for immediately attacking and trying to kill Lord Kira, even though he had reinforced his security, and they would surely die in the attempt. While they may have disagreed about the proper response, they all believed:

> a man may not live under the same heaven as the murderer of his Lord.[2]

Ultimately, Kuranosuke and the ronin decided that they would surrender Lord Asano's castle, pretend to disperse, and plot to kill Kira.[3] They became farmers, drunkards, pleasure seekers, and beggars, all biding their time until their enemy let down his guard.

Kuranosuke had the hardest role to play. He was the leader, and he knew that Kira's spies would be watching him closely. He left his home, divorced his wife, moved into the red-light district, and immersed himself in a life of utter debauchery.

His performance was so convincing that one night, as he lay drunk in the street, a man from Satsuma came up to him and spit in his face, decrying him as a faithless beast, unworthy of the name "samurai."[4]

The Night Raid by Kuniyoshi (WILLIAM PEARL / THE KUNIYOSHI PROJECT)

One year and nine months passed. Kira became convinced that the ronin were no longer a threat and relaxed. Then, on the night of December 14, 1702, Kuranosuke and his fifteen-year-old son, Oishi Chikara, at the head of Forty-Seven Ronin, attacked and conquered Lord Kira's castle, killing sixteen men and wounding twenty-two.[5]

They found Lord Kira hiding in a coal shed, pulled him out and offered him the chance to redeem his honor by committing seppuku, using Lord Asano's sword.

When he refused, Kuranosuke cut off his head.

The Forty-Seven Ronin, as they came to be known, put Kira's head in a bag, and walked the nine miles from his castle to Sengaku-Ji, a Buddhist temple in Takanawa, where Lord Asano was buried. They washed the head in a well located on the grounds, and laid it at their master's grave.[6]

Having completed their mission, they immediately laid down their arms, turned themselves in to the authorities, and awaited sentencing.

47 Ronin (2013) (PHOTO 12 / ALAMY)

It did not come quickly. The shogun and his advisers were torn: the Forty-Seven Ronin had fulfilled their duty to their lord. They had been loyal, faithful, and true. They had exhibited the highest virtues of a samurai. Public sentiment was strongly in their favor. But they had broken the peace and the law.

In the end, their punishment was death, not as criminals but as samurai, and by their own hands. On February 4, 1703, all forty-seven committed seppuku, asking only to be buried with their lord.

Their group suicide shook the country. In a land that had been at peace for one hundred years, the Forty-Seven Ronin had shown that the samurai warrior spirit still lived. They had become stars that, though invisible by day, shone brightly at night.[7] They were no longer ronin, they were *gishi* (righteous warriors).

Less than two weeks after Kuranosuke and the others died, *bunraku* (puppet plays) sprang up in Tokyo to tell the story. After only three performances. the government closed them down. Why? The shogun worried the plays would incite people to rebel.

The plays returned quickly but were set in a different time and place, with ever so slightly different characters. For example, Kuranosuke was no longer "Oishi Kuranosuke": he became "Oboshi Yuranosuke." The theme, however, was still the same: loyalty, honor, and duty.

In time, the puppet plays were replaced by more dramatic and stylized *Kabuki* productions, in which actors sang, danced, and stomped their way through the story. In 1748, *Kanadehon Chushingura*, an eleven-act play, became the standard.[8] Its performance lasted an entire day, but audiences brought their own food and stayed for it all. As for actors, the single most desired role in all of Kabuki was that of Oboshi Yuranosuke, the leader of the Forty-Seven Ronin.

Three hundred years later, *The Story of the Loyal Retainers* is still so universally loved that struggling Kabuki theaters often perform it in order to save their finances. So beloved, in fact, that during the American occupation of Japan after World War II, it was banned because it glorified, honor, loyalty, and revenge.

The Forty-Seven Ronin became stars of nineteenth-century Japanese woodblock prints. Artists such as Hokusai, Hiroshige, and Kuniyoshi not only depicted the story *(Kuniyoshi's "Night Raid" is shown above)* but also offered individual portraits of the heroes.[9] For a list of their names, see Appendix III.

The literature about them, even in English, is almost never ending. Beginning with Mitford's "Story of the Forty-Seven Ronin" in *Tales of Old Japan* (1871), it has continued through graphic art depictions such as *Ehon Chushingura Jikki* (1886), and translations by Jukichi Inouye (1910) and his son Tozo (1937), Sakae Shioya (pre- and post-World War II) and Donald Keene (1971).[10]

And the movies, the movies. There were at least thirty-four Japanese productions during the twentieth century. Three American films recently joined them: *Ronin* (1998) starring Robert De Niro, *47 Ronin* (2013) with Keanu Reeves, and *Last Knights* (2015) with Morgan Freeman and Clive Owen.

People just can't get enough of this story. And why should they, for to know *Chushingura* is to know Japan.

Takanawa is an unassuming area on the outskirts of Tokyo. If you take the Asakusa subway line and get off at Stop A 07, Sengaku-Ji, it is a short, one-block, uphill walk to the temple. We had to go. It's why we went to Japan in the first place.

Sengaku-Ji (Spring Hill Temple) is quiet, empty, and reserved. When we visited, no more than a dozen people were there. Most of them had sticks of burning incense, which they left after praying at each grave. We could buy postcards, a stamp confirming our visit, and souvenirs in a shop just outside.

As we entered the grounds, we were greeted by a statue: noble, dignified, and confident. It was Kuranosuke, welcoming us to his lord's temple. There we stood, staring up at him. Cast in bronze, he wears a traditional coat and a furrowed brow. In his hands, he holds a scroll bearing the names of the forty-seven.

TAKANAWA, JAPAN | *131*

TOKYO

TAKANAWA, JAPAN | 132

The Sengaku-Ji Temple Main Gate (SENGAKU-JI TEMPLE)

Oishi Kuranosuke (COWARDLION / SHUTTERSTOCK)

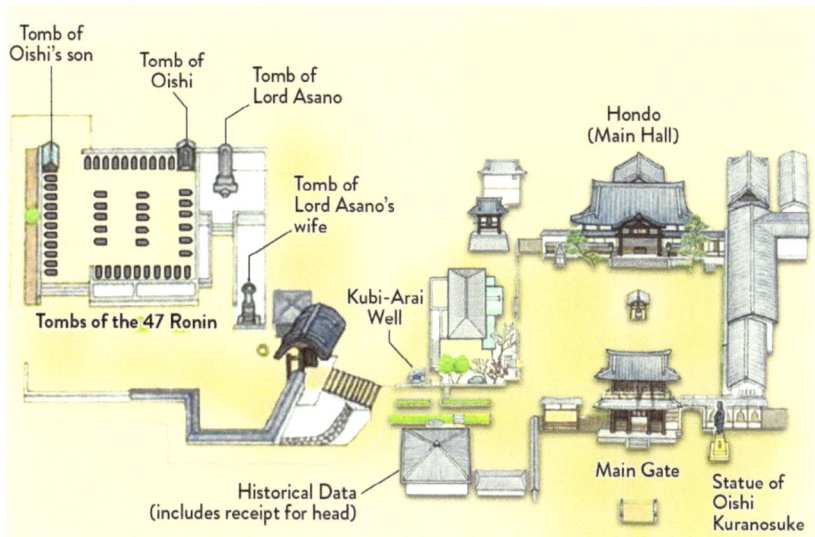

Sengaku-Ji, Burial Site of the Forty-Seven Ronin (DRAWING BY ERIN GREB)

Tomb of Lord Asano (PUBLIC DOMAIN)

The Graves of the Forty-Seven Ronin (TRAVEL/ALAMY)

We passed him. We passed the well where Kira's head was washed. We passed the headstones of Lord Asano and his wife.

To the left in the back, inside a small fenced-in square, we found the Forty-Seven Ronin, resting in peace.[11]

We took plenty of time paying our respects, and asking ourselves . . . could *we* ever be as loyal and brave as they? [12]

Could *you*?

VILLNÖSS, SOUTH TYROL

Two yetis in the high mountains
were sitting around talking,
when Reinhold Messner walked by.
"See," said one yeti to the other, "he does exist."

— PETRA ÜBERBACHER

Villnöss / Val di Funes (BRIAN JANNSEN / ALAMY)

Here. How could you grow up here and *not* dream of becoming a mountain climber?

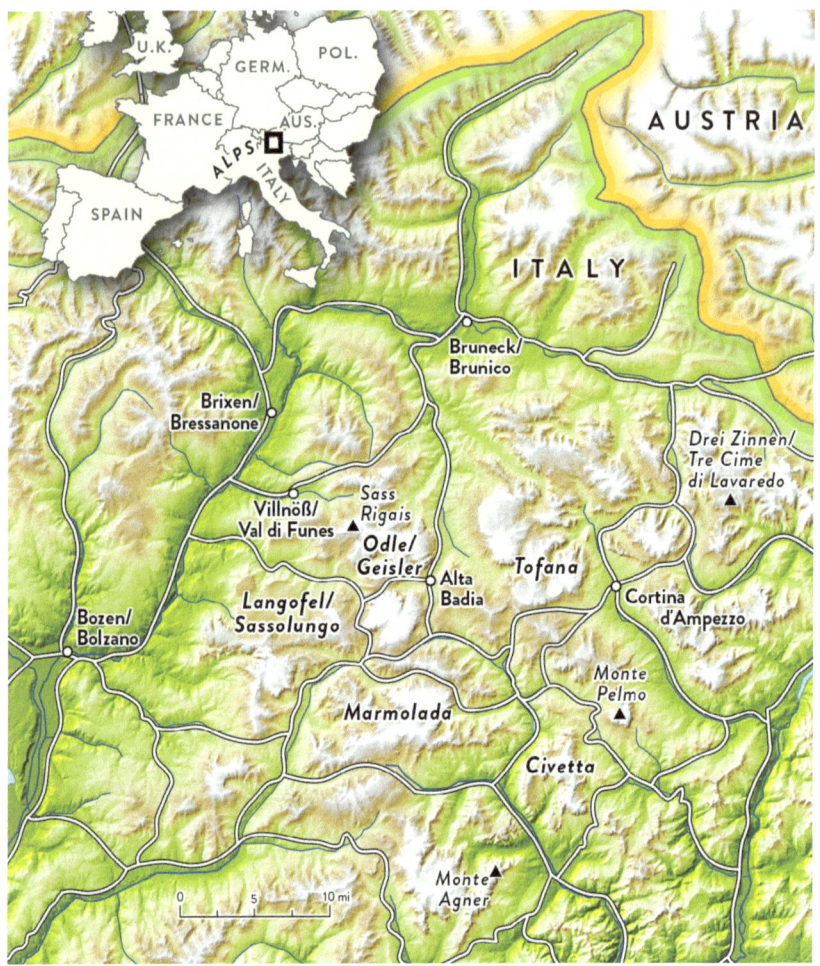

THE DOLOMITES

Here is where Reinhold Messner, the greatest mountain climber in history, was born and raised.

Here is where he learned to climb. For him, it was quite simple: always have three firm holds, two hand holds and a foot, or two foot holds and a hand. He practiced anywhere he could, at home on the stairs, on a churchyard wall, or on a rock in a streambed.[1]

Here is where he climbed his first mountain, at age five. It was Sass Rigais, the one with the rounded peak just to the left of center in the opening photo. It was right in his backyard.

Here are the Dolomites, a series of strange and spectacular spires *(see the photo again)* in Northern Italy *(now see the map)*. Think of them as a continuation of the Alps, only better.

Here is where you can be in two places at the same time. If you speak German (as 70 percent of the people do) you are in Villnöss, South Tyrol. If you speak Italian, you are in Val di Funes, Italy. Every city, every town has two names: "Bozen" and "Bolzano," "Brixen" and "Bressanone," "Bruneck" and "Brunico."

Here is where you can climb two mountains at once. Sass Rigais is part of the Odle or the Geisler, take your pick. You can climb Langofel or Sassolungo. You can summit Drei Zinnen or Tre Cime di Lavaredo, the most famous rock formation in the Dolomites *(shown below)*.[2] Just remember, even though you can climb two mountains at once, you can never climb the same mountain twice.

left: Drei Zinnen (ROBERTO MOIOLA / SYSAWORLD / GETTY IMAGES)
right: Tre Cime di Laverado (BUENA VISTA IMAGES / GETTY IMAGES)

Here is where Messner began to think about mountain climbing. Reaching the summit was not enough. He had to get there the right way. This could be by taking the hardest route, up an unconquered face, over an uncrossed edge, along an untouched ridge. This could be by using the simplest equipment, climbing quickly in "alpine style" rather than slowly as if making a "siege." Above all, this had to be by "fair means." [3]

Here is where he tested himself. He followed the classic routes and then found his own way. He followed the line that the mountain offered, instead of forcing a new one upon it. He looked for the *direttissima*, the most direct way to the top. He climbed solo, untying his rope and risking all. He climbed the hardest side of the mountain. He climbed during winter, in the worst conditions.

By 1969, at age twenty-five, he had made fifty first ascents and twenty solos. People thought he was crazy. He thought he was ready.[4]

There. To become the greatest mountain climber, one must climb the greatest mountains. There are none greater than those in Pakistan and Nepal. And, of these, there are none greater than the "Fourteen Eight-Thousanders," the fourteen mountains higher than eight thousand meters (i.e., 26,247 feet), the fourteen tallest mountains in the world above sea level. For a list of them, by height, see the map. For their climbing chronology, see Appendix IV.

Why are they called "eight-thousanders?" History and aesthetics. It was the French who first climbed an "eight-thousander," Annapurna (in 1950), and they used meters, not feet, as their standard of measure. In addition, which is the more attractive and memorable number: eight thousand or 26,247?

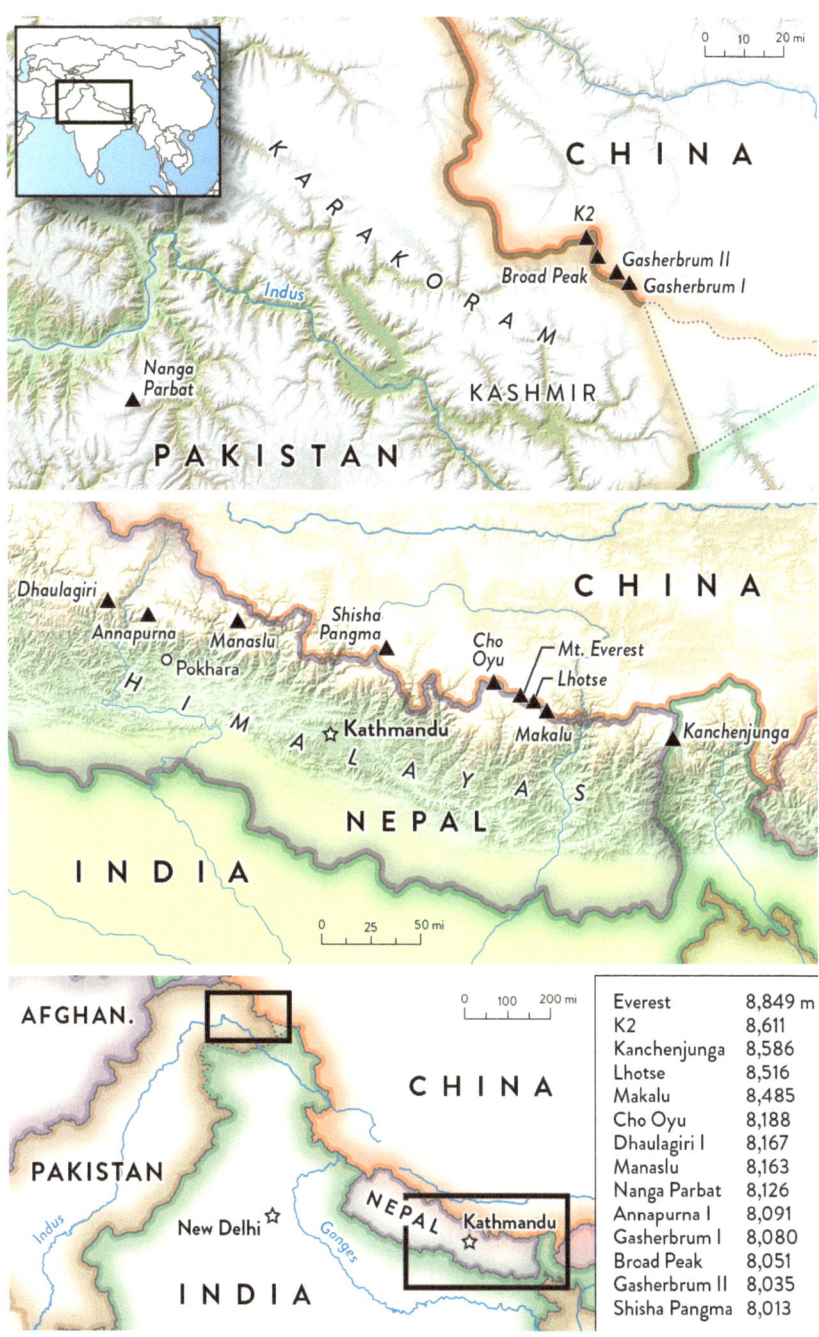

THE FOURTEEN EIGHT-THOUSANDERS

There. Messner had not given much thought to climbing an eight-thousander. He knew that the Alps and Dolomites had become too small for him, but he was a South Tyrolean, not a German, not an Austrian, not an Italian. He doubted that any national expedition, the way that the big mountains were climbed then, would invite him along.

As a result, he was surprised, when, in 1970, he was asked to join a German group preparing to climb Nanga Parbat, the "German" eight-thousander, so called because its first climbers had been German. He was even more surprised, and happily so, when his brother Gunther was invited as well.

Reinhold might not have gone if he had known what would happen. He and Gunther climbed the dangerous "Rupal Face" on the south side of Nanga Parbat, the highest ice and rock wall face in the world, almost three times the size of any face in Europe. They were the first to summit this way. But, during the descent, Gunther was lost in an avalanche, Reinhold was stuck on the mountain for five nights, two of them madly searching for Gunther, and, by the time he was finally saved, he had lost seven frost-bitten toes and three fingers.

And then he was blamed for Gunther's death.[5]

It took Reinhold six months to recover, during which time he realized that, after the amputations, he no longer could get footholds and thus wasn't any good on rock. He would have to be a mountain climber . . . and he would go back for the big ones.

He did. He went back, and back, and back. One by one, he climbed each and every eight-thousander. He climbed them in his own style, alpine, quickly, without a ton of supplies, without a caravan of porters. The less the better, the fewer the better, the faster the better.

He climbed solo. He climbed without oxygen. Indeed, in 1980, when he climbed Mount Everest for the second time, he climbed it solo, without oxygen, and in the middle of a monsoon. In fact, conditions were so bad that he was the only person even on the mountain.

There. It took him sixteen years, sixteen years of repeated failure and fresh starts, sixteen years, beginning in 1970. When he finally climbed Lhotse in October 1986, he became the first person in history to have climbed all fourteen eight thousand meter mountains.[6]

And everywhere. If you are going to climb the greatest mountains in the world, you have to climb not only the greatest mountains *in* the world, but also the greatest mountains *all over* the world (i.e., the tallest mountain on each and every continent). That would be seven.

THE SEVEN (?) SUMMITS

The "Seven Summits," then, is the second great mountain-climbing paradigm. These peaks may not be as tall as the eight-thousanders, but they offer a global challenge, with travel and logistical issues as great as, if not greater than, the climbs themselves. For a list of these and their climbing chronology, see Appendix V. Could Messner do two things at once? As he climbed the Fourteen, he scaled the Seven. He worked six months a year, lived on nothing, raised money, and then climbed.

Not surprisingly, when he climbed, he refused to take the easy way. For Mount Aconcagua, the tallest mountain in South America, it had to be a first ascent up the South Buttress to the highest face in the New World. In January 1974, he struggled to the top, passing a mummified llama and the remains of a fallen climber.[7]

Messner was not alone in his quest. Others were also trying to be the first to climb the Seven Summits. Chief among them were Dick Bass and Frank Wells, two American self-funding millionaires, and Pat Morrow, a quiet Canadian.[8]

Messner also knew that there was a debate as to which mountains really were the Seven Summits. In Europe, if the line with Asia were drawn politically, its tallest mountain was Mont Blanc in France. However, if a geological border were used, the tallest was Mount Elbrus, even though it was in the Caucasus (i.e., Russia). Messner's solution: climb them both.

In Australia, the issue was similar: what is a "continent?" Is it the Australian mainland, in which case the tallest mountain is Mount Kosciuszko, a relative walk in the park? Or is it the entire Continental Shelf, which includes Papua New Guinea, with its highest mountain, the far more treacherous Carstensz Pyramid?[9] Again, when in doubt, Messner topped them both.

Everywhere. No matter how one defines "continent," when Messner climbed Antarctica's tallest mountain, Mount Vinson, in December 1986, just two months after finishing off all the fourteen eight-thousanders, he became the first person in history to have climbed *both* the Fourteen *and* the Seven.

Nowhere. Reinhold Messner was sitting on top of the world. He was the King of the Mountains. What would he do next?

He would find the yeti, whether he existed or not. Beginning in 1986, he spent twelve years searching, first in Tibet, then in Nepal, in the Hindu Kush, in Bhutan, in Mongolia, and then back in Tibet.

Reinhold Messner (MAURITIUS IMAGES GMBH / ALAMY)

What was he looking for? The Abominable Snowman, a demon, a monster, a Himalayan King Kong. A snow-covered animal that climbs up rock faces and glaciers, that survives in the high-altitude wilderness, that's wild and hairy and thick-skinned and leaves huge footprints, even though the toes may have been amputated.

Nowhere. Messner was the man who kept asking everyone about the yeti, only to discover, at the end, that he was looking for . . . himself.[10]

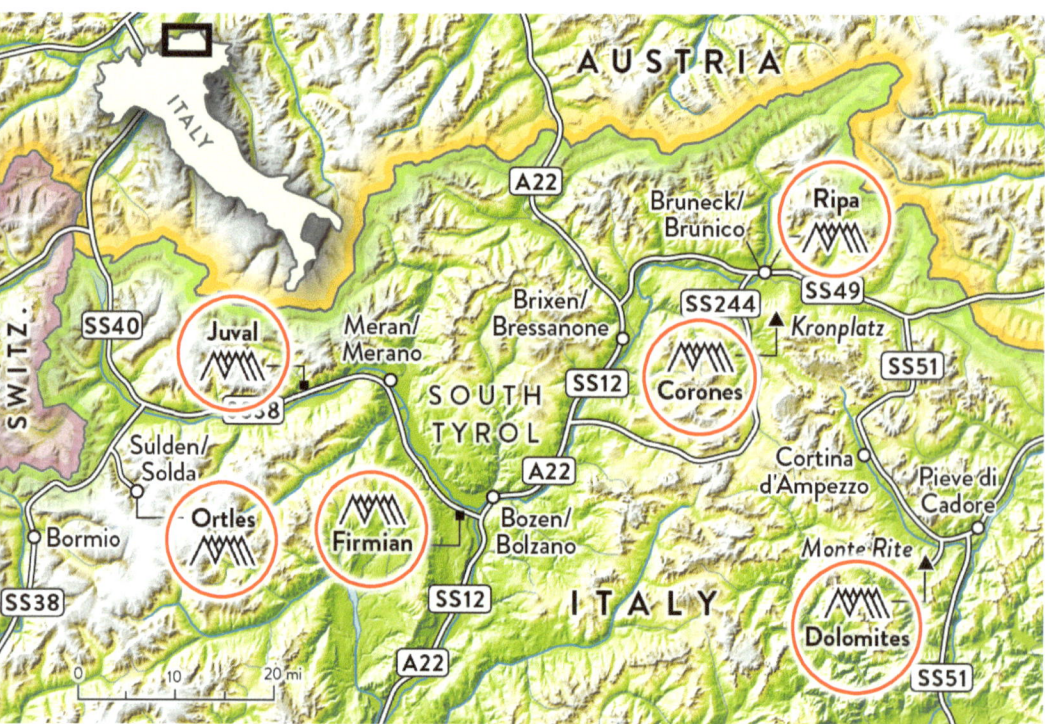

The Six Messner Mountain Museums (MMM) in South Tyrol

The Castle on a Hill (IMAGE PROFESSIONALS GMBH/ALAMY)

Back again. Reinhold Messner is back in South Tyrol. He says he's just a storyteller now, but he's built six Messner Mountain Museums (MMM) to tell his tales.

We visited them as a way to organize our trip through the Dolomites. MMM Juval, our first stop, is a castle on a hill that doubles as his summer residence. Opened in 1995, it focuses on mountains as places of magic and mystery. We had been told he was so crazy that he had hand and foot holds on his living room ceiling so he could climb across it upside down. He wasn't that crazy; they were on his basement ceiling, in the room where he kept his climbing equipment.

To our surprise, Messner was home. He was quite gracious and gave us a personal tour. He even told us how he came to buy the place. When he learned it was for sale, he hired an agent to represent him, fearing that if the seller knew he wanted it, the price would only go up. Instead, his agent found that the seller was unwilling to sell to just another guy with money; he wanted to sell to a South Tyrolean, and, in fact, there was only one South Tyrolean he wanted to sell to, and that was Reinhold Messner. It made for a happy transaction.

Each of the other Messner Museums has its own particular theme. MMM Dolomites, opened in 2002, is a museum in the clouds devoted to rock. MMM Ortles (2004), an underground museum, is devoted to ice. MMM Ripa (2011), a hauntingly beautiful castle, focuses on mountain peoples. The centerpiece of his museums is MMM Firmian, located at Sigmundskron Castle in Bozen, also known, of course, as Bolzano. It opened in 2006 and focuses on the history and art of mountain climbing. Finally, Messner's most recent museum, MMM Corones (2015), is devoted to the discipline of mountaineering.[11]

Do we have a favorite artwork of all those displayed? Absolutely. It's in MMM Ortles. Should you visit, look for a window with a wooden shutter covering it. Open the shutter, and it triggers the video of a raging avalanche, quickly advancing, just about to overwhelm you. The artwork's title? *Shit Happens*.

Messner considers his museums to be his "Fifteenth Eight-Thousander." It makes for a good story. We think, however, that his life is a better one.

AL-AIN, UNITED ARAB EMIRATES

I went there with a belief in my own racial superiority, but in their tents, I felt like an uncouth, inarticulate barbarian, an intruder from a shoddy and materialistic world.

— WILFRED THESIGER, *ARABIAN SANDS*

The Al Jahili Fort (F1ONLINE DIGITALE BILDAGENTUR GMBH / ALAMY)

*I*t looks just like a sandcastle, doesn't it? Only we weren't at the beach, we were in the desert. In the small oasis-town of Al-Ain ("the spring"), at the border of the United Arab Emirates (UAE) and Oman.

The Al Jahili Fort is a testament to the great friendship between Sir Wilfred Patrick Thesiger, an English explorer and traveler, and Sheikh Zayed bin Sultan Al Nahyan, the emir of

Abu Dhabi, and the founder and first president of the UAE. We went looking for Mubarak bin London, as Thesiger was known, and were pleased to have also found the sheikh.[1]

Let's provide a little background.

The Arabian Desert covers more than a million square miles. Its southern half stretches nine hundred miles from Yemen in the west to Oman in the east and five hundred miles from the Gulf of Aden in the south to the Persian Gulf in the north.

THE EMPTY QUARTER

At its heart is a quarter of a million square miles of sand, enormous and desolate. A desert within a desert. No people, no animals, no food; it is empty. Empty, that is, except for sand dunes towering one thousand feet high, miles of gravel plains, treacherous salt flats that turn into deadly quicksand, and deep, hidden wells that are often a two-week camel's ride apart. The Arabs call it *Rub'al Khali*, the Empty Quarter.[2]

By 1930, people had reached the North and South Poles, almost climbed Mount Everest, searched the Amazon, and braved the inner spaces of Asia and Africa. No one, however, had yet mapped this uninviting little corner of the world. It was "terra incognita," a place to avoid, beyond the beyond.

For an explorer, it was irresistible.

Leave it to the British; they had to be the first, particularly two men who were already in the area. Bertram Thomas was the Finance Minister to the Sultan of Oman. In October 1930, he secretly left his post in Muscat and made his way to Salalah on the southern coast. From there, he crossed the middle of the Empty Quarter, taking the shortest and easiest path, where the dunes were small and the water holes frequent and well known *(see the red line on the map on the next page)*. He was, indeed, the first Westerner to cross the "Sands," as they were known, taking fifty-eight days to go from the south to the north, ending up in Doha, in what is now Qatar.[3]

H. St. John B. Philby also wanted to be the first, but he was the Chief Adviser to Ibn Saud, the King of Saudi Arabia. As such, he dared not depart until he received his King's permission. He was delayed, then, until January 1932. Denied the initial crossing, he settled for the first crossing from the north to the south. He departed from Al Hofuf, again traveling through the relatively easy central sands, and reached the well at Shanna. However, he refused to follow Thomas' tracks south and turned west, running out of water and almost dying. Somehow, he made his way to Sulayil at the edge of the Sands *(see the map's orange lines)*.[4]

That left the eastern and western Sands unexplored. They remained so until the late 1940s, when a certain locust hunter came along.

CROSSING THE SANDS

During World War II, a species of locust called "the desert locust" threatened the Middle East with famine. What began as lonely, common grasshoppers became social and gregarious when their numbers grew after a rainy season created plentiful vegetation. Then, when the land dried and the vegetation died back, confining them to a smaller and smaller area, the grasshoppers swarmed and migrated, changing into desert locusts.

Swarms increased rapidly, as each locust laid one hundred eggs at a time, which hatched in just three weeks. Swarms covered two hundred square miles, devouring everything in front of them. Then, when disease hit them, they vanished as quickly as they had appeared, going back to being lonely, common grasshoppers.

Desert locusts had breeding grounds where the water runoff from the mountains met the Sands. Scientists believed that if you could restrict or eliminate these "outbreak centers," you could control the locusts.[5]

But first you had to find the centers.

The Middle Eastern Locust Control Center of the British Food and Agricultural Organization was looking for someone willing to travel into the Empty Quarter to collect information about locust movements.

And Wilfred Thesiger was willing to collect information about locust movements in order to travel into the Empty Quarter.

Born in Addis Ababa, Ethiopia, the son of a British diplomat, Thesiger was educated at Oxford and returned to Ethiopia, where he first began his travels. During World War II, he served with the British forces in North Africa. With the war over, he was looking for an opportunity. To him, the

Empty Quarter was a dream come true; it offered the mystery and adventure of unmapped routes, unknown wells, uncontrolled tribes, and non-existing boundaries.

The Locust Control Specialist met Thesiger for dinner and, before coffee was served, the job of surveying locust movements in the Empty Quarter had been offered and accepted.

Sir Wilfred Thesiger, 1949 (PITT RIVERS MUSEUM / BRIDGEMAN IMAGES)

During the 1945–46 winter season, Thesiger prepared for his work by learning Bedu ways and desert travel. He wore a loin cloth, walked barefoot, squatted when going to the bathroom (the cloth did provide privacy), and sat, ate, and slept by the fire. He had to be careful wearing a loin cloth when sitting at the fire, though, because he could expose himself. If this happened, the Bedu would politely whisper "your nose." When told this for the first time, Thesiger thought the comment actually was about his nose.[6]

As for travel, Thesiger practiced loading and unloading the camels (his saddle bags filled with money, ammunition, medicines, and photography equipment) and learned how to mount, dismount, and ride them, although he never could ride kneeling, sitting on the soles of his feet.

He learned that Bedu only rode females. There were two reasons. First, the females gave milk and Bedu could not afford to feed an animal without getting a return. Second, bull camels were expected to service any female that was offered and, consequently, were often too tired to travel.

Thesiger had found the life he sought. On one journey, he and the Bedu had been eight days from a well and twenty-four hours without water. When, at last, he and part of the group reached a water hole, he went to drink, but no one else would. They — and he — sat and waited five hours until the others joined them. No one drank until everyone drank.[7]

During the 1946 to 1947 winter season, Thesiger made his First Crossing of the Eastern Sands *(see the blue line on the map)*. To succeed, he had to climb the great dunes of Uruq al Shaiba, endure gritty sand cold as frozen snow, dodge scorpions, snakes, and spiders and, of course, make it to the next water hole. It took forty-eight days.

The return had its own challenges. To avoid the quicksand of Umm al Samin, he rode across the gravel plains and low hills of Oman, which exposed him to enemy tribes and starvation. Yes, he ate dates to survive. It took fifty-four days.

Thesiger prepared his report for the Locust Control Center. The working theory had been that riverbeds drained from the Oman Mountains and flooded enough to produce vegetation and breed locusts. The reality was that floods were rare and, if they did occur, the water drained into sterile salt flats, where nothing grew.

The Center so liked Thesiger's work that it offered him a new job with a better salary, paid expenses, and the prospect of long-term employment. He turned it down. He wanted to cross the Western Sands and, with the money he had saved, he could pay for it himself. He knew that King Ibn Saud would not approve, so he did not ask for permission; he hoped, instead, for forgiveness.[8]

Thesiger planned his Second Crossing for the 1947–48 winter season *(see the green line)*. Departing from Mukalla on January 6, 1948, he went north to Manwakh, resupplied and then rode through the Dawasir Valley to Sulayyil, a journey of four hundred miles with no well in between. The trip took sixteen days.

After arriving in Sulayyil, Thesiger, as he expected, was promptly arrested by agents of the king. However, H. St. John Philby still was Ibn Saud's adviser and, after he interceded, Thesiger was, indeed, forgiven.[9]

Released after five days in captivity, Thesiger set off to cross the Northern Sands. His caravan traveled 160 miles north to Layla and then six hundred miles east to Abu Dhabi *(see, again, the green line on the map).*

It took them twenty-four days to reach the Dhiby Well, only to discover that its water was too brackish to drink. Survival was in doubt and their only chance was to keep going. After another six days — and one hundred miles — they saw the sands of the Liwa Oasis and were saved.

They rested for three days. The camels were worn out, as were they. Refreshed, they set off again and, a week later, on March 14, 1948, arrived safely in Abu Dhabi. They had done it.[10]

Thesiger and his companions were welcomed by Sheikh Shakhbut, the ruler of Abu Dhabi. Thesiger, however, wanted to move on. He wanted to explore Oman. He knew he could not attempt it until the 1948–49 winter season but, still, he wanted to make inquiries.

The Sheikh sent him to his younger brother, Zayed bin Sultan Al Nahyan, who ruled a group of small villages at the Oman border, now called Al-Ain. He had been born there, and the family maintained it as a summer residence.

Thesiger liked Sheikh Zayed the minute he saw him. Powerfully built, Zayed had a strong, intelligent face with steady observant eyes. He was informal and friendly, but had a quiet, masterful manner.

Zayed liked Thesiger as well, hosting him for a month and taking him falcon hunting the following year.[11]

AL-AIN, UNITED ARAB EMIRATES | *156*

And, as you can see, Sheikh Zayed was quite comfortable riding on his knees, sitting on his feet.

Sheikh Zayed bin Sultan al-Nahyan, 1949 (PITT RIVERS MUSEUM / BRIDGEMAN IMAGES)

Falcons are beloved in the Emirates. Historically used to capture game, they enabled Arabs, before the discovery of oil, to survive in the desert. Today, falcons are symbols of the country and falcon hunting is its national sport.[12]

We visited the Dubai Falcon Heritage and Sports Center, a huge shopping mall devoted solely to falcons. As advertised, falcons and all kinds of falcon paraphernalia were for sale. There were many varieties of hoods (*burqas*), some quite beautiful, and we bought a few.

From there, we went to the Abu Dhabi Falcon Hospital, the largest falcon hospital in the world. We watched two basic procedures, one for the eyes and one for the claws. Each falcon eye has three eyelids. If sand is caught between two of them, it is quite painful and debilitating, and hard to remove. Falcon claws grow and, if not shortened, are sharp enough to dig damaging holes in their paws. At the hospital, we saw doctors remove the sand and cut the claws. That's right, we saw an eye job and a nail cut, just like in a beauty salon.

Thesiger and Zayed were going in different directions when they met. For Sir Wilfred, time in Arabia was coming to an end. He had made his two great Crossings, climbed the dunes of Uruq Al Shaiba, explored the Liwa Oasis, risked the quicksand of Umm al Samin, and studied the interior of Oman.[13] He had drawn maps, filled notebooks, and taken thousands of photographs.[14] However, the borders were closing, and he had brought with him the very civilization he fled.

For Sheikh Zayed, life was just beginning. The oil men had arrived. In 1958, oil was discovered and, starting in 1962, exported. In 1966, Zayed replaced his older brother as the

Sheikh of Abu Dhabi. In 1971, he led the unification of the Arabian emirs, creating the United Arab Emirates. He became its first president and was reelected four times.

Sheik Zayed modernized his country, building roads, schools, hospitals, and cities. He became one of the richest men in the world. But he and his countrymen never forgot their first Western friend.

In 2008, the Al Jahili Fort in Al-Ain was renovated in honor of this friendship. It now holds a permanent photography exhibition devoted to Sir Wilfred and Sheikh Zayed.

Of course we went. You can't visit Dubai and Abu Dhabi without going to Al-Ain, they're all right next to each other.

DUBAI, ABU DHABI, AND AL-AIN

LHASA, TIBET

> I can still hear the wild cries of geese and cranes
> and the beating of their wings
> as they fly over Lhasa in the clear cold moonlight.
>
> — HEINRICH HARRER, *SEVEN YEARS IN TIBET*

The Eiger, the Mönch, and the Jungfrau (JON ARNOLD IMAGES LTD / ALAMY)

> Their wing-beat sounds say "Lha Gye Lo,"
> "The Gods will prevail."
>
> — HEINRICH HARRER, *RETURN TO TIBET*

There are three conjoined mountains in Switzerland that have long attracted lookers, hikers, and climbers: from left to right (and east to west), the Eiger, the Mönch, and the Jungfrau. Their names tell the story: the ogre, the monk, and the young maiden.

It is the Eiger, however, that has captured the most attention. Just look at its north face. It is concave, bending back over a climber. It does not hold snow and it is, accordingly, famous for avalanches and rock falls. It is a death trap. As such, it simply had to be climbed.

The mountain was first summited in 1858, but by the far safest route, the northwest ridge. It was then topped by the southwest ridge in 1874, the south ridge in 1876, the Mittellegi Ridge in 1921, and the northeast face in 1932.

Still, no one dared the unclimbable, impossible north face.[1]

By the mid-1930s, the Eiger remained the last "unsolved problem" in the Alps. It was a philosophical and psychological riddle:

> Is not the irrationality of its very lack of purpose
> the deepest argument for climbing?[2]

Two men tried in 1935. Four nights they spent on the face, disappearing in the mist. They were eventually found by a military plane, standing knee deep in snow, frozen upright. The site became known as the "Death Bivouac."

Four more tried in 1936. Unable to retreat after the weather changed, only one of them was still alive, hanging on a rope. He died, in harness. "I'm finished," he said, just as a rescue party reached him. As for the three others, they were officially "missing and never found."

And then, at the 1936 Olympics in Berlin, climbing the north face of the Eiger became a political issue. Its conquest was declared a German goal, symbolizing man's triumph over nature, worthy of its own gold medal.

All Heinrich Harrer ever wanted was to be a mountaineer. Born in Austria in a hillside mining cottage with no running water or electricity, he studied geography and sports, climbing in summer and skiing in winter.

Heinrich Harrer with Ropes (HEINRICH HARRER MUSEUM)

Harrer was a good enough skier to make the Austrian Olympic Team for the 1936 Winter Games and to win the downhill event at the World Student Championships the following year.

In 1938, Harrer graduated from college. He found a teaching position at his old grammar school, which gave him time to climb. His goal was the Himalayas, but he knew he had to do something special to get there. That's it: he would be the first to climb the north face of the Eiger.

It sounded crazy. A kid just out of school who thought he could climb the north face? It wasn't. Harrer not only dreamed it, he did it.

Harrer and a partner began at 2 a.m. on July 21, 1938. They climbed all day, water pouring onto them from the melting ice above. They spent a wet night, too, unable to change clothes, nailed to the mountain side.

Still, they carried on, their clothes drying in the second day's sun. They met another pair of climbers and spent a second night, perched on a ledge barely as wide as a window sill. But they cooked some food and were content.

On the third day, they reached the part of the mountain known as "The Spider." Through the snow and mist they could barely see each other. The wind began to howl, but there was a different noise as well: an avalanche. They weren't wearing helmets, but they improvised. With one hand, they held their rucksacks on their heads, with the other, they grasped the mountain. They survived . . . to enjoy another night out, once again sleeping on their feet.

The following morning, Harrer and the other three roped up as a single, united group of four. Onward and upward, together. They knew the risk. If the lead man fell and number two couldn't hold him, all four might fall.

They forged on. The lead man, fighting the wind and snow, could not see anything ahead. Suddenly, he stepped into — *down* into — a dark patch below him. The second man pulled him back . . . and kept him from falling off the *south* side of the mountain. It was 3:30 p.m. on July 24, 1938. They had done it.³

Heinrich Harrer had spent eighty-five hours on the north face of the Eiger.

───────

The north face would see faster times. On August 14, 1974, the team of Reinhold Messner and Peter Habler summited in exactly ten hours, leaving Clint Eastwood and the other actors making the movie *The Eiger Sanction* speechless. Flash forward to November 16, 2015, when Swiss speed climber Ueli Steck reached the top in only two hours, twenty-two minutes, and fifty seconds. We, ourselves, have ascended it, in less than two minutes, but then, we *were* in a helicopter.

───────

Again, Harrer had spent eighty-five hours on the north face of the Eiger. There had to be *some* reward. There was. Just eight months later, in the spring of 1939, he was invited to be a member of the four-man German-Austrian Himalayan Expedition, which would explore the possibility of climbing Nanga Parbat. He happily accepted.

The expedition left Munich for Bombay in early April. Led by Peter Aufschnaiter, they made one stop along the way, in Cairo. There, to the surprise of guides and camel drivers, they climbed the great Cheops Pyramid in just eight and one-half minutes, yodeling as they reached the top.

From Bombay, the expedition went by train through

Karachi and Lahore to Rawalpindi, the end of the line. They marched through forests of cedar trees and villages that got smaller and smaller. They were efficient, finishing their survey work and returning to Karachi by mid-August. There, they waited for a ship to return to Europe.

They never left. On September 3, 1939, England declared war on Germany. World War II had begun. Since India was British territory, the German-Austrian group was promptly arrested and became prisoners of war.

They were first taken to a camp near Karachi, and then moved to one near Bombay. Finally, they were taken to the largest prisoner of war camp in India, located just outside of Rawalpindi, in the foothills of the Himalayas.[4]

Harrer had married just before departing on the expedition. Obviously, he couldn't return to his wife. Then, it took over a year to learn she had given birth: he had a son. Finally, he lost her to divorce. She couldn't stand the uncertainties of war and had met another man.

He was hurt, but he wasn't broken. Indeed, he prepared for a possible escape. He learned Hindi, Tibetan, and Japanese. He studied maps. He kept in shape, playing football, handball, and winning the camp decathlon competition.

He tried and tried and tried again to escape before he finally succeeded. On one occasion, when he had been caught following a month of freedom, the camp commandant, Colonel Williams, lectured him:

> You made a daring escape Mr. Harrer. I admire you, but I still have to give you twenty-eight days solitary confinement in accordance with the Geneva Convention.[5]

Harrer spent almost five years as a prisoner. Finally, on April 29, 1944, along with Peter Aufschnaiter and five others, he escaped for good. They painted their faces, shaved their heads, wore turbans and white robes, carried ladders, barbed wire, and tar pots, and, escorted by two appropriately dressed "English overseers" bearing rolls of blueprints and waving their swagger sticks, simply walked out of camp on their way to "repair" fence posts.

Years later, Harrer gave a speech about his adventures at the Royal Festival Hall in London. There, on the podium, he found a note from the same Colonel Williams:

> As Commander of your Camp, I had to take the blame for your successful escape. Tonight, to add insult to injury, I had to pay to listen to you tell how you did it.[6]

OK, they were free, but where to go? They had two choices. There was India, through thickly populated areas where one needed to have money and speak English. Or there was Tibet, where foreigners were not allowed, but spaces were empty and mountains were high. Besides, it was still a magical land, unknown and mostly uncharted. And, maybe, just maybe, they could somehow make it all the way to Lhasa. They chose Tibet.

As the map shows, it was a long, long way from Dehradun to the Forbidden City.

The journey took them almost two years.

First, they had to reach Tibet. Traveling only at night, avoiding the roads, facing down apes, leopards, and bears, getting lost along the way, fighting off altitude sickness and the cold, they mounted Tsangchokla Pass in mid-May. At last, they were beyond British control.

LHASA, TIBET | 166

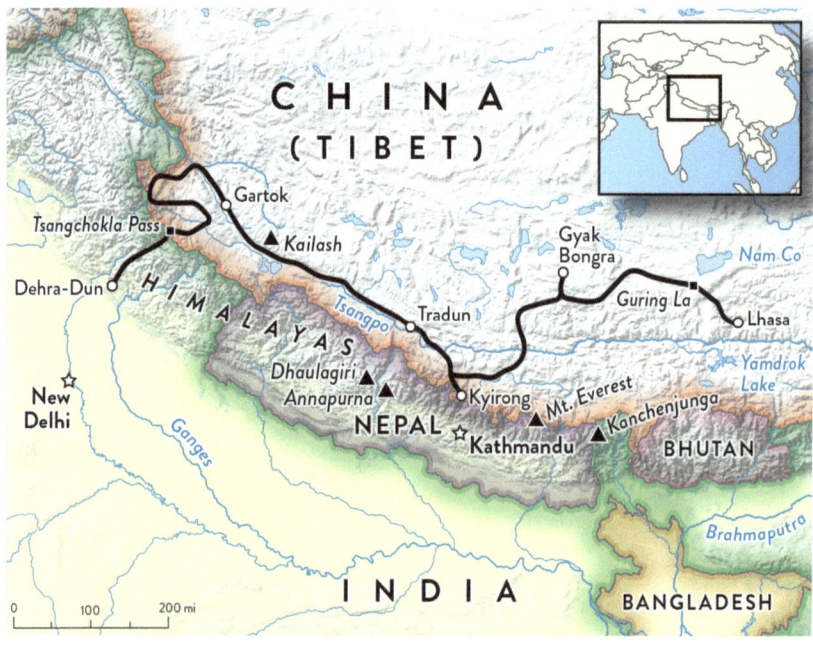

HEINRICH HARRER'S ESCAPE ROUTE

Thankfully, the Tibetans had no border patrols or frontier posts. As it was, Harrer and his companions kept meeting local officers who ordered them to return to India. They pretended to obey but circled back, hoping to find another official who would be more accommodating.

When they reached Gartok, the celebrated capital of western Tibet, they were surprised. It consisted of only a few tents, some mud-brick huts, and a lot of stray dogs. Still, they found an official willing to give them travel passes and transportation to Nepal, *provided* that they promise not to go to Lhasa. Promises, promises.

They crossed wide plains and hill country. They grew beards to protect themselves from the sun. With no tents, they slept out in the open. They reached Tradun (if you look, you can find it on the map).

There they begged for asylum and were permitted to petition the authorities in Lhasa. It took almost six months for a response. By then, only two of the original seven escapees remained: Harrer and Aufschnaiter.

Their answer: NO. They were still forbidden to travel deeper into Tibet and were ordered to head directly to Nepal.

This led them to Kyirong, only eight miles from the border. They were the first Europeans ever to visit and were welcomed to the "Village of Happiness." They stayed ten months.

Summer came. World War II was over but still they feared being imprisoned if they went back to India. Moreover, they had long ago given up hope of ever returning home.

Summer went. It was time to make their move. "On to Lhasa" became their motto, but they didn't really know how they would get there.

The challenges were many. Robbers followed, lurking, always hoping for the right moment to strike. Mountain passes blocked them—all in all, they overcame twenty-five.[7] They faced hunger, poverty, wind and cold, you name it, but they did not give up.

And so, on January 15, 1946, they staggered into Lhasa, bare-footed, half-starved, penniless. They were given refuge, they were granted asylum. In time, they became useful.

Lhasa was a medieval place. Superstition and religion were everywhere. They met oracles, rain makers, mediums, astrologers, faith healers, mystics, and pilgrims.

Lhasa needed their help. They planted a forest to provide fuel. They built a canal to water the crops. They built a dike, so the crops would not be flooded.

They introduced sports, swimming in the summer (boy, was the water cold), and skating, "walking on knives," in the winter. They even built a tennis court, laying down a level of very fine gravel and covering it with yak dung. It worked.[8]

They made a map of the city . . . which was so accurate that it became the starting point for all subsequent surveys.[9] However, it contained so many buildings that have since been destroyed and so many streets that have been straightened, closed, or widened, that it is now almost useless.

That didn't matter, we had our own.

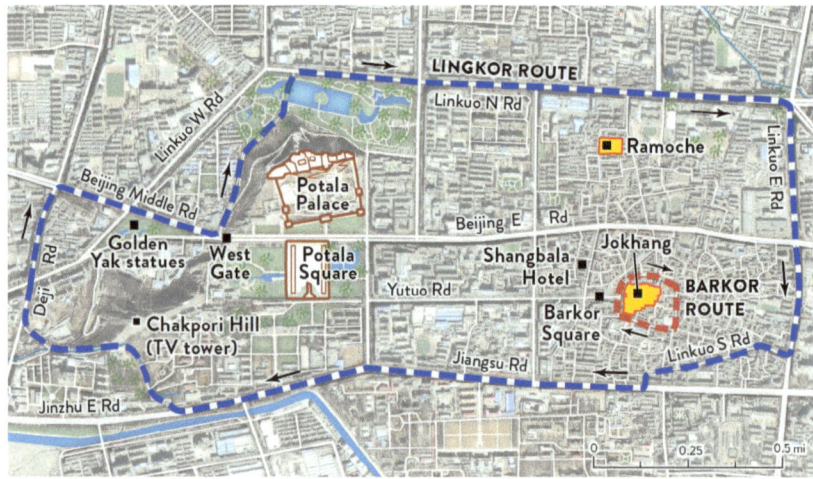

LHASA OLD TOWN

Lhasa is a holy city, defined by its pilgrim routes. The first, the Lingkor *(shown in blue on the map)* set the town's original boundaries. At just under five miles around, it is quite walkable, but not until you've acclimatized. Unfortunately, it has lost its magic, as karaoke bars and brothels have found a home along the way. Still, a walk *(always go clockwise)* gave us a good sense of the place. Don't miss the "post-liberation," Chinese-built landmarks such as the Golden Yaks and the restored West Gate.

There is a second Pilgrim circuit, the Barkor *(shown in red)*. It surrounds the *Jokhang,* the most sacred Temple in Tibet. This route is both religious and commercial, for it is lined with shops selling devotions, local necessities, and souvenirs. It is short enough that we went round and round *(again, always clockwise)* and, when we did, we saw something new and different every time, and something the same all the time. We found a golden silk hat with four fur flaps that we liked, and we found it over and over again.

The Jokhang has a sister temple, the *Ramoche.* Their relationship can be traced to Lhasa's founding as Tibet's capital. They were both built in the seventh century by the first recorded ruler of Tibet, King Songtsen Gampo, when he moved his court from the countryside to Lhasa. The temples were intended to honor the homelands of his two foreign queens. The Ramoche faces east, to honor Princess Wen Cheng, his bride from China. The Jokhang faces west, for Princess Bhrikuti from Nepal.[10]

King Gampo also built a small palace for himself on top of the most prominent hill in town. It kept expanding, and eventually grew into the Potala Palace, the seat of Tibet's government and the residence of the Dalai Lama. It's still there, but it's just a museum now.

Back to Harrer. In time, he became tutor to the fourteen-year-old "living buddha."

It was the honor of Harrer's life. The boy's favorite subject was geography, but he also had talent for technical things and languages. He was a hard worker; given ten sentences to translate, he would do twenty.

LHASA, TIBET | *170*

Heinrich Harrer with the Young Dalai Lama (HEINRICH HARRER MUSEUM)

The Dalai Lama with the Old Heinrich Harrer (DBA PICTURE ALLIANCE ARCHIVE / ALAMY)

Harrer bore witness to a passing way of life. He wrote what he saw, he wrote what he lived, producing *Seven Years in Tibet* (1954), *Return to Tibet* (1985), and *Beyond Seven Years in Tibet* (2007). Here's how he summed it up:

> I shall never forget the hospitality of those happy people, their joyous laughter or the politeness they showed at every meeting. Instead of shaking hands, they place their palms together in front of their chest: Instead of kissing, they greet those closest to them by touching foreheads. The nicest custom, and the one I came to love best, is the giving of a white silk scarf for good luck. This is offered with both hands, as is everything one receives.[11]

Heinrich Harrer and the Dalai Lama remained lifelong friends. They shared the same birthday, the sixth of July. Once, Harrer asked if this was fate, divine providence, luck, or coincidence. "All of these," His Holiness replied with a smile.[12]

Not finished yet, would that we were. Harrer, even if he had escaped his prison camp and found freedom and happiness in Tibet, remained a prisoner of war. Back in 1938, in order to qualify for that teaching job at his old grammar school, he had joined the Nazi Party. He never served in the German military, he never marched, he never fired a gun, he wore a uniform only one time. And the day World War II broke out, he was immediately arrested and put behind barbed wire.[13]

Still, no matter all the good he did in his life, and despite his loving relationship with one of the great peacekeepers of the twentieth century, he had been a Nazi.

Sixty years later, in 1997, when the movie about his life,

Seven Years in Tibet, was being released, that fact emerged. The world neither forgave nor forgot. Heinrich Harrer, at age eighty-five, was disinvited from the film's premiere, and its portrayal of his life was altered, not for the better. A young man's compromise had become an old man's burden.[14]

Was it fair?

You tell us: if the gods had prevailed, what would they have done?

BYGDØY PENINSULA, NORWAY

I shall call her the "Fram" — "Forward."

— FRIDTJOF NANSEN

The Fram Ship Model (MICHAEL CZYTKO, WWW.MODELSHIPS.DE)

*I*t began with an idea.

In 1884, wreckage from a ship that had been crushed by ice near the New Siberian Islands just north of Russia in 1881 was found floating off the east coast of Greenland. Scientists in Norway argued that the wreckage must have been carried by a current that flowed from Siberia across the Arctic Ocean to Greenland, passing over the North Pole on its way.

At the time, explorers were trying to reach two unknown and uncharted parts of the world, the North and the South Poles, and were looking for ways to do it.

The idea (the true test of a great idea is how obvious it is in hindsight) was to get a boat stuck in the ice above Russia and then drift with the current as it carried the ice — and the boat — *over* the North Pole. In this way, one would be working *with* the forces of nature, not *against* them. In this way, the boat and its passengers would all reach the pole.[1]

It's one thing to have an idea, and it's another to act on it. In this case, however, the idea-man and the risk-taker were the same person: Fridtjof Nansen.

And why not? Nansen had just returned from a great adventure. He had crossed Greenland, the first person ever to do so, and on skis.

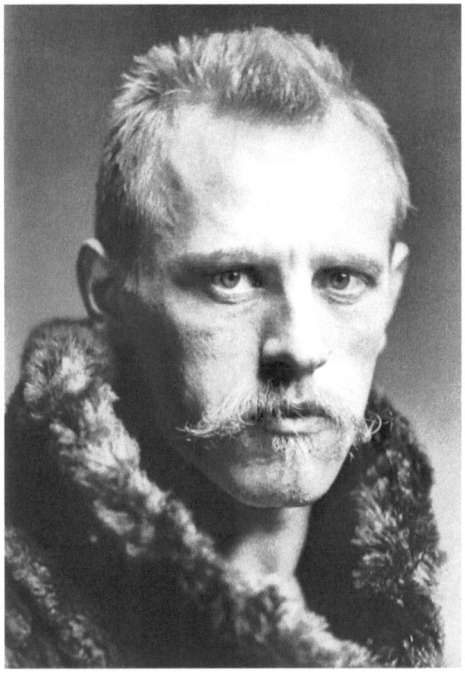

Fridtjof Nansen (ARCHIVIO GBB / ALAMY)

He succeeded because he followed another one of his ideas. He noticed that all the previous attempts to cross Greenland had started from the settled, west side of the island. This meant that expeditions were always able to retreat to safety and that, if they made it through the unexplored desert of ice in the middle to the east coast, they had to turn around and repeat their journey in order to get home. Of course they failed.

Nansen's idea: land on the desolate, ice-bound east coast and cross Greenland from east to west. In front would be the attractions of civilization, behind would be nothing:

> There was no choice of routes: "Forward" being the only word.[2]

Nansen also knew that, with skis, one could cover a long distance in a short time. His use of them, which he later described in *The First Crossing of Greenland* (1890), led to an explosion in the popularity of skiing and its adoption as a universal sport.[3]

What Nansen needed for the North Pole was a boat that could withstand the pressure of encroaching ice. He wanted two things that had never been tried before. First, the boat had to have sloping sides and a smooth, rounded bottom, like an egg cut in half. This way, instead of being crushed by the ice, it would be pushed up by it. Second, the boat had to be good at sea, able to stand the trip to Siberia, *and* be good near land, able to navigate shallow coastal waters. No existing ship fit these criteria, so Nansen set out to build one.

He found just the naval architect to do it, Colin Archer. Archer knew how to design a boat according to specifications. He knew how to combine seaworthiness with shallow draft.

He knew how to combine the right materials: American Elm for the keel, Italian Oak for the frames, Norwegian Pine for the deck.

Archer built a double sternpost that allowed the rudder and the propeller to be raised or lowered, as required by conditions. He provided triple insulation, two gaps filled with cork shavings, reindeer hair, and thick pelts, and the third with an air pocket. The bow and the stern were equally sharp, making the craft a double-ender, able to prevent ice from gripping the boat. When finished, it looked just like the model.[4]

The boat was named the *Fram*. As noted, the word means *forward*, which, just like in Greenland, was the only direction that Nansen wanted to go. Once caught in the ice, there could be no retreat.

Nansen stocked the boat with all sorts of new products: a primus stove, the first cooker to use liquid fuel, and a combination sporting gun with two barrels, one for bullets, one for shot, enabling him to use the same rifle for game and birds. There were extra-long skis for cross-country skiing. And, not to be forgotten, enough food and fuel for five years.

Nansen then selected his crew. He wanted educated men for company, good skiers with knowledge of the sea, and scientists who could also work a ship. He knew it would be difficult to find men willing to be in the Arctic for an indefinite amount of time. He knew they had to be special.

Two stood out. Otto Sverdrup, who had been with him in Greenland, agreed to captain the ship. He would take complete control if Nansen left for an individual try for the Pole. Hjalmar Johansen would be Nansen's companion if he did.

The *Fram* departed from what is now Oslo on June 24, 1893. It sailed up the coast of Norway to Tromso. There it restocked, and set off for the Barents Sea.

BYGDØY PENINSULA, NORWAY | 177

The map below shows the path of the wreckage *(in blue)*, the voyage of the *Fram (in red)* and Nansen's attempt at the North Pole and retreat therefrom *(in green)*.

**FRIDTJOF NANSEN'S ATTEMPT AT THE NORTH POLE
1893-1896**

The map also shows *(at the top)* the Bering Strait *(black arrow)*, another way to enter the pack ice in order to reach the pole, a route that Nansen thought about but rejected.

By late September 1893, the *Fram* was in the ice, and, as planned, was pushed up rather than crushed. The drift began.

The crew kept regular hours: 8 a.m. for breakfast, 1 p.m. for lunch, 6 p.m. for dinner. After their chores they entertained themselves playing cards, telling stories, making music, and reading books. They knew it would be a long, dark winter, but the boat was snug and warm, and the Northern Lights gave them their own private show.

By April 1894, the *Fram* had floated to 80 degrees, 44 minutes north. The expedition was thus a scientific success: Nansen had proved the existence of a current crossing the Arctic Ocean. However, the current was not as strong as predicted and Nansen's calculations showed that the *Fram* would not drift farther north than 85 degrees.

As spring came with the sun, outdoor activities beckoned: long walks with snow shoes, sledging with dogs, and even some scientific work, such as temperature readings and location measurements. But the monotony was wearing. For men of action, the hardest thing to do was nothing. There was time for reflection. There was time for homesickness. There was too much time.

The *Fram* reached 83 degrees north on Christmas Day 1894 and remained there until March 1895. During this time, Nansen debated whether or not to leave the boat and make an individual try for the pole. He knew it was vanity. He knew he had promised not to, but he really, *really* wanted 90 degrees north.

Bored on the Ship (HERITAGE IMAGE PARTNERSHIP LTD / ALAMY)

Nansen reviewed the situation: he had kayaks, sleds, and dogs. He had food and supplies. He had Hjalmar Johansen. He knew the risks, but he just couldn't *not* go. So, on March 16, 1895, after two failed attempts, he made his move and left the *Fram*.

From the beginning, it was a mistake. The temperature was a constant 40 degrees below zero. The terrain was exhausting. The ice drifted in all directions. By April 8, they could go no further. Still, they had reached 86 degrees 13 minutes, 6 seconds north, the farthest north anyone had yet been.[5]

BYGDØY PENINSULA, NORWAY | 180

Nansen Saved (HISTORIA / SHUTTERSTOCK)

The return had its own problems. Nansen and Johansen didn't reach land until August, when they realized they would have to stay through the upcoming winter. They built a hut and moved in. The hunting was good; they shot polar bears and they shot walrus. Soon, they began sleeping twenty hours a day.

They survived.

The spring of 1896 came. Nansen knew they must go south and he knew it would be difficult. One time the kayaks, filled with all their provisions, floated away and Nansen jumped into the water to save them. He almost died from the cold. Another time, the kayaks were attacked and sunk by a walrus.

The outlook was grim. But, on June 17, 1896, they heard dogs barking.

Nansen went to look. Rather be lucky than good. He was greeted by an English expedition, and in a Stanley and Livingston moment, they were saved.

The English boat delivered them back to Norway on August 13, 1896. In a moment of perfect timing, the *Fram* broke loose from the ice that very same day. Otto Sverdrup had done his job. On August 21, Nansen and the crew were together again.

The *Fram*'s trip down the coast of Norway was a triumphant procession, and they were greeted by the cheers of thousands when they docked in Oslo. Nansen had joined the immortals of Norse exploration.

Still, Nansen had *not* reached the North Pole.

Close, but no cigar.

In time, another Norwegian explorer, Roald Amundsen, would try. His prior exploits certainly qualified him. For example, in June 1903, as captain of the *Gjoa*, Amundsen had been the first person ever to sail through the Northwest Passage. He was smart. He was fearless. He was adaptive.[6]

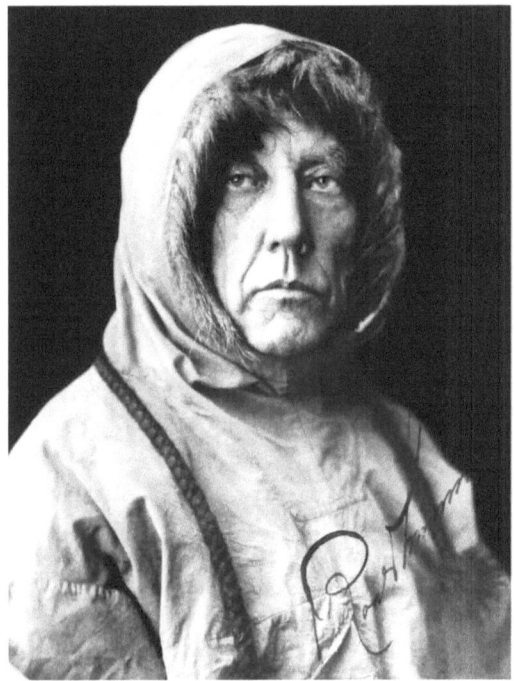

Roald Amundsen (EVERETT COLLECTION HISTORICAL / ALAMY)

He had learned of Nansen's consideration of the Bering Strait as an entrance to the North Pole ice fields and believed that starting from there would be the key to success. He was willing to sail the long way around, from Norway down to Portugal, across the equator to South America, around Tierra del Fuego, at the tip of Argentina, and then back up the Pacific side of South and North America to the strait. The only thing he wanted for this trip was the *Fram*.

Amundsen asked for permission to use the boat. Nansen gave it. Amundsen asked for the blessing of the king and queen. They gave it. With this support, he set off in June 1910 for the North Pole. However, he knew two Americans, Frederick Cook in 1908 and Robert Perry in 1909, had already claimed to have been there. He also knew he was heading south.

Did we say that Amundsen was adaptive? In September 1910, while at harbor on the Island of Madeira, located four hundred miles off the coast of Africa, he announced changed plans to the crew. Instead of going for the North Pole, they would go all the way south. Anyone who wanted could leave. No one did.

Amundsen informed Nansen and the king of his changed plans and got their consent. He telegrammed Robert F. Scott, leader of a British expedition already on its way to the South Pole, that he was coming to join him. All of a sudden, it was a race.[7]

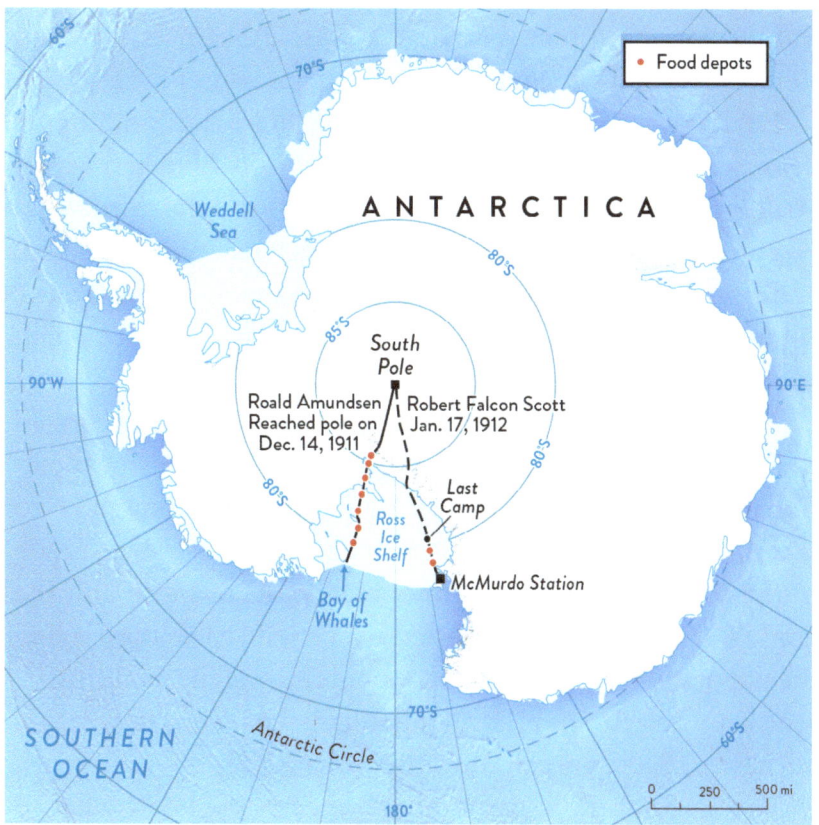

RACE TO THE SOUTH POLE 1911-1912

It wouldn't be much of one.

The *Fram* performed masterfully, delivering Amundsen and his crew to the Bay of Whales on January 14, 1911, one day ahead of schedule. Meanwhile, Scott had landed at what is now McMurdo Station. Both are shown on the map.

The run for the South Pole proved to be a battle of judgments.

Location. Scott thought he had the better one. From his camp, he would follow a path previously mapped by another British explorer. Amundsen would face unknown obstacles, but his camp was seventy miles closer to the pole. That's a 140-mile saving on a round trip.

Preparation. Amundsen and Scott spent most of 1911 waiting for the *warm* weather that would begin in October. Remember, summer comes to Antarctica as winter comes to us.

But Amundsen did not just wait. He set up food and supply depots, and he set them up very methodically. The first was at 80 degrees south, the second at 81 degrees and the third at 82. His plan was to take provisions from each location and set up additional depots at every different degree along the route. All in all, he established seven depots on the Ross Ice Shelf. Scott only set up two. It cost him his life.

Methods of transport. Scott started with four: motorized sleds, ponies, dogs, and humans. Like earlier British expeditions, he was opposed to skis; he didn't even know how to use them. And what happened? The motorized sleds failed in the cold, the ponies were hobbled by deep snow, and the dogs, which Scott never trusted, were sent back after laying the depots. In the end, Scott adopted the one method consistent with his experience: man hauling. That's right, wearing harnesses, Scott's men pulled their own sleds.

For Amundsen, it was almost too easy. He knew what to do in the snow. It was skis and dogsleds, all the way. Dressed in warm furs, with well-marked food depots at regular intervals, Amundsen and his crew made the nine-hundred-mile trip to the South Pole in *only* fifty-seven days. They arrived on December 14, 1911.

They spent two days at the pole confirming and marking their location. And then, at last, they celebrated. Everyone was given the chance to talk, but one crew member did more than that. As Amundsen recounted:

> My amazement reached its culmination when, at the conclusion of his speech, he produced a cigar-case full of cigars and offered it round. *A cigar at the Pole!* What do you say to that?[8]

Then it was time to go, but not before one glorious photo.

Norway at the South Pole (PICTORIAL PRESS LTD / ALAMY)

The return was uneventful. Since they knew their way, Amundsen and crew made it back to their base in only forty-one days. They never missed a trick, even skiing at night so the twenty-four-hour sun was at their backs.

Amundsen did make one mistake: he lived. When the world learned Scott had died on his way back from the pole, and only ten miles from a food depot, it overlooked his mistakes. After all, he had died "like a proper English Gentleman." As a result, Scott became the ascendant cultural hero and Amundsen drifted into the background, a most unhappy fellow.[9]

And the *Fram*? What became of the *Fram*?

The Fram Museum (MAURICIO ABREU / ALAMY)

It stood, and still stands, alone in the annals of Polar exploration. Under the command of Otto Sverdrup, while Nansen made his dash for the North Pole, the *Fram* floated to 85 degrees 57 minutes north. Under Amundsen, it sailed to 78 degrees 41 minutes south. It carried the Norwegian flag both farthest north and farthest south. It brought all its men back alive. To this day, no other boat in the world can match it.

During the 1930s, in gratitude for its service to the country, Norway renovated the *Fram* and built a museum around it. That's right, a museum for a boat. A museum to honor Nansen and Amundsen, and Sverdrup, too. A museum located on a peninsula just outside of Oslo. A museum that draws four hundred thousand visitors a year.

Including us, and, we hope, someday, you.

Just remember, to get there, don't take a bus, take the boat.

ISLA NEGRA, CHILE

Puedo escribir las versos más tristes esta noche.
Tonight, I can write the saddest lines.

—PABLO NERUDA, "POEM TWENTY,"
FROM *TWENTY LOVE POEMS AND A SONG OF DESPAIR*

Bombing of the Presidential Palace (ASSOCIATED PRESS IMAGES)

The day: September 11, 1973.
The place: Santiago, Chile.
For the first and only time in the country's history, its Air Force was called into action. The mission: to bomb its own Presidential Palace and kill its democratically elected president.

Walk into any souvenir shop in the Santiago Airport and you can't avoid three figures: General Augusto Pinochet, who ordered the bombing, President Salvador Allende, its victim, and the poet Pablo Neruda. Together, they lived out the defining drama of their country, a nervous breakdown still resonating today.

Let's start with the poet.

Pablo Neruda's life was a map of Chile.

Born in 1904, he grew up in the south, in Temuco, a pioneer town at the edge of civilization. What he remembered most was that it always rained . . . every day, for a month, for a year. It just always rained.

Young Pablo Neruda (ARCHIVO FUNDACIÓN NERUDA)

ISLA NEGRA, CHILE | *190*

CHILE

He went to university in the center, in Santiago, the capital city. There his days were filled with poems and dreams, and his nights with parties and play.

In time, he became a politician, a Communist representing the north, where it never rained . . . even for a day, in any month, in any year. It just never rained.

Then, he became an exile, escaping east over the Andes, to become a citizen of the world.

In the end, he returned to find happiness in the west, in a sailor's beach house by the sea.[1]

As a young man, Neruda was pensive, melancholy, and romantic. In 1924, at just twenty, he wrote of love, and of loss.

> Tonight, I can write the saddest lines.
> I loved her, and sometimes she loved me too . . .
>
> To think that I do not have her. To feel that I have lost her . . .
>
> What does it matter that my love could not keep her.
> The night is starry and she is not with me . . .
>
> I no longer love her, that's certain, but how I loved her.
>
> Another's. She will be another's. As she was before my kisses.
> Her voice, her bright body. Her infinite eyes.
>
> I no longer love her, that's certain, but maybe I love her.
> Love is so short, forgetting is so long[2]

Twenty Love Poems and a Song of Despair (1924) became the best-selling book of poems ever written in Spanish. Since its publication, it has sold over twenty million copies. And "Poem Twenty," abridged above, is its single most beloved poem.

At the time, though, poetry brought Neruda only celebrity. He still had to make a living. He had a friend who had a friend at the Foreign Ministry. He arranged an introduction, which led to an interview, which led to an offer, which Neruda accepted. Thus began his career as a consul in the Chilean Diplomatic Corps.

Neruda started at the bottom and his first postings were miserable: Rangoon in Burma (now Myanmar), Colombo in Ceylon (now Sri Lanka), Batavia in Java (now part of Indonesia), and Singapore. The pay was terrible, the duties minimal, the life hot and boring. In Java, he was so lonely that he married the first of his three wives.[3] In 1932, Chile abolished his post and recalled him.

The following year, Neruda was reassigned, this time to Buenos Aires. Life got better. He was a man of affairs and had many of them. He loved the nightlife and his new friends, most of all the Spanish poet Federico García Lorca. Yet, even though he worked for the government, Neruda still considered himself an outsider.[4]

That would change with his next postings in Spain. In 1934, he was appointed to Barcelona and then transferred to Madrid. There, his great friend García Lorca introduced him to everyone who was anyone, especially at party time. Neruda did okay by himself, though, meeting the woman who became his second wife.[5]

But soon, the music stopped. Spain, which had recently become a democratic republic, held elections in 1936. The leftist Popular Front won by a narrow margin. As a result, these "Republicans" found themselves supported by the Communists and Anarchists. As for the "Nationalists" who lost, General Francisco Franco launched a military coup but failed to take control. He was backed by the Nazis and Fascists. And so, the Spanish Civil War began.

One of its first victims was García Lorca, who was assassinated. Neruda responded with poetry, writing *España en el Corazón (Spain in My Heart)* (1937) to declare his support for the Republicans:

> You will ask: and where are the lilacs
> and the metaphysics petalled with poppies? . . .
>
> You will ask: why doesn't his poetry
> speak to us of dreams? . . .
>
> Come and see the blood in the streets,
> come and see
> the blood in the streets,
> come and see the blood
> in the streets![6]

The Chilean government tried to remain neutral but couldn't control Neruda. So, it closed down its consulate. Without income, Neruda returned home. Still, he continued to fight for the Spanish Republicans, trying to raise funds.

One night changed him forever. He went to address a porter's union in Santiago's central market. Nervous, frozen, he looked out over the workers, men with hard features and huge hands, and he couldn't begin his speech. He just couldn't. Instead, he read the poems from *Spain in My Heart*. When he finished, there was silence, a long silence, followed by the sounds of men weeping. Neruda decided that, from then on, he would write, not for the intellectuals, but for the workers. He was no longer just a lover, he was also a fighter.[7]

In 1938, Chile held new elections. It had its own Popular Front, and Neruda joined them. Together, they narrowly won. The new government sent Neruda to Paris, to work with Spanish refugees.

Franco had won the Civil War and half a million men, women, and children had fled to France, living in squalor, desperately needing help. Neruda organized a ship, the *Winnipeg*, that carried two thousand people to safety, landing them all at Valparaiso, Chile.

Neruda's immigration efforts were not without the usual debate: Will the refugees be honorable, hard-working people, or will they be vagrants? Should they be intellectuals, or should they be manual laborers?[8] It was all so tiring.

Neruda needed a rest and a place to write. He had always loved the ocean, so he found a place on the Pacific coast, south of Valparaiso. The owner, a retired sea captain who approved of what Neruda had done for the Spanish refugees, sold him the property.

The house had a lot of problems, no road into it (even today it's just dirt), no electricity, and barely any hot water. But Neruda turned it into one of the most famous locations in all of South America, expanding it room by room. He called it "Isla Negra," not because it was an island but because of the large black rocks he could see from his bedroom.[9]

And he loved his bells. When he arrived, they celebrated his presence. If the weather changed, they gave warning. If he were out walking, they called him for lunch or dinner. Here, he found, was home.

What is the perfect beach? Is it smooth sand, warm water, and an infinite view? Not for Neruda. He liked action. Sand, of course, but just enough to rest and walk on, containing treasures and surprises, with a path to the sea. Rocks, big enough to climb, with hiding places for discoveries. Waves, crashing onto the shore, inviting and dangerous. And, as we learned when we got our feet wet, he loved his water freezing cold.[10]

What is the perfect beach house? When we visited, Isla Negra was chockablock with seashells, bottles, and rocks, all celebrating Neruda's collection of large, wooden, bare-breasted women, who, in former lives, had been ship figureheads. Ah, women.

The Bells at Isla Negra (HEMIS/ALAMY)

Still, for years, Isla Negra was a construction site and money pit. Neruda's guests didn't care. After the food and wine were gone and the party was over, they could always leave.

Back to the struggle. In 1940, Neruda was posted to Mexico. There, he began to understand who owned what and what that meant. Peru: the United States controlled 80 percent of its oil production and almost 100 percent of its mineral output. Venezuela: the whole country might as well have been owned by Standard Oil. Colombia: the same thing, but by the United Fruit Company. And Chile, with the largest copper reserves in the world, providing one-third of the world's annual production: Anaconda Copper.[11]

Neruda began to tire of the diplomatic duties he saw as superfluous and ineffective. In 1943, he took a leave of absence. He wanted to go home and get involved.

Politics in Chile was complicated. Even the names were deceiving. The Conservatives and Liberals had grown close together as defenders of the Right. The Socialists and Communists fought them from the Left. And the swing vote in the middle? Not the *Rationals* (no such political party has ever existed) but the Radicals.[12]

In 1944, the Communist Party asked Neruda to be its candidate for Senator, representing the northern part of Chile. The district encompassed the Atacama Desert, the highest, driest desert in the world *(shown on the map of Chile)*. It held all the rich copper mines, including Chuquicamata, the world's largest open-pit copper mine, three miles long, one mile wide, and one-half mile deep.

And it was where the poorest, most miserable people in the country — the miners — lived.

The Chuquicamata Open Pit Copper Mine (AVALON CONSTRUCTION PHOTOGRAPHY / ALAMY)

He ran. They voted. He won. He was now "Senator Neruda," thank you very much.[13]

In 1946, Neruda had his first involvement in a presidential election. Gabriel Gonzáles Videla, a Radical running for president, asked him to be his information manager. Neruda ran up and down the country, singing Videla's praises. He won.[14]

Videla formed a cabinet with a mixture of Liberals, Communists, and Radicals. When they couldn't get along, Videla ordered the Communists to step down. When they refused, he fired them.

Neruda was furious: the man he helped get elected had turned on him. He was the victim of broken promises and deliberate lies.

The tipping point came in 1947, when government forces arrested striking miners and sent them to military prisons or concentration camps. Among those in charge was a young Augusto Pinochet.[15]

Senator Neruda exploded. He called the crisis in Chile a "dramatic warning for the continent." He called President Videla a traitor. He accused the government of treachery, bowing to the dictates of the North American owners, rather than representing its own citizens.

He exposed the terrible conditions in which coal miners worked, particularly the "Warm Bed" system. Let us explain: The walk from bed to work took miners four hours, none of it paid. They worked for twelve hours, walked back, and returned to bed for four. Then they woke up and did it all over again. Do the math. Each day, six miners took turns using the same bed. For years, the bed never went cold.[16]

In response, Videla filed a "Desafuero Petition," demanding the revocation of Neruda's senatorial status. The lower court approved it; Neruda appealed. He knew what would follow if he lost his senatorial immunity from prosecution.

Still Neruda spoke out. In "Yo Acuso" ("I Accuse"), a dramatic speech in the Senate, Neruda attacked Videla for his political persecutions. He then read the names of the 628 people — men and women — who, without being interrogated or informed of the charges against them, had been sent to concentration camps.[17]

In early 1948, the Supreme Court upheld Videla's petition and issued an order for Neruda's arrest. Just like that, he was an outlaw.

Neruda began hiding in Santiago, moving from place to place, always one step ahead of the police, a fugitive on the run. He continued to write, words pouring out of him. He was not writing just for Chile; he was writing for the soul, the land, and all the people of South America, calling them to rise up and fight their oppressors. His *Canto General* (1950) was an epic song. In the end, he linked the continent's situation to his own, standing defiantly against his pursuers.

In June, he fled to Valparaiso, staying for forty days while planning to escape on a banana boat, disguised as a traveling salesman. However, at the last minute, he deemed it too risky and stayed put.

In September, things got worse. The Communist Party itself was declared illegal.

And so, by February 1949, the only option left for Neruda was to sneak across the Andes.[18]

PASO DE LILPELA / ANDES

He planned to travel south from Santiago, through the land of his childhood, and take a smuggler's path over the mountains to San Martín de los Andes in Argentina.[19] He grew a beard, gave himself a new name, and carried a fake passport.

Neruda passed alongside two lakes—Lago Ranco and Lago Maihue—to reach a timber estate whose absentee owner supported Videla. As such, it seemed the perfect hiding place, beyond suspicion.

Until, all of a sudden, unannounced, the owner showed up for an inspection. When told about Neruda, he demanded to see him. Neruda feared the worst: arrest and imprisonment. Instead, the owner greeted him with open arms, reciting his poetry. They talked until two in the morning.

Neruda on Horseback, 1949 (JORGE BELLET/COLECCIÓN ARCHIVO FOTOGRÁFICO, ARCHIVO CENTRAL ANDRÉS BELLO, UNIVERSIDAD DE CHILE)

As he prepared to leave, the owner turned to his estate manager and said:

> This has been one of the most beautiful nights of my life. I have just met the greatest poet of this century. What do I care if he's a Communist? Make sure he is given everything he needs.[20]

Neruda thought he was ready to cross the mountains . . . until he learned he would have to do it on a horse. Could he ride? Not really. He looked like a sack of potatoes in the saddle and could barely hang on. At his first river, he was almost swept away. As he climbed, his horse stumbled on rocks or tripped over tree roots and downed branches. Off he went, sprawled on the ground. Finally, after four days, he reached the Lilpela Pass and the border to Argentina. He had escaped, and with the nearly completed manuscript of *Canto General* tucked safely in his saddle bags.

There, he wrote another poem, this one in the cruder, *cuarteta* form, and carved it on a tree:

> How good the air smells
> in the Lilpela Pass
> because the shit has not yet arrived
> from traitor Videla's ass.[21]

What began as a three-year exile turned into an awards tour and holiday. Neruda was presented by Picasso at a Peace Conference in Paris. Then, he was presented, with Picasso, a Peace Prize in Poland (where he learned it was better to be paid in caviar than in cash). He spent months at a villa in

Capri. All while he juggled two women: his second wife and she who would be the third.[22]

Meanwhile, back in Chile, the political left was reasserting itself. In 1951, a man named Salvador Allende was running for president on the Socialist ticket, calling for the nationalization of Chile's basic resources. It was his first of four attempts.

In June 1952, the arrest warrant issued for Neruda was dropped: he could return. He took a break from politics and began focusing on the simple day-to-day things in life. He wrote odes: to joy, to gratitude, to solitude, but also to artichokes, to birdwatching, to laziness, to lemons. And, of course, he never stopped writing love poems. Ah, women.

During the 1960s, Neruda gave readings in many different countries. One night in Venezuela, he read to over six hundred people. When he finished, the audience had requests. First, would he please read *Poem Twenty*. Neruda apologized, saying that he didn't memorize his poems and hadn't brought that one. In response, the audience stood up and recited it back to him.[23]

In 1970, politics beckoned again. The Communist Party asked Neruda to be its candidate for president of Chile. He was the country's most famous person but even he did not believe a Communist could be elected. He deferred to Salvador Allende, and with Neruda's support, Allende won, becoming the world's first ever democratically elected Marxist head of state.[24]

They made a good team, Allende (on the left) nationalizing key industries (including the Chuquicamata Mine) in Chile, and Neruda (yes, he went bald; yes, he got fat) defending him to the world.

Salvador Allende and Pablo Neruda (ARCHIVO FUADACIÓN NERUDA)

Neruda was named ambassador to France and in 1971 was awarded the Nobel Prize for literature. Life was good. Until it wasn't. He had one operation, then another for prostate cancer. He told all his Parisian friends that his country needed him and was calling him back. But really, he was going home to die.[25]

He would see his dream die as well. In Santiago, people were afraid to go out into the streets, people were afraid to be seen, people were just afraid. Neruda could sense that Chile was becoming what Spain had been before its Civil War.

The political scene was chaotic. How does one hold a six-party ruling coalition together, anyway? And is there anything worse than a room full of smart people, each trying to outsmart the other?

Allende was coping, but the country was collapsing. In June 1973, an attempted coup was crushed. In response, Allende appointed General Augusto Pinochet as defense minister and commander of the army. It was quite the mistake.[26]

Neruda, however, was tired and sick, resting at Isla Negra. He wrote, he listened to the news, he feared for the end.

The day: September 11, 1973.

The place: Isla Negra, Chile.

It was a bright, sunny morning. Neruda watched Pinochet's bombing of the Presidential Palace on television. His friend, Allende, was gone, either murdered or a suicide — what difference did it make?

Three days later, Pinochet's men came for him. Yes, even though Neruda was dying of cancer, Pinochet's men came. Late at night, soldiers appeared, knocking at the door. Guns in hand, they marched upstairs. Neruda rose from his sick bed to meet them, and said:

> Look around — there's only one thing of danger for you here — Poetry.[27]

He died nine days later.

ST. PETERSBURG, RUSSIA

> In the ... years of the Great Terror,
> I spent seventeen months in the prison lines ...
> Once, someone "recognized" me ...
> A woman ... whispered in my ear
> (everyone spoke in whispers there):
> "Can you describe this?"
> And I answered, "Yes I can."
> Then something that looked like a smile
> passed over what had once been her face.
>
> —ANNA AKHMATOVA, *REQUIEM*

The Stray Dog Cabaret (MATTEO OMEID / ALAMY)

*I*t opened on New Year's Eve, the last day of 1912, and was shut down by the Russian government two years later, a casualty of World War I. During its brief life, however, the Stray Dog Cabaret was the center of bohemian life for St. Petersburg's artists and writers.

Located in a basement, down the outside stairs from the street, the Stray Dog didn't open until midnight. Its windows were closed and covered, and its walls and ceilings were painted with evil French flowers and fantastical birds, done, as you might expect, by one of the regulars.

On its stage, actors, poets, and musicians performed, entertaining themselves, their friends, and the paying customers. They flaunted the fact that, in polite society, they were considered "stray dogs." [1]

Foremost among them was a tall, thin woman with regal bearing and sad eyes. She was a real looker, but so were we, and we were looking for her.

Anna was her name, and she always knew she'd be a poet. Her father, however, was opposed. He saw poetry as frivolous and self-indulgent. He thought such an activity would bring shame upon him. So, she changed her last name. She became "Anna Akhmatova" after a maternal great-grandmother who was said to be a descendant of Genghis Khan.[2]

Anna's poems were confessions. In *Evening*, her first book, she wrote about love, from its awakening to its fulfillment to its disillusion. More often, she wrote about "non-love," where the woman loves but is not, or is loved and doesn't.[3]

Portrait of Anna Akhmatova by Nathan Altman, 1914 (PETER BARRITT / ALAMY)

Anna's poems were prayers. Her second book was devoted to pain, and suffering, and endurance. Her voice, her verses, her beauty, all made her a rock star. Women recited her *Rosary* to each other, with one person starting and the other one finishing.[4] She was easy to memorize and easy to imitate. Women wanted to look like her, sound like her, be her.

But nobody could write like her, especially when she was having a good time at the Stray Dog.

> All of us here are hookers and hustlers.
> We drink too much, and we don't care.
> The walls are covered with birds and flowers
> that have never seen sunshine or air.
>
> You smoke too much. There's always a cloud
> of nicotine over your head.
> Do you like this skirt? I wore it on purpose.
> I wanted to show lots of leg.
>
> Sometimes I feel this awful pain,
> as if someone were breaking a spell.
> Take a good look at the one over there!
> She's dancing her way into hell![5]

What Anna didn't realize was that hell was pretty much where she would spend the rest of her life.

Indeed, Anna's Russia became one big killing field: World War I, the Revolution and Civil War, Stalin's regime, and World War II. The death toll would be staggering and, of course, it's been debated. We will use round numbers and try to err on the low side, but "necrometrics" is hard to talk about.[6]

During World War I (1914–17), Russian military casualties were 1.5 million dead, five million wounded, and 2.5 million imprisoned or missing. That's nine million soldiers, give or take.[7] As for civilians, 1.5 million died.[8]

But nobody could kill Russians like Russians could kill Russians. During the Revolution and Civil War (1917–22), it was safer to be in the military than to be a civilian. Sure, the opposing Red and White forces killed each other, almost one million, but eight times as many civilians (eight million), died, from massacres caused by the "Red Terror," the "White Terror," and their side effects: disease, drought, and famine.[9]

Stalin's regime (1924–53) just added to the misery. About fourteen million people were sent to *gulag* forced-labor camps, four million to less remote labor "colonies," and another three million to labor "settlements." [10] Among these victims were 3.3 million dead: 800,000 million by execution, 1.7 million in the gulags, 400,000 million in the colonies and another 400,000 in the settlements.[11] Forget the White and Red Terrors, this was the "Great Terror."

And finally, World War II (1939–45). Of the Russian military, 8.7 million were dead or missing, 15 million were wounded, and four million were prisoners of war.[12] As for civilians, 13.7 million were killed, 7.4 million outright, 2.2 in forced labor camps and 4.1 million by disease and famine.[13]

In round numbers?

Anna Akhmatova lived through more than twenty million civilian arrests and imprisonments, more than twenty-five million conflict-related civilian deaths, and more than thirty million military injuries and deaths.

All of this made Anna's love poetry slightly irrelevant. For the Soviets, however, it was also decadent, an expression of bourgeois, private sensibility that should be outlawed. So it was. In 1925, the Central Committee banned her poems — and we mean *banned*. She wasn't just censored — she couldn't publish in any form, and she was forbidden even to write.[14]

She had no income; she had no assets. How was she going to live? Where was she going to live?

The Sheremetev Palace was built in 1712 on land Peter the Great granted Field Marshall Boris Sheremetev as a reward for his military service. Grand and noble, it was so famous for its fountains that it was also known as Fountain House. It became the ancestral home for the Sheremetevs who, by the end of the eighteenth century, were the richest people in Russia, not counting the Czars.

After the revolution, however, the last surviving family owner "gave" it to the government. Part of it became The Museum of Feudal Living, with exhibits about peasant labor. Another part was turned into Soviet *kommunalka*, communal apartments, where strangers were forced to live together, one room per person, with communal kitchens, bathrooms, and hallways.[15]

The Sheremetev Palace (RUSS IMAGES / ALAMY)

No one could have expected that Anna Akhmatova would become its most famous resident, living there on and off for almost thirty years.

She arrived in 1918. Though still married to someone else, she moved into the northern wing with a man who became her second husband. He was a brilliant scholar but a very difficult person. Nevertheless, she stayed with him as she lived through a series of disasters. Her first husband was arrested as a counter-revolutionary conspirator and shot without trial. Her mother was indigent, denied a pension as the widow of a Czarist officer. Her older sister died of tuberculosis, her younger one was in its final stages, one brother disappeared and another killed himself. Even so, husband number two was impossible, so in 1921 she left, and became homeless.[16]

Meanwhile, the man who would become Anna's third husband lived in the southern wing, together with his wife, young daughter, and stepmother. The apartment was not large. It had an entrance hall, a kitchen, a corridor, and four rooms: a study, a dining room, and two bedrooms. As the layout shows, the rooms flowed into each other, and while not grand, the place was comfortable.

This would not last. In 1924, the housekeeper and her son moved in. They slept in the kitchen. Then, in 1926, Anna joined her new man. There was no room for her, so she slept on a sofa in the study and he joined her there. As for his former wife, she and their daughter remained in their bedrooms (they had to live somewhere). In 1929, Anna's only son moved in, creating a "room" for himself in the corridor. Then, a year later, the housekeeper's son brought his wife and two children and took over the former dining room.[17]

As shown below, the gracious openings were closed, and the rooms could be entered only from the corridor. Also as shown below, Anna ended up living in three of them.

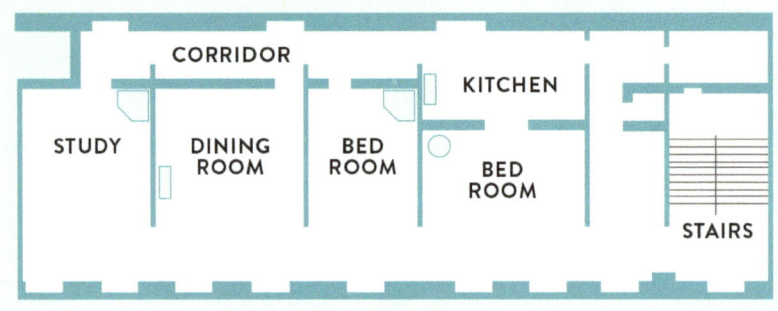

SHEREMETEV PALACE APARTMENT
1918 TO 1925

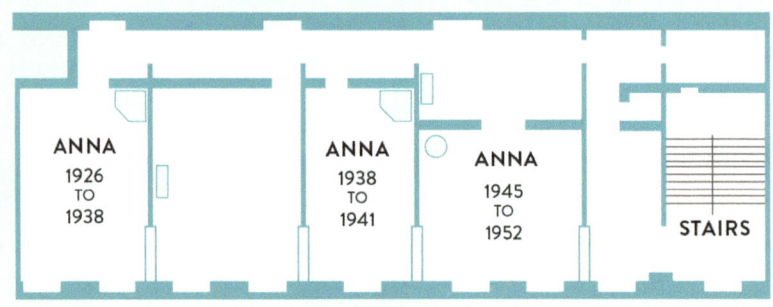

1926 TO 1952

And then the arrests began.

Kresty Prison (MAURICE SAVAGE / ALAMY)

Kresty Prison sits on the north bank of the Neva River, across from the historic heart of the city. It has two main buildings, each shaped in the form of a cross (*kresty* means "crosses"), with a domed church in between. The crosses have a religious meaning, offering salvation for penance, but their true purpose is to enable guards to observe all the corridors from a single vantage point in the middle.

Built in the late nineteenth century, Kresty was considered the most "advanced" prison in the world (it had electricity, it had central heating) and it still is the largest one in Europe. Reportedly, its architect was so proud of his creation that he told the Czar, "Your Majesty, I have built a prison for you."

"No," came the reply, "You have built it for yourself." And the architect was never seen again.

Kresty has 960 cells, with a planned capacity of 1,150 inmates. During Stalin's reign, however, the place was horribly over-occupied. Cells designed for solitary confinement held fifteen to twenty inmates at a time. And why not? It was the perfect nearby holding pen while authorities decided a prisoner's fate.[18]

In December 1933, Anna's son was arrested but released after questioning. In October 1935, he was arrested again after reading an anti-Stalin poem, betrayed by a fellow student. Anna took his case directly to Stalin. No, she pleaded, he is not a political criminal, he is just a child. He was released.

In March 1938, Anna's son was arrested for the third time and held for interrogation at Kresty. There were beatings, torture, and attempts at forced confession. Was he a counter-revolutionary, a conspirator, a terrorist? For seventeen months, Anna stood outside, waiting to learn his fate and offering up scraps of bread for any information she could get. She was not alone:

> "Can you describe this?"
> I answered "Yes I can."
> Then something that looked like a smile
> passed over what had once been her face.[19]

Anna, remember, had been banned. So began a ritual: Write, memorize, burn; write, memorize, burn. Anna would write a poem. Her friends would recite it over and over again until they knew it by heart. Anna would then set her poem on fire, burning it in her ashtray. Eleven friends learned her work and not one of them betrayed her.[20]

Anna became the Witness, the Poet of Memory: her words would prevent those who had been killed from dying a second time... by being forgotten.[21]

Meanwhile, the housing situation was crazy. During 1938, Anna left her third husband, sort of. How did she do it? Simply by changing rooms with his former wife, the two of them continuing to live together in the same apartment. But the housing situation wasn't crazy. Everyone knew that, if someone they knew left, they would be replaced by someone they didn't.

At last, World War II arrived. Anna would have one more rendezvous at the Stray Dog. In August 1941, she was walking in the street when a German air attack began. As the sirens roared, she ran down steps into the nearest bomb shelter, opened her eyes and, once again, saw flowers and birds who, like her, yearned to be free.[22]

With this war came the Siege of Leningrad (as St. Petersburg had been renamed), nine hundred days enduring the German blockade. Anna, even though outcast and scorned, remained a patriot:

> We know what's at stake, and how great the foe's power,
> And what now is coming to pass.
> Every clock shows the same time — it's courage's hour,
> And our courage will hold to the last.[23]

Just like that, she was back in favor, but not for long. After the war, returning from an evacuation of the city, she had nowhere to go except back to the apartment at Fountain House. But she made the mistake of entertaining a member of the British Embassy without prior government approval.

Soon, her room was bugged, and she was followed wherever she went. That was just the beginning.

She was expelled from the Union of Soviet Writers. She was labelled "half nun, half harlot, running between the chapel and the boudoir." A new printing of her works was seized and destroyed. Her son was arrested for the fourth time and sent to the gulag. He survived. Husband number three was arrested and also sent to the gulag. He didn't. Then she was evicted.[24]

There she was: a tired, downtrodden old woman. She had lost her looks, her height, her figure. She had witnessed madness, suicide, execution, starvation. She was so poor that she could put all her possessions in one suitcase, except the locks on it were broken and she needed a rope to keep it closed.[25] Worst of all, she had lost her home. But she was still the voice of her people and she had never been more noble.

Most importantly, she had outlived Stalin.

In time, toward the end, Anna received the international acclaim she long deserved. Dignitaries, admirers, fellow poets, they all came to visit. She greeted them well, but with ironic detachment. Once, Robert Frost, America's Poet Laureate, came to call. She couldn't help but think:

> Here you are, my dear, a national poet.
> Every year your books are published . . .
> they praise you in all the newspapers and journals,
> they teach you in the schools,
> the President receives you as an honored guest.

left: Anna Akhmatova (BRIDGEMAN IMAGES)
right: Robert Frost (AMERICAN STOCK ARCHIVE / GETTY IMAGES)

> And all they've done is slander me!
> Into what dirt they've trampled me!
> I've had everything – poverty, prison lines, fear,
> poems remembered only by heart, and burnt
>   poems.
> And humiliation and grief.
>
> And you don't know anything about this and
> wouldn't be able to understand it if I told you . . .
>
> But now let's sit together, two old people,
>   in wicker chairs.
> A single end awaits us.
> And perhaps the real difference is not actually
>   so great.[26]

We've been to St. Petersburg twice. The first time was in 2003, for the three hundredth anniversary of the founding of the city. All the buildings were clean and freshly painted. Usually, they're dull and tired because of the sea air and dampness. Remember, the city was built on a swamp at the edge of the Gulf of Finland, which leads into the Baltic Sea, not far from the Arctic Circle.

It has lots of small canals and two main water ways, the Neva and Fontanka rivers.

We ran around trying to see everything, the State Russian Museum, the Church of the Spilled Blood, and of course, the Hermitage. We spent a full day there, looking at all of its paintings, only to find out there was one whole building we didn't even go into. But the real discovery of our trip was Anna.

We went back sixteen years later, looking just for her. In the meantime, we had read her poems and every biography we could lay our hands on.

The historic part of the city is a small town with wide streets and, if you know where to look, Anna is everywhere.

We stayed at the Belmond Grand Hotel Europe, on the city's main street, Nevsky Prospect. Our room was beautiful. The restaurants were great. One featured its own private ballet. The other, the best caviar we've ever had. But our favorite spot was the lobby bar. It had a signature drink: the "Anna Akhmatova." It was made with gin, elderflower liqueur, Lillet Blanc, and dry vermouth. We tried it without the gin (we are short hitters) and it was so good, we had it every night.

ST. PETERSBURG, RUSSIA | 219

BALTIC SEA

ST. PETERSBURG

One morning, we walked out the back of the hotel to Italyanskaya Ulitsa (Italian Street). We crossed it and, there, down a flight of stairs, was the Stray Dog. It had reopened in 2001.

The Stray Dog Logo (MSTISLAV DOBUZHINSKY/PUBLIC DOMAIN)

During our first visit, we had attended a midnight acrobat show. The ceilings were so low, we could touch them with our hands, and we kept waiting for the acrobats to hit their heads. Somehow, they didn't. This time, we stayed for lunch and a poetry reading. We couldn't understand the words, but we didn't care.

In the afternoon, we walked across the square to the State Russian Museum. We were looking for Room 72, where the sitting portrait of Anna is usually displayed. It wasn't there. Instead, it hung in a special exhibition, together with portraits of her painted at other times in her life, figurines of her made by the Imperial Porcelain Factory, and a bust of her in old age.

The next day was dark, dreary, and wet. It was just right for a visit to the Sheremetev Palace to see Anna's old apartment. It has been turned into a museum and we wandered through it, asking ourselves if we could ever live there.

The Ashtray (ANNA AKHMATOVA MUSEUM AT FOUNTAIN HOUSE)

Among the displays, one item jumped out at us. It was the ashtray in which Anna had burned her poems.

There are four statues of Anna in town, and we visited two of them. One is small and discreet, sitting in a lovely private garden. The other isn't really a statue, it's a monument.

It was built in 2006 to honor the fortieth anniversary of Anna's death and sits on the south bank of the Neva River.[27]

There she is, tall and thin and young again, with her head turned over her shoulder, looking back across the water at Kresty Prison, waiting for her son to be released. We would have stayed longer, communing, but down came the rain and soon we were soggy and sad. It was perfect.

Monument to Anna (SERGI AFANASEV / DREAMSTIME.COM)

STAVROS BEACH, CRETE

A man needs a little madness or else...
he never dares cut the rope and be free.

—NIKOS KAZANTZAKIS, *ZORBA THE GREEK*

Zorba's Dance from *Zorba the Greek* (1964), directed by Michael Cacoyannis
(ALLSTAR PICTURE LIBRARY LIMITED / ALAMY)

Crete is an island in the middle of the Mediterranean Sea and, as you might expect, it is surrounded on all sides by... beaches. There are cosmopolitan beaches with sophisticated, international clientele; trendy beaches for the party crowd; family beaches where the water is shallow and kids rule; secluded beaches perfect for lovers; wild beaches with rough water; calm beaches, quiet, protected, and safe;

smooth beaches with soft sand; rugged and rocky beaches for risk-takers; and nude beaches, lots of them. Whatever your preference, Crete has a beach for you.[1]

By one count, the island has 219 beaches, offering a different swim for every day during even the longest summer.

Yes, we have favorites. Hippies "discovered" two of them: Matala, a semicircular beach where they lived in caves; and Preveli, ten minutes from a monastery, where a river runs to the sea.[2]

Three others have special features: Vai, with five thousand palm trees and lots of sand dunes; Frangokastello, with shallow water in front of a castle; and Agia Roumeli, at the mouth of the Samaria Gorge, the longest gorge in Europe, with sand reachable only by boat or an eight-hour hike through the gorge.[3]

But we went to Crete to visit one very special beach, Stavros, so that we could pretend, if just for a moment, that we have the same spirit, the same joy, the same madness as Zorba. After all, who else but a madman would dance after a catastrophic business failure?

Zorba the Greek was a man who inspired a novel (1952), which became a movie, a Broadway play, and then a legend, and we were looking for him.

The story is simple. A shy young writer, a man of thought, meets an old flame-thrower, a man of action. They find love. For the writer, she's a mysterious widow. For Zorba, she's a faded courtesan. Both women die. The men are entrepreneurs and attempt a logging operation. It fails "splendiferously," and they are ruined. The young man asks the old one to teach him to dance, and they dance on the beach.[4]

STAVROS BEACH, CRETE | 225

CRETE IN THE MEDITERRANEAN SEA

CRETE

STAVROS BEACH, CRETE | *226*

Nikos Kazantzakis (THE NIKOS KAZANTZAKIS MUSEUM, KAZANTZAKIS ARCHIVE)

Of course, it was madness. But what kind? Because, for the Greeks, there are two. *Trela* is your everyday madness, nuts, crazy. *Kouzoulada* is the madness we all aspire to, the great, glorious enthusiasm, the grand lust for life.[5] This is what Zorba gave to the writer, Nikos Kazantzakis. This is what Nikos gave to the world.

Ah, Nikos, we were also looking for you.

Nikos Kazantzakis was a traveler, a pilgrim, a seeker. Born in Heraklion, the largest town on the island, he grew up at the end of the nineteenth century. It was a time of revolution, and he dreamed of being a hero and a saint. One day, his father taught him what those words meant. He took Nikos to see Cretan freedom fighters whom the ruling Turks had just hung from a tree, and made him kiss the dead men's feet. Freedom wasn't just a right; it was a duty.[6]

For young Nikos, Crete, with its location in the Mediterranean, was the crossroads of the world. Here he saw everyone: Christians, Muslims, and Jews; British and French; Greeks and Turks; sailors and ship owners; politicians and military men.

When he grew up, he kept looking. He went to Athens for the law, to Paris for Nietzsche, to Assisi for St. Francis, to Moscow for Lenin, to East Asia for the Buddha.[7] He wasn't just visiting places, he was trying on ideas. But he began to understand;

> As a child, I had almost fallen into the well. When grown up, I nearly fell into the word "eternity," and into quite a number of other words too: "love," "hope," "country," "God." As each word was conquered and left behind, I had the feeling I had escaped a danger and made some progress. But no, I was only changing words and calling it deliverance.[8]

Nikos may have portrayed himself as shy, but he sure had nerve. How else to describe someone who wrote his own *Odyssey* and called it *A Modern Sequel?* (1958)[9] How else to describe someone who went to Mount Athos and then created his own religion? It wasn't God who saved men, it was men who were *The Saviors of God* (1960).[10] Indeed, he was so good at the religion thing that the Greek Orthodox Church wanted to excommunicate him.[11]

> "The idea's everything," he said.
> "Have you faith? Then a splinter from an old door becomes a sacred relic.
> "Have you no faith? Then the Holy Cross itself becomes an old doorpost to you."[12]

Finally, how else to describe someone who imagined that *The Last Temptation of Christ* (1955) was the chance to live a normal life, to marry, to have children, to be loved and respected, and to grow old with grace and dignity?[13]

No wonder the Church couldn't stand him.

Still, Nikos kept coming back to Zorba. Yes, he was a real man, flesh and blood. And he cleaned up pretty well.

His name was Georgios Zorbas, and Nikos met him in 1915. Together, they worked a lignite mine. It failed, but Zorbas taught Nikos to abandon the safe haven of prudence and dare the great folly, the risk of life. He called Nikos "boss," over and over he called him "boss," and laughed. Next, he called Nikos "pen-pusher" and laughed.[14] In the Beginning was the Word. Ha, ha, ha. Before Action? Ha, ha, ha.

Zorba knew life is a battle between now and forever. Plan, plan, plan. Save, save, save. Or live! Because someday, now *is* forever. Why not make it today?

Georgios Zorbas (THE NIKOS KAZANTZAKIS MUSEUM, KAZANTZAKIS ARCHIVE)

Zorba got the joke:

> Look, one day I had gone to a little village. An old grandfather of ninety was busy planting an almond tree.
> "What, granddad!" I exclaimed. "Planting an almond tree?"
> And he, bent as he was, turned round and said: "My son, I carry on as if I should never die."
> I replied: "And I carry on as if I was going to die any minute."
> Which of us was right, boss?[15]

Kazantzakis loved Zorba. And so do we. That's why we went to Crete, just to dance on his beach.

LAST WORDS

Like Zorba, Kazantzakis loved freedom. The need was basic, the need was stark. And it found no better voice than his own tombstone. Sitting tall on the ramparts, looking out over the Mediterranean Sea, it proclaims:

> I hope for nothing,
> I fear nothing,
> I am free.

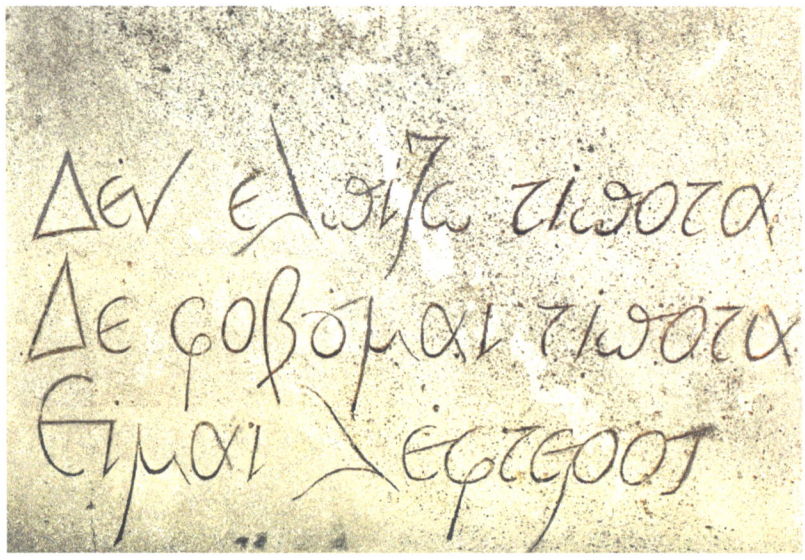

Epitaph of Nikos Kazantzakis (CONSTANTINOS PLIAKOS/ALAMY)

KALADHUNGI, INDIA

*A tiger is a large-hearted gentleman
with boundless courage.*

—JIM CORBETT, *MAN-EATERS OF KUMAON*

The Kumaon Foothills (FERNANDO QUEVEDO DE OLIVEIRA / ALAMY)

*Go after a man-eater that has killed a hundred people?
Not on your life.*

—JIM CORBETT, *THE MAN-EATING LEOPARD OF RUDRAPRAYAG*

Up until the beginning of the twentieth century, Kumaon, a region in northern central India, was covered with forest, grass, and wetland. Located in the Himalayan foothills (the *bhabar*) and the plains just below (the *terai*), scrubby undergrowth and swampy bushes made it a jungle teeming with wildlife.

In this jungle the tiger was king. In this jungle, the greatest of them all, the Bengal tiger, was home.[1]

Some might think we went there looking for the tiger. Not really. We were looking for the man who spent his entire life looking *for*—and then looking *after*—this king of beasts.

Jim Corbett was born in Kumaon in 1875. Growing up, he lived in the hill town of Nainital during the summer and in the lowland of Kaladhungi in winter *(yes, there will be a map)*. He was an outsider, by birth and by preference. His family was English but had lived in India for three generations. As such, he was *country-bottled*, neither a Britisher serving a term in a far-away land nor a native. But the outside was what Jim loved and the outside was where he would make his mark.[2]

Jungle Folk. At an early age, Jim created his own system to classify birds and animals. He didn't do it by species, he did it by function. First, there were those that beautify: orioles and sunbirds, deer and antelope, just a pleasure to see. Second were those that sing: thrushes and robins, providing background music. Next came those that regenerate the ground: hornbills, pigs, and porcupines, digging up and aerating the soil. Then, those that warn of danger: red fowl and babblers, monkeys and squirrels, sounding the alarm. Some *were* the danger: eagles and hawks, tigers and leopards, maintaining the balance of nature. Finally, some cleaned up after everyone else: vultures, crows, jackals, and hyenas.[3]

Jim's was a good, practical system that considered each creature's role in the jungle. Yes, tigers were at the top of the food chain, but they killed only to eat or in self-defense, not for sport or pleasure.

Jungle Talk. Jim learned the language of the jungle folk. Birds and animals call for a reason. Those who call to sing may simply sing. But they and others will also call to summon or warn, to convey excitement or fear. It is all in the intonation. Over time, Jim learned to identify the bird or animal as well as the purpose of their call. Jim became fluent and could imitate them as well.[4]

In particular, Jim learned the calls of tigers. They roared, growled, whined, hissed, spit, and purred, depending on the situation. Jim could tell the difference between a mating call and a warning growl, and imitate them both.[5]

Finally, Jim learned to hear the silence: was it anticipation or contentment, preparation or repose? Sometimes, things were as they appeared to be. Sometimes, they weren't.

Jungle Tracking. Jim learned how to follow the jungle folk. Oh, the stories that tracks can tell! Animals that stalk their prey have big pads and small toes, and animals that chase have small pads and big toes. It's logical when you think about it.[6]

Just look at the tracks of your dog or cat. Now you know how they would hunt if they had to.

Jim could see a track and know whether the animal was tiger or leopard, male or female, young or old, big or small, injured or healthy. Soon, he could tell whether the track was fresh or stale, depending on its location in the sun or shade, and the time when the winds blew or dew fell.[7]

Big Pad, Small Toes. Small Pad, Big Toes. (OXFORD BOOKS, ENGLAND/ERIN GREB)

He didn't know it, but Jim was learning to be a *shikari* (a big-game hunter). As he advanced, so did his weapons, and they increased the size of his domain. He went from sling shot to bow and arrow to shotgun to rifle and, at that point, the entire jungle opened up to him.[8] As you might imagine, he became a crack shot.

Jim's education was interrupted by only one thing: school.

Whenever he could, though, he was back outside, doing more homework:

> *Jungle Lore* is not a science that can be learned from textbooks; it can, however, be absorbed a little at a time and the absorption process can go on indefinitely, for the book of nature has no beginning, as it has no end.[9]

Jungle Hunting. Ultimately, Jim began to hunt tigers. The most basic method was to *stalk* them on foot, never forgetting, of course, that, while he was stalking the tiger, the tiger, most likely, was stalking him.¹⁰ Indeed, he quickly developed *jungle sensitiveness*, an intuition warning of unseen but approaching danger. It would save him many times.¹¹

Jim learned all the tricks. He followed the *pug marks* (paw prints) of the tiger. He followed the *drag* or the *blood trail*. In the former, the tiger would take the kill (human or otherwise) and carry it to a safe, secluded place to eat. If the prey were too large to be carried cleanly, the tiger would drag it, leaving a trail of marks to follow. And, if the prey were bleeding, there would be blood to show the way.¹²

Hunting a tiger was dangerous. It was far safer to *sit up* over bait or a kill, and wait for the tiger to appear. This involved a lot of patience and endurance. The hunter would set out a small animal, a goat or a cow, tied to a stake in the ground near a tree. He would climb up the tree and sit, hoping the tiger would take the bait. Alternatively, the hunter would find a partially eaten kill and sit up near it, waiting for the tiger to return and finish the meal. Either of these could take all night and lead to nothing.¹³ So, the hunter would stay out for another night, and another and another . . . unless, of course, the tiger attacked the tree.

If it were mating season, Jim might *call up* the tiger. He would cup his hands around his mouth and give the roar that every male or female longs to hear.¹⁴ It worked.

Hunting was not always a solitary affair. Jim learned how to *conduct a beat* to force a tiger out of cover. Natives would stand together creating a linked wall of noise, banging on pots and pans, throwing stones or shooting rifles into the air. The wall would close in on a tiger hiding in the bush, forcing it to move in the direction of a hunter waiting to take the shot. In some cases, the natives would *burn* the tiger *out*, using fire instead of noise.¹⁵

Imagine tigers on the prowl. They're big, four hundred to five hundred pounds. They're fast, three times as fast as a human. They're strong, with jaws that can crush one thousand pounds per square inch. They're smart, able to sneak up behind their victims.[16]

Now imagine the attack. First comes the impact, boom. Then ten sharp claws, carving you up, scraping off your skin. And, finally, four large canine teeth, sinking into your neck, ending it all.[17]

Little wonder that tigers have the respect of every animal and every human living within or venturing into their range. However, if they become man-eaters, that respect turns into fear, and the worst kind of fear: terror.

Relax, humans are not a tiger's natural prey. All things being equal, they would rather avoid us. But sometimes they can't.

> A man-eating tiger is a tiger that has been compelled, through stress or circumstances beyond its control to adopt a diet alien to it.[18]

What were these circumstances?

Loss of habitat for one. The British were modernizing India. But, in order to do so, they were cutting down the forests for railroad ties, building materials, and fuel. They were turning wild grasslands into farms. And, they were squeezing tigers into a smaller and smaller jungle, encroaching on their space.

Loss of prey for another. People eat meat, too, and there were just so many deer (whether they be *sambar*, *chital*, or *kakar*) to go around.

Loss of ability for a third. Like all animals, tigers get wounded or old and lose their edge. They are then forced to look for easier, domesticated, and increasingly closer food sources.[19]

And so the terror would begin. Natives were killed working in the fields, walking between villages, and just sitting at home. No place was safe, and the natives were defenseless. In order to prevent rebellion, owning guns had been forbidden.

It was up to the British authorities in Kumaon, therefore, to kill the man-eaters. They posted rewards. They hired regular and special shikaris. They sent out soldiers. They pleaded for calm. After no success, they turned to an untried, local young man: Jim Corbett.

Jim became the most successful hunter of man-eaters in history. Between 1907 and 1938, he killed eleven tigers and two leopards, who, together, were responsible for over twelve hundred human deaths. X marks the spots on the map *(see next page)* where Jim killed them, and there is a brief description of all his hunts in Appendix VI.

Jim killed the man-eaters by using the skills he had learned as a boy: stalking, tracking, sitting up, conducting a beat, and for his last one, a tigress in heat, calling her up and shooting her at point-blank range. Every kill was a life-or-death proposition. Time and time again, he took the ultimate risk in order to protect the lives of the Indian villagers. They loved him for it. He was more than a hunter, he was a savior.

Man-Eaters of Kumaon Killed by Corbett. X Marks the Spots Where Jim Killed Them.

There were two kills that established Jim's reputation: the Champawat Man-Eater, the most prolific killer in history, and the Man-Eating Leopard of Rudraprayag, the most famous leopard in the world.

Just look at the Champawat Man-Eater. Half of her right upper tooth has been lost and the entire right lower one is missing. Still, she killed two hundred people in Nepal before being driven across the Sharda River into Kumaon. There, beginning in 1903, she killed another 236.[20]

The Champawat Man Eater (RAVI DAYAL PUBLISHER/ERIN GREB)

In 1907, after years of failed attempts by others, Jim was asked to hunt this tigress. He imposed two conditions: all rewards must be cancelled, and all other shikaris withdrawn from the field. Made sense. He didn't want to be a bounty hunter and he didn't want to be accidentally shot. After all, this was probably the first man-eater ever known in Kumaon — and definitely the first one for Jim.[21]

Notified of a new attack, Jim marched three days to the site of the victim. Once there, he sat *out* (not *up*) all night, without success. Well, actually, he had sort of a success. He had made the mistake of spending the night on the ground. And survived.

During the next two days, Jim looked for tracks, guarded the wheat harvest, and shot three wild goats for the pot: two for the village and one for his men. He spent three more days visiting any place where there had been a tiger sighting. He suspected, however, that the tigress would not kill twice in the same location and would not return to her kill. She had a domain of hundreds of square miles, and Jim believed that finding her would be like finding a needle in two haystacks.[22]

Jim spent his ninth day walking fifteen miles to Champawat. The following day he went on a wild goose chase, finding a cow that had been killed by a leopard. On day eleven, the man-eater struck again, this time a young girl. There were pug marks, a drag, and a blood trail. They all led into a stream that fed into a small, blood-filled pool. Jim found the remains of the young girl's leg. Suddenly, he sensed great danger and turned to see the tigress about to spring. His movement stopped her and she retreated, still carrying the remains of the girl. Jim tracked them for more than four hours, but the fading light forced him to return to the village.[23]

Once there, Jim asked the villagers to help him organize a beat. Despite their fear, on the following day, almost three hundred men appeared. They lined themselves across the top of the ridge above the tigress's hiding place. Down they came, making noise any way they could, with drums, shouting, even using illegal firearms.

When the tigress broke into the open and ran into the riverbed, Jim was waiting for her. He fired once and missed. He fired two more times, and both shots found their mark. But the tigress refused to go down and Jim was out of bullets. He shouted for another gun, grabbed it from the village leader and, at twenty feet, ended four years of terror.[24]

Rudraprayag is a hill town ten days march northwest of Nainital. Here, two rivers that lead into the Ganges merge. Since ancient times, Hindus have made Rudraprayag a stopping place for pilgrims going up one river, the Mandakini, to the Temple of Kedarnath, or up the other, the Alaknanda, to the Temple of Badrinath.[25] These are all shown on the prior map.

In 1918, a deadly pandemic (the Spanish flu) made its way to northern India and swept through Rudraprayag, claiming so many victims that people died faster than could be cremated, as was the usual practice. Instead, a live coal was placed in a deceased person's mouth, the body was carried to the edge of a hill, and then thrown into the valley below. A leopard found these bodies and soon acquired a taste for human flesh. When the pandemic ended, he refused to change his diet.[26]

The Rudraprayag Leopard (RAVI DAYAL PUBLISHER/ERIN GREB)

Behold the Man-Eating Leopard of Rudraprayag. Isn't he cute? And deadly. Between 1918 and 1926, a span of eight years, this leopard killed at least 125 people and terrorized not only the fifty thousand villagers who lived within his range, but also the sixty thousand pilgrims a year who made their way to the shrines of Kedarnath and Badrinath.

This leopard became one of the most publicized animals that ever lived. His every kill was reported by the daily and weekly newspapers in India. His threat to pilgrims was news all over the world.[27]

The government offered rewards, granted three hundred special gun licenses, appealed to sportsmen all across India, and permitted soldiers on leave to take their rifles with them. Jim followed the news, and was sure his services wouldn't be needed. Unfortunately, in late 1925, they were.[28]

In the fall of 1925, Jim spent ten weeks searching for the leopard, mostly at night. The leopard's territory was huge, five hundred square miles, roughly divided in half by the Alaknanda River. Jim closed off one of the two bridges crossing it and spent twenty nights sitting up in a tower overlooking the other, hoping for a shot. No chance. He set out a fierce metal trap, only to catch and kill the wrong leopard. He even tried lacing bait with cyanide, but the man-eater seemed to like it. After ten weeks of around-the-clock hunting, Jim was exhausted. He withdrew from the field, promising to return in the spring.[29]

In March 1926, Jim went back. He spent another five nights on the bridge tower, without success. He set out a goat that the leopard ignored. He poisoned the leopard's next kill but arsenic and strychnine were as ineffective as cyanide had been. Jim then tied up a goat as bait and sat up in a pine tree overlooking it. When the goat fell asleep, Jim tried to call up the leopard, using his mating call. He got an answer. Unfortunately, he got a second answer and, while both leopards probably got lucky, Jim didn't.[30]

The pilgrimage to Kedarnath and Badrinath is seasonal and, as March turned to April, the snow was melting, the road was opening, and the pilgrims were coming. It was time to stop the leopard.

In past years, the man-eater had taken to patrolling the pilgrims' road, and was brazen enough to pull them out of their shelters as they slept. Jim realized that the leopard had a fixed route around which he would circulate during a five-day period. As a last attempt, he decided to tie a goat with a bell around its neck in the middle of the road close to one of the shelters, and sit up over him in a mango tree.

Jim gave himself ten nights, after which he would quit. The ten passed uneventfully and he was ready to leave. However, 150 pilgrims arrived and wanted to stay at the shelter, so Jim agreed to spend one more night. It was meant to be. The leopard attacked the goat, the bell tinkled, Jim shot the leopard. The goat lived and was a hero for the rest of its life.[31]

As for the leopard:

> . . . the best-hated and the most-feared animal in all India, whose only crime — not against the laws of nature, but against the laws of man — was that he had shed human blood . . . was peacefully sleeping his long last sleep.[32]

After kills like these, Jim Corbett became the go-to man for hunting tigers in Kumaon. He was a friend to the high and mighty, from local governors to the viceroy himself. But he was a better friend to the underdog Indians whose lives he protected. They called him "Carpet Sahib," twisting his name with their accents.[33]

Jim's life, however, was about to change. While he had

started out saving the natives from the tigers, he would end up saving the tigers from the natives.

It was a gradual but logical move. Growing up in the jungle, Jim knew that tigers were not "cruel," or "blood thirsty." Instead, humans were the problem. When he led hunts, he found that his clients didn't want one tiger skin, they wanted ten.

Still, if there were a "moment of conversion," it was the day Jim went hunting with three British military officers. They came across a lake filled with thousands of waterfowl. The officers started shooting, kept shooting, and just kept shooting. Finally, after killing over three hundred birds, they stopped. It wasn't hunting, it was slaughter. There was no way they could ever carry out all those birds; they had killed merely for the pleasure of killing.[34]

It was then that Jim took up photography and "shooting" took on a whole new meaning:

> The taking of a good photograph gives far more pleasure to the sportsman than the acquisition of a trophy; and further, while the photograph is of interest to all lovers of wild life, the trophy is only of interest to the individual who acquired it.[35]

Indeed, while trophies lose their hair, become moth-eaten, are stored in the attic, or thrown away, photos can last forever.

In the early 1930s, Jim began thinking about conservation, not as a way to protect tigers *for*, but as a way to protect them *from* hunting. He had seen their decline firsthand. In 1907, when he hunted the Champawat Man-Eater, there were an estimated forty thousand tigers in India. By the 1930s, only one in ten was left.[36]

Jim Corbett at Camp (CONSTABLE, LONDON)

Without help, he could see the end:

> A tiger is a large-hearted gentleman with boundless courage and when he is exterminated — as exterminated he will be unless public opinion rallies to his support — India will be the poorer by having lost the finest of her fauna.[37]

Jim was close friends with the governor of the province and one of their favorite spots was on the Ramganga River west of Ramnagar. The fishing was good and so was the scenery and wildlife. They considered turning the area into a preserve.

In 1934, over one hundred square miles was deemed a sanctuary, with no hunting allowed for five years. In 1936, it was established as India's first national park. In 1957, ten years after independence, to honor and thank Jim, India named the park after him. In the 1960s, Corbett National Park was expanded to over two hundred square miles. Today, including the core and buffer zones, it is almost five hundred square miles.[38]

As we prepared to visit the park, we read all of Jim's books: *Man-Eaters of Kumaon* (1946), *The Man-Eating Leopard of Rudraprayag* (1948), *My India* (1952), *Jungle Lore* (1953), and *The Temple Tiger and More Man-Eaters of Kumaon* (1955). It was clear that, as much as the people of India loved Jim, he loved them more.

"Corbett," as the park is known, has tigers, Asian elephants, and almost six hundred different kinds of birds. Little wonder that it is called the "Land of Roar, Trumpet, and Song." Close your eyes when you get there, listen, and hear for yourself.

Corbett is not only India's first national park, it is also the country's first tiger reserve. In April 1973, the government founded Project Tiger, in a meeting held at the Dhikala Forest Rest House *(see Dhikala FRH on the map)*. The project's purpose was simple: to save the tiger from extinction. It designated nine safe havens throughout the country for tigers and their prey. In these reserves, there would be no human interference, no forestry, no grazing, no agriculture, no hunting. Today, India has fifty such reserves.[39]

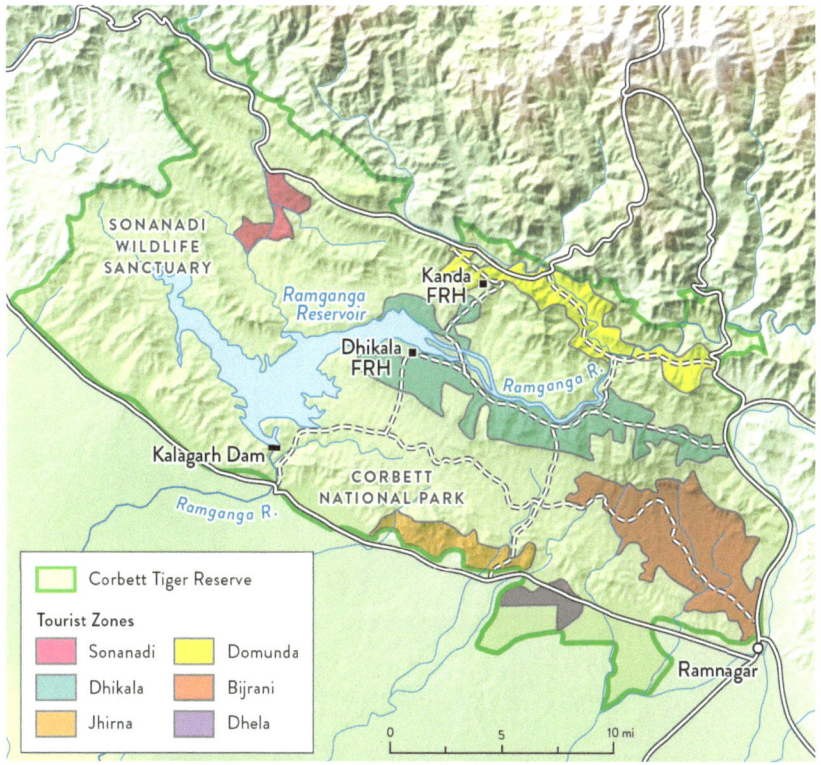

TIGER RESERVE AND TOURIST ZONES

Corbett offers the best of Kumaon: thick green forest, steep hills and ravines (*nullahs*), white-rocked rivers, and wide, sprawling grasslands (*chaurs*).

It has been divided into six tourist zones, as shown on the above map. Dhikala is its heart, with the Ramganga River running through it. Jhirna on the south side is open all year round. Bijrani to the east is dryer than the other zones, with only seasonal springs. Sonanadi is located in the wildlife sanctuary on the western side of the Ramganga Reservoir. Domunda to the north is leopard country. Nearby is the

Kanda FRH, located at the highest point in the park. Dhela, the most recently added zone, is quickly returning to the wild from its previously cultivated state.[40]

Corbett is home to more tigers than any other reserve in India and, wherever we went, we felt Jim looking over our shoulder.

Shoot Nothing But Pictures. (R. J. PRICKETT/SANGAN BOOKS, LONDON)

MARRAKESH, MOROCCO

> *He was the Eagle of Telouet, the Black Panther,
> the Mountain Gazelle, the Last of the Lords of the Atlas.*
>
> —GAVIN MAXWELL, *LORDS OF THE ATLAS*

T'Hami El Glaoui (HISTORICAL COLLECTION / ALAMY)

Please meet El Hadj T'hami El Glaoui, Pasha of Marrakesh. The son of a Berber warlord and his Ethiopian concubine, he was, in Europe, a myth: "a knight like Sir Galahad, a saint like Saint George, a sage like Solomon." He was noble, brave, kind, unselfish, faithful, and true. He was the epitome of Oriental splendor and romance, hosting vast banquets, bestowing priceless gifts. His manners were exquisite, his clothes refined, and his diplomacy delicate.[1]

He was an astute businessman, using power to advance his financial interests. He cornered the local market in basic commodities: almonds, saffron, dates, mint, olives, and oranges. He controlled four of the five French-Moroccan newspapers. And the famed brothels of Marrakesh? They all paid him a commission.[2]

T'Hami was a voracious sexual athlete, with two wives, four concubines, three harems, and talent scouts posted at the country's railroad stations, looking for unaccompanied, attractive, and adventurous European women traveling south.[3]

He was a scratch golfer with his own course, a Hadji who made the once-in-a-lifetime pilgrimage to Mecca, a heroic warrior with many victories . . . and the owner of active dungeons.[4]

He was, especially for the French, a dream come true.

In 1890, Morocco had no roads and, even though it had boundaries, it was barely a country. Indeed, just because someone was the "Sultan," it didn't mean he ruled, and the greatest risk of going off to conquer anyone was to return and find someone else occupying your place or pretending to your throne.[5]

The country was divided in two parts: the *Bled el-Makhzen*, where the Arab sultan's government supposedly was in control; and, as shown on the map, a much, much greater *Bled es-Siba*, where Berber tribes owed no allegiance to the sultan or anyone else.[6]

Enhancing this political division were the Atlas Mountains, running down the middle of the country like a spine. The sultan might be master of the lowlands, north, from Fez and west, from Marrakesh. But the mountains, the great deserts east, and the trading routes south belonged to the warlords.

MOROCCO IN 1890. BLED EL-MAKHZEN (GREEN)
AND BLED ES-SIBA (RED).

With an occasional exception. Then, the sultan would embark on an expedition to the desert oases, looking to collect taxes and tribute along the way. In the summer of 1893, he crossed the Atlas from Fez and made for Tafilalt *(again, on the map)*, the oasis that had been the origin of his family's dynasty. Historically, these types of expeditions were viewed as *harkas* (burnings) because that's what royal entourages did. They burned through the countryside, taking food and fodder and fighting as they went.[7]

On this trip, however, the results were meager: food was lacking, water was bad, heat was great, and rebellion was everywhere. It was almost winter when the sultan finally arrived. His army was fever-stricken and demoralized. He himself, although he didn't know it, was dying.[8]

The sultan realized Tafilalt could not support his troops during the winter, but it was too late for the long march back to Fez. So, he headed for Marrakesh, knowing that he would, again, have to cross the Atlas.

Looking at the mountains, he saw only three passes *(once more, on the map)*, each controlled by a different Berber tribe. To the south was *Tiz-n-Test*, ruled by the M'tougga, who had grown so powerful that the sultan had recently stripped them of all their lands except the mountains. They commanded six thousand rifles and would probably not be helpful. The center, *Oued Nfis*, was controlled by the Goundafa. The sultan considered them friends, but still, they could raise five thousand armed men, and all warlords were opportunists.

The northernmost pass was *Tiz-n-Telouet*. There, the Glaoui commanded. The leaders were young, their father having recently died: Madani El Glaoui was twenty-seven and his brother T'hami, only fifteen. They were unique, however, for they owned a profitable salt mine and didn't have to rely on piracy, tolls, or violence for their fortune. And, besides, they could only raise two or three thousand men.[9]

Telouet was the obvious choice, and not just for military reasons. It was the most direct route to Marrakesh, and the sultan had no time for delay. By the time he reached the foothills, the snow had begun. As his troops marched higher, their transport, camels, mules, and horses, faltered and died. Injured soldiers were left behind, buried alive, so enemies couldn't cut off their heads. Men too weak to carry their own rifles were forced to haul the sultan's major weapons, one of which was a seventy-seven-millimeter bronze Krupp assault cannon.

This cannon would change the history of Morocco.

The Glaoui Cannon (GEOFFWIGGINS.COM / ALAMY)

As the sultan and his defeated troops staggered into the *kasbah* (castle) at Telouet, the Glaoui gave them a three-day royal welcome . . . with extravagant banquets befitting a conquering hero. There were chickens and pigeons, sheep and kabob, couscous everywhere, pastries and mint tea, with women swaying and young boys dancing. The brothers had saved the sultan, but they were acting as if *he* had granted *them* the pleasure of his company.

When the time came for the sultan to leave, he rid himself of arms too heavy to carry, including the cannon. He gave it to the Glaoui and made Madani his personal *khalifa*, with nominal control over all the tribes between the Atlas Mountains and the Sahara Desert. With their new weapon, the only one outside the Royal Army, the brothers soon made that control real.[10]

The 1890s brought something else to Morocco: tourists. They came from many countries, Scotland, England, America. They travelled on horseback, as there were no roads. And safety was in numbers. One party, for example, consisted of three male and two female travelers, fifteen servants, five soldiers for protection, ten tents, and forty animals.[11]

This group found the country fascinating, "from the wildest and most rugged scenery to the tamest of tame landscapes." As for its natural inhabitants, they were intrigued: beautiful green beetles, lizards of all colors and sizes, and locusts, so many locusts. In fact, the locusts were a dietary specialty, whether fried, roasted, or maybe even boiled ... and they supposedly tasted like shrimp.[12]

They set out from Tangier and visited the coastal towns, including Casablanca (with its "white houses"). They made their way to Marrakesh, met the sultan, and went shopping in the *souks*. But the goal of their trip was the Atlas Mountains, where they hoped to hunt for wild sheep. At last, they reached their destination: the kasbah at Telouet.[13]

T'hami personally welcomed them, and after they were settled and rested, took them hunting. On the way, he gave them a special treat:

> He suddenly put his horse — a great big powerful black Barb — into a gallop, twisted and turned about at full speed, and then without rhyme or reason, fired off his

gun, and with the same suddenness, and for as much reason as he started, brought his horse to a full stop. Whether it was to exhibit the sure-footedness of his horse or his skill as a rider we did not know. But . . . it seemed to afford him and his followers an enormous amount of pleasure.[14]

This was a solo performance of a mock battle charge that has since become the classic Morocco tourist attraction: the *Fantasia*. Also known as the *Tbourida* or *Lab al Baroud*, the "gunpowder game," it celebrates Morocco's equestrian heritage and was originally intended as a military training exercise.[15]

The *Fantasia* (RUDI ERNST / SHUTTERSTOCK)

There would be plenty of opportunities to use that training between 1900 and 1912. After the sultan died, his thirteen-year-old son acceded to the throne. While the Glaoui were pacifying the Bled-es-Siba, the Bled el-Makhzen descended into chaos. Corrupt advisers encouraged the child sultan to spend extravagantly, while they enriched themselves and bankrupted the country. One pretender after another claimed his throne. Two replacement sultans were crowned. Madani was named Grand Vizier and T'hami, Pasha of Marrakesh, and then both were dismissed. This game of musical chairs ended in 1912 when the French military moved into Morocco to "protect" it and reappointed the Glaoui brothers to their positions.[16]

Two years later, in 1914, World War I began. The French troops were needed at home and strained to stay. The Glaoui came to their rescue. Madani pledged:

> We are the friends of France, and to the very end we shall share her fortune, be it good or bad. That is my sworn word.[17]

When Madani died in 1918, it was France's turn to be faithful. They replaced him with T'hami and together they ruled Morocco until 1955, sidelining and then exiling the sultan.

T'hami combined households. He married one of Madani's widows. They had two sons, one of whom, slightly to his father's dismay, dreamed of becoming a painter. He also absorbed Madani's harem. Still, with all his power, T'hami did not control his ancestral home, Telouet. Madani had given its rule to his favorite daughter's husband, who was strongly anti-French.

Let's go back to the map. Today, twenty miles west of Telouet, lies the pass of *Tiz-n-Tichka*. This is the modern road, tortured and twisted as it may be. It was completed by the French in 1935 as a way to cross the Atlas without fighting over Telouet, the much easier, more natural route.

How ironic that T'hami helped to make his family's stronghold irrelevant. And then, how unnecessary. Just before the new road opened, his niece's husband died, T'hami merged her family into his, absorbed another harem, and consolidated the Glaoui empire.[18]

Don't you just love maps? When you learn how to read them, they tell the story without telling the story.

It is fitting that T'hami El Glaoui was the Pasha of Marrakesh. He was a fairy-tale man in a fairy-tale land: a marketplace for camel caravans, a party town for the innocent, the experienced, and even the jaded, and a tourist attraction beyond compare.

By daylight, the central square is a disappointing, hot-baked, empty, boring parking lot. But, as the sun goes down, the *D'Jemma el-Fna* (the "Assembly of the Dead," as the square is known), comes to life.

The Magical D'Jemma el-Fna (MLENNY / GETTY IMAGES)

If there is anywhere in the world that might be the "Center of the World," it is here. Snake charmers, acrobats, and fortune tellers. Lepers, beggars, and dervishes. Water sellers, cymbal beaters, and pickpockets. Sword swallowers, henna artists, and fire eaters. Storytellers and scribes. Come one, come all, let the show begin.[19]

With this circus comes the food: just snap your fingers and the stalls magically appear.

The delicacies include lamb and couscous, snail soup, kebabs, sheep brains, skewered hearts, and, of course, locusts. Yes, they do taste like shrimp.

The food looks good but, somehow, you just know it will make you sick. Go ahead, take a chance. You don't have to use the dirty utensils and plates, use bread or your hands. One night, just one night, it will last a lifetime.

If that's not for you, or when you want to get away from the crowd, we have just the place: Dar Moha.

Dar Moha (COURTESY OF DAR MOHA RESTAURANT)

It's not only private, it's beautiful, and it serves the best pigeon and almond *pastilla* (pigeon pie) we've ever had.

Where is it?

Just around the corner, or up through the souks, on Rue Dar El Bacha, directly across the street from *Dar El Bacha*, the palace of T'hami El Glaoui, the Pasha.[20] You knew we'd bring you back.

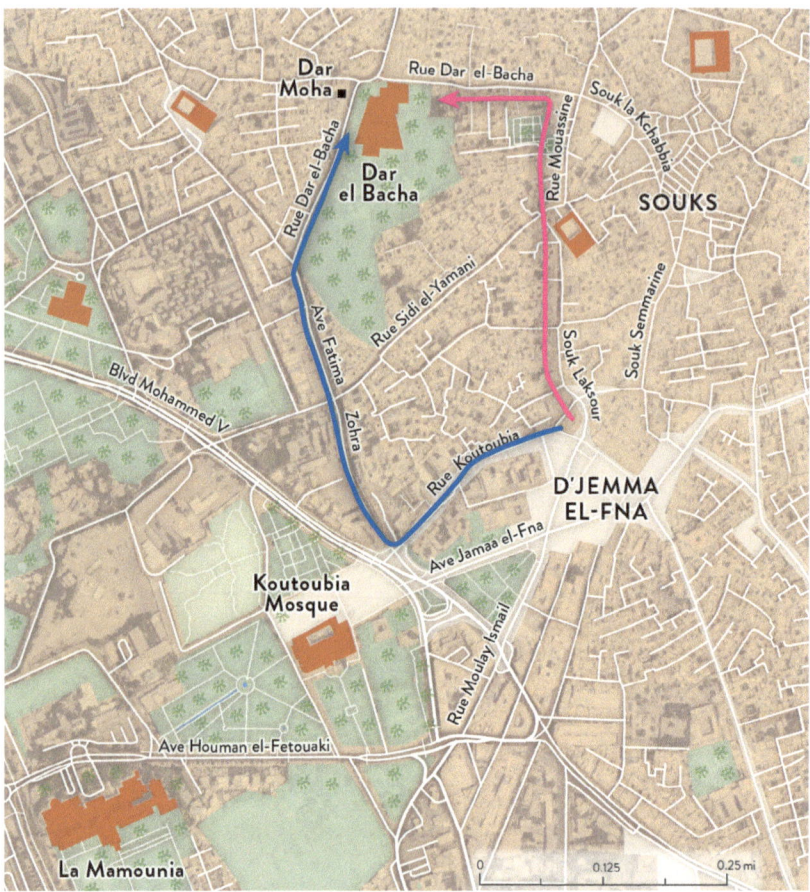

From D'Jemma el-Fna to Dar Moha: Around the Corner or Up Through the Souks

---

During the 1930s, T'hami was in his glory, entertaining dignitaries on an almost unimaginable scale. On one occasion, he accompanied the new French Resident General from Marrakesh to the mountain pass at *Tiz-n-Tichka*, about fifty miles away. He lined the road with men on their best horses, women in their finest clothes, all voices raised in song, all accompanied by musicians playing their favorite instruments. When they arrived at the pass, they were greeted by ten thousand horsemen, each firing their rifles twenty times in salute.[21]

T'hami also became great friends with the British, particularly Sir Winston Churchill. Churchill visited Marrakesh six times, almost always staying at *La Mamounia*, then (and now, in our opinion) the best hotel in the world. He would walk in the gardens, work on his books, and paint landscapes. He was a good painter and recognized that T'hami's son, Hassan, had talent. He convinced T'hami to send him to Paris to study art.[22]

With World War II came the collapse of France. Germans arrived. Then, in 1942, allied troops landed in North Africa and drove them out. And, with the weakening of France, came calls for independence, led by a reinvigorated sultan. Forget the new ports, roads, and mines, the French were not "protecting" Morocco. They were "colonizing" it.[23]

The French had a simple response: set T'hami off against the sultan, a move that enabled them to hold on for another thirteen years. It was all intrigues, with made and broken alliances, followed by curfews, arrests, torture, and terror. In the end, however, the French withdrew, and independence came.[24]

Abandoned, T'hami had no choice but to submit. This he did, kneeling at the feet of Sultan Mohammed V, paying homage, begging for forgiveness and mercy.

Mohammed V gave it:

> Let us forget the past. We have need of you both for our person and for our people. It is not what you have done that matters, but what you do in the future.[25]

T'hami himself was to have no future. Two months later, he died. It was his son, Hassan, the shy artist, who carried on the Glaoui name. His paintings have brought the romance, the history, and the glory of Morocco to the world.[26]

His inspiration is clear.

Fantasia Sur Fund Bleu, a Painting by Hassan El Glaoui
(COURTESY OF THE ESTATE OF HASSAN EL GLAOUI AND BRIAN BEXTER)

BANGKOK, THAILAND

Hallo there ... Come on up.

— JIM THOMPSON

Jim Thompson with Cocky (THE JAMES H. W. THOMPSON FOUNDATION)

So might begin a dinner party, which would turn out to be, even if the food was bad and drinks poor, one of the best nights of your life.[1]

Jim Thompson's World: Bangkok, Thailand, and the Cameron Highlands

You never knew who you'd meet: politicians, aspiring young actors, high society, even ordinary, everyday people who had somehow caught his eye. Jim Thompson was a salesman, a soldier, and a spy. He was an architect, a collector, and a wonderful host. Most of all, he was a mystery.

It began simply enough. Jim grew up in Delaware on the East Coast of the United States. His family was wealthy; he could have coasted through life. And that's pretty much what he did, up until the late 1930s. He was a society architect in New York City, attending parties with rich friends and designing their country houses.[2]

Then, he saw World War II coming and changed. He wanted to do something more substantial. In 1941, at age 35, he enlisted as a private in the Delaware National Guard. After basic training, he went to officer candidate school. When the war began, he joined the Office of Strategic Services (OSS), the predecessor of the Central Intelligence Agency (CIA).

He served in North Africa, Italy, and France. He then volunteered for the Pacific, to fight in the India-to-China zone. In 1945, he was assigned to Thailand, and, after survival training in the jungle, prepared to parachute into the country. While on the plane, however, a radio message arrived: Japan had surrendered and the war was over. A few days later, Jim flew more conventionally into Bangkok, not sure of what to do next.

Once there, however, he assumed the duties of OSS station chief, working to set up a temporary American Consulate. The social demands were never-ending, and Jim quickly came to love the work, the people, and the city.[3]

CENTRAL BANGKOK

Discharged from the service, he decided to stay on and looked around for something to do. He found the Oriental Hotel, a building of faded grandeur. As shown on the map, it sits on the banks of the city's main passageway, the Chao Phraya River. Today, this hotel is one of Asia's most famous and one of the world's best. But when Jim first saw it, the place was a dump.

He joined a group to renovate it, using his architectural skills and experience. When construction was finished and the hotel reopened, Jim had worked himself out of a job. While he continued to live there, he began a new search. What he eventually found was right in front of him: silk.[4]

Weaving was an ancient handicraft in Thailand, but

machine production had largely replaced it. Jim, however, saw that both the color and the texture of handmade silk was far superior. He introduced color-fast Swiss dyes and foot-operated looms and contributed his design skill and enthusiastic salesmanship. Indeed, he often wandered around the hotel lobby with bolts of silk draped over his shoulder, tempting the tourists.[5]

We stayed in the new wing of the Oriental, as it is endearingly called, high above the water. The building is beautiful and the air conditioning divine, but when the sliding glass doors opened for breakfast on the riverside terrace, it was as if we had stepped into a steam bath. We had only one day when the temperature and humidity dropped to a comfortable level and, while we were relieved, the locals walked around in parkas.

Jim certainly could sell. He dressed the queen of Thailand. He convinced *Vogue* magazine to showcase his work. And then *The King and I* opened on Broadway. He provided the silks for the costumes and the stage sets. The play was a hit, running for more than 1,200 performances. It was turned into a movie, and both the silks and Jim became world-famous. Orders poured in for the costumes in the movie *Ben-Hur*, for the suites at the Savoy Hotel in London, even for Windsor Castle.[6]

But Jim wasn't just a salesman. He was a designer, a creator. He found inspiration for his silks in local sculptures, paintings, and ceramics. It was only natural to begin to buy them and, before he knew it, he had assembled a staggering collection: Buddhas in stone and bronze, from the eighth to the thirteenth centuries, sitting, reclining, standing, or walking.

This Buddha, sitting at the end of a hallway in his house, was our favorite. Quiet, peaceful, and profound, it made us feel the same way.

Sitting Buddha (THE JAMES H. W. THOMPSON FOUNDATION/LUCA INTERNIZZI TETTONI)

Jim also collected paintings from the various Thai "schools" of art: Ayutthaya, Sukhothai and Bangkok. And ceramics: blue and white, Bencharong, and Lai Nan Thong.[7]

Jim had moved from the Oriental Hotel into a house, but soon it was too small. So, he sat down and designed himself a new one: large enough to hold his collection and entertain his friends, private with a jungle-like garden, and classically located on a *khlong* (canal).

Indeed, Bangkok is a city of khlongs. Traditionally dug for defensive purposes, the canals became short-cuts to get from one side of town to the other. Just look at the map. During the twentieth century, however, many of them were filled in to make roads. Ironically, automobile traffic is now so impossibly congested that water, once again, is the fastest way to travel.

Jim absorbed the country's aesthetic, adopting the spires, swooping roofs, and paneled exterior walls of Thailand's temples and palaces.[8] He searched the countryside for individual teak houses but found they were too small, often being just a single room. His solution: he didn't buy one house, he bought six, transported them to the city, and combined them all into one glorious residence.

Take a look at Jim's layout.

His drawing room came from Bangkrua, a village just across the khlong where many of his weavers lived, and he reversed the walls to bring their beautiful exterior carvings inside. His entrance hall, dining room, and master bedroom came from buildings found in the countryside village of Pak Hai. The kitchen was found in Banglamphoo, another district in Bangkok.

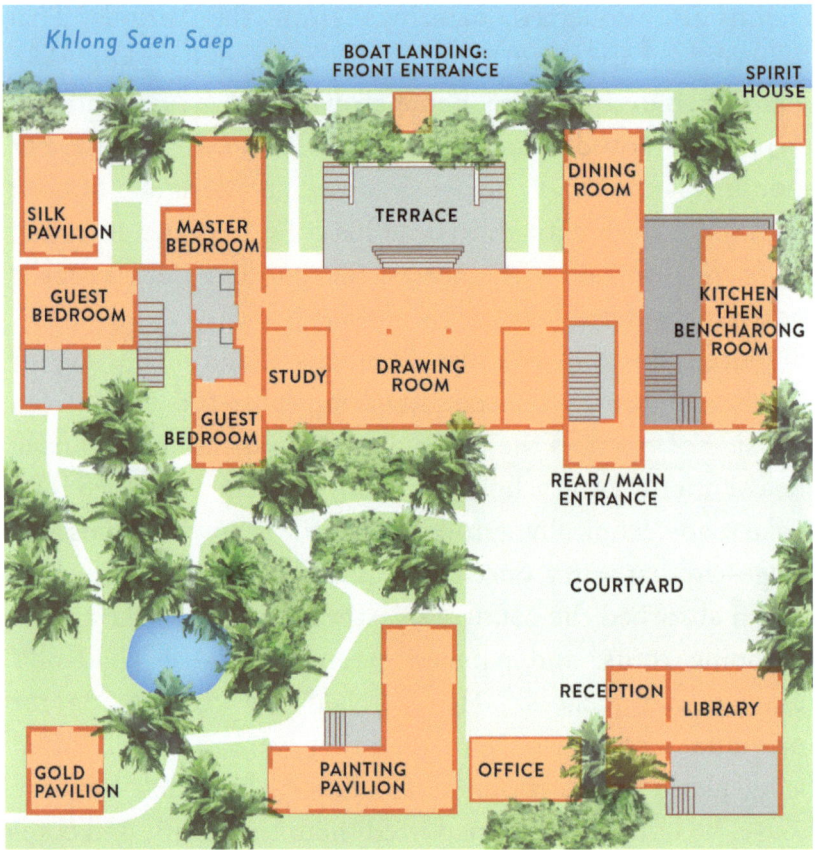

The Jim Thompson House: Six Houses in One

Putting the houses together was complicated. Jim didn't know the intricacies of Thai construction and neither did his Bangkok workers. So, he brought in carpenters from the countryside, where they still built traditional homes. He knew that houses on the khlong face the khlong. His front entrance, therefore, was on the water, but his main entrance was in the rear, opening to a courtyard where romantic roofs greeted his guests.[9]

The Jim Thompson House: Rear, but Main Entrance (JOERG HACKEMANN / ALAMY)

Jim was sensitive to local religious traditions. Buddhist blessings were required on three occasions: when construction began, when the spirit house was sited (the shadow of the main house must never fall on it, as shown in the layout), and when the main house was completed and ready for move-in.[10]

It was from this House on the Klong that Jim, with his pet white cockatoo on his shoulder, became the most famous *farang* (foreigner) in Thailand: wining, dining, entertaining, and, some would say, spying.[11]

Indeed, he was so well known that a letter addressed simply to "Jim Thompson, Bangkok" was delivered without a problem.[12]

By 1967, Jim seemingly had it all: a successful business with a brand-new store in the most fashionable part of town, a fabulous art collection, and an extraordinary home. But he was unhappy.

The United States had begun using Thailand as a staging point for its bombing raids into Laos and Vietnam.[13] Jim wanted America to be a liberator, not a conqueror. Did this make him a communist sympathizer? Some people thought so.[14]

And Thailand was becoming more difficult. Jim had revived a moribund silk industry, only to face resentful local competitors. He had rescued priceless antiquities from destruction and decay, only to be accused of stealing them. He needed a break.[15]

Most people are remembered for the way they lived. For some, however, their lives are overshadowed by their deaths. So it was with Jim.

Friends invited him to spend Easter weekend in the Cameron Highlands, a resort in the mountains of Malaysia. It sounded perfect.

Jim flew from Bangkok down to the island of Penang, crossed over to the Malaysian mainland and drove up into the highlands. At six thousand feet above sea level, it was a golf-course community carved out of the jungle. It was known for its walking trails, beautiful gardens, and lovely, cool weather.[16]

Jim stayed at Moonlight Cottage, overlooking the golf course, next to the trails.

Moonlight Cottage (ATLANTIDE PHOTOTRAVEL/GETTY IMAGES)

His hosts, longtime friends, sensed he was restless, edgy. After church services, they went on a Sunday picnic. Jim, however, wasn't in the mood, and wanted to return. They arrived back at the cottage in time for a nap and, as his hosts rested, they thought they heard Jim's footsteps "going down the gravel leading to the road." [17]

He was never seen or heard from again.

At first, Jim's friends weren't concerned. After all, the highlands were filled with trails and, if anybody knew his way around the jungle it was him. He'd trained in it, he was experienced in it, and, on the day before his disappearance, he'd been temporarily lost in it, and greatly enjoyed finding his way out.[18]

But then Sunday evening came, and he still hadn't returned.

On Monday, one hundred people began an official search.

On Tuesday, the number grew to three hundred, at that time the largest manhunt in Malaysian history. It lasted for ten days and found nothing.

Speculation soon ran wild. Jim must have gotten lost, had an accident, or been attacked by an animal. But there were no footprints or tracks, no clothes, no blood stains, no body, and, most tellingly, no vultures hovering overhead.

Was Jim kidnapped for ransom? Nobody ever made a demand.

Was he taken by the Thai government, by business competitors, or by the communists? Maybe, maybe, and maybe.

Was he a drug dealer who had made his escape?

Better yet, and most fittingly, was he captured and killed by the CIA? After all, "once an agent, always an agent." [19]

On the other hand, perhaps he just ran away from it all, and was living in Tahiti.[20]

The "search" attracted a vast array of investigators: astrologers, destiny scientists, spiritual consultants, soothsayers, clairvoyants, and even witch doctors. "Finding Jim Thompson" became almost a game.[21]

And, of course, there was the missing will.

Let's explain. Jim Thompson loved Thailand and wanted to help. When he formed the Thai Silk Company, he made sure that 51 percent of its stock was owned by Thai citizens, and he kept just 18 percent for himself. Even though he was known as the "Silk King," his goal was not to make a fortune in an underdeveloped country, but to make a contribution to its improvement. Indeed, he once described his job as being "like a missionary, but with better visual results." [22]

Jim tried to do the same in his estate planning. He was a member of the governing council of the Siam Society, a local nonprofit dedicated to preserving the country's culture and history. Remember, the country of Thailand was previously the Kingdom of Siam. In order to keep his art collection intact, he prepared a will leaving it, along with his house and his interest in the Thai Silk Company, to the society.[23]

Shortly thereafter, in 1962, the Thai Government recognized Jim's leadership in reviving the silk industry. It awarded him The Order of the White Elephant, a decoration given to people for their service to Thailand.[24] Jim thought he was being welcomed home.

The Order of the White Elephant—First Class—Knight Grand Cross (XIENGYOD/WIKIMEDIA COMMONS)

Maybe he missed the point. Historically, white elephants have been a mixed blessing. Yes, the elephants were a high honor bestowed by sovereigns. But they were expensive to maintain and didn't have much practical use. Rulers, in fact, often gave them to their biggest challengers as a way of burdening them and thus preventing them from becoming an even stronger threat. So, an award named after a white elephant was ironic.

In any case, within a year, the government's Fine Arts Department accused Jim of accepting five beautiful stolen limestone heads and demanded their return. Jim was shocked and infuriated: "First they decorate me, and then they raid me." [25]

But, as requested, he took the heads to the national museum, where they are still on display. He never asked for or was offered any reimbursement for his costs.[26]

That wasn't the end of it. Jim resigned from the Siam Society. He made a second will leaving all his property not to the Society, but to his nephew.[27]

And he even threatened to dispose of his collection and leave the country. Jim felt he wasn't at home anymore, that he was being treated as if he were just another farang.

This second will was lost. When Jim disappeared, the Siam Society, which had a copy of the first will, quite naturally claimed his assets. But the second had been witnessed and all three witnesses testified that it left everything to his nephew.

It was a difficult and embarrassing situation that could have led to a fight. Fortunately, a settlement was reached. The society and the nephew would jointly administer the property until Jim was declared legally dead (they had to wait for seven years after his disappearance). At that point, the collection, house, and company stock would all be donated to a charitable foundation as a permanent memorial.[28]

However, two years later, the second will was found, stored in the blueprints for Jim's house. That secured the nephew's claim, but he still wanted the collection and house to remain in Thailand, and, after all, he'd made a deal.[29]

In 1974, Jim was officially declared dead and the second will was probated. Since he had remained an American citizen, up rose a new threat: the United States Treasury. This was all about death and taxes. If Jim had left everything to a charitable foundation, his gift would not be subject to U.S. estate tax. However, he had left it to his nephew and, even though the nephew had agreed to contribute it, the property had still been left to him. Estate taxes, therefore, were due, and they were so great that the collection would have to be sold in order to pay them.

"Not so fast," argued a bright young lawyer administering his very first estate. Since the nephew had agreed to donate everything to the foundation while Jim was still legally alive, when he was later declared dead, his property passed to the nephew, not as an individual, but as an agent of the foundation. It took a while, but the U.S. Government agreed. No taxes were imposed, the collection was saved, and Jim was finally, and truly home.[30]

Today, the Jim Thompson House is one of Bangkok's major tourist attractions. It is not to be missed.

And the Jim Thompson Thai Silk Shop on Surawong Road is thriving. It's a great place to find gifts and souvenirs. We bought a set of cotton, elephant-printed napkins. White elephants, of course.[31]

KATHMANDU, NEPAL

Scribere necesse est, vivere non est.
Only that which is written about has really happened.

NEPAL

Himalaya is a Sanskrit word meaning "abode of snow." Since 1950, when Nepal opened its borders, the Himalayas have attracted a vast array of adventurers: explorers, climbers, trekkers, white-water rafters.

When they've had their fun and return to Kathmandu, their first stop was often at this historic watering hole, Rum Doodle.

"Climb Mount Everest and you can eat here free for the rest of your life."

Now, that's great advertising!!!

Rum Doodle Sign (RUM DOODLE RESTAURANT)

That's right, all you have to do is climb Mount Everest, at 29,032 feet, the tallest mountain in the world (from sea level). It's easy. Not that we've done it, or will. Compared to the beginning, however, it *is* easy. But you be the judge.

It started in the 1920s, when the British made three attempts to climb Everest from Tibet on the northern side. Their efforts were recorded in monumental tomes: *Mount Everest: The Reconnaissance, 1921*, *The Assault on Mount Everest: 1922*, and *The Fight for Everest: 1924*.

All three attempts failed . . . or did they? For in 1924, George Mallory, who had been in the climbing party each of the three years, was last seen "on the summit ridge . . . moving expeditiously . . . before being enveloped in a cloud." [1]

This was the same George Mallory who, when asked by a pestering newspaper reporter why he wanted to climb Mount Everest, responded quite succinctly: "Because it's there." [2]

Soon, however, the world became preoccupied by depression and war. Until the late 1940s, Mount Everest was left alone. Almost. In 1949, the Chinese invaded Tibet and closed the northern side. In 1951, Nepal opened its borders to foreigners, permitting climbs from the south.

That year, the British sent an expedition to look for a possible southern route to the top. They found one, up the icefall of the Khumbu Glacier. This route was particularly dangerous, however, for the icefall moved as much as three to four feet each day. At that speed, large crevices opened in seemingly solid blocks and ice towers suddenly collapsed. Still, the route looked doable.

In 1953, the British sent another expedition, this one to climb. It was organized in military siege-style by John Hunt, who selected ten climbers, two doctors, a cameraman, a reporter, one guide, and five reserves. He supported them with 350 porters, 34 Sherpas, and tons of supplies. The expedition left Kathmandu on March 10, and, after acclimatization, reached base camp on April 12.[3]

Let's interrupt for a little terminology. A "glacier" is a river of ice that flows down from a mountain. At Everest, the Khumbu Glacier begins at the bottom of the "face" of its neighbor, Mount Lhotse. It wanders through a broad, flat valley named the Western Cym, *cym* being the Welsh word for "valley." It then makes a steep drop, becoming an "icefall," before moving on. At the bottom of this icefall, the British set up their base camp.

1953 MOUNT EVEREST EXPEDITION

To climb Mount Everest, then, one must march to base camp, climb the icefall, traverse the cym, scale the face, and take a left to reach the South Col. A "col" is the low point along a ridge between two mountains. You might also think of it as a "saddle." Just look at the map.

From the South Col, one must climb past the South Summit, the second highest mountain in the world, except that it doesn't qualify as one, because it's part of Everest.

You are almost there, just one more step. This "step," however, would be a vertical rock wall about forty feet tall, with an eight-thousand-foot drop on one side and a ten-thousand-foot fall on the other.[4]

How would anyone climb this? We don't know, but on May 29, 1953, Edmund Hillary and Tenzing Norgay did.

The Hillary Step in 1953 (ROYAL GEOGRAPHIC SOCIETY / GETTY IMAGES)

Hillary, himself, took this photo. Then what did he do? He looked left and thought he might lower himself to get around, but he couldn't see any way back up. He looked right and found a crack between the wall and overhanging ice (a "cornice"). He wedged himself into it, grabbed onto the rock and, using his crampons (spikes on the bottom of his boots), walked backwards up the ice, reaching for every hold he could find. Somehow, wriggling and jamming, he made it to the top. Norgay then forced his way up and, together, on the same rope, they climbed to the summit.[5]

They were heroes, and received parades, awards, and worldwide fame. The rock wall, itself, became known as "The Hillary Step." Still, the ultimate honor didn't come until 1956, when *The Ascent of Rum Doodle* was published.

───────

What is the greatest compliment? Is it silent admiration or bottomless praise? No. It is friendly repartee, loving insult, and well-intended mockery.

───────

We knew from the start that the book was a spoof. The Rum Doodle massive was in the shape of "a reversed M." We can understand an upside-down "M," but what do you get when you reverse an "M?"

Two summits, of course: Rum Doodle, at forty thousand and one-half feet above sea level, and North Doodle, slightly lower and to the west.[6] Compared to them, Mount Everest is a walk in the park.

The climbing team bore appropriate names. Jungle, the route-finder, was always lost. Shute, the cameraman, didn't know how to take photographs, and Dr. Prone, well, you can imagine his position.[7]

The Ascent of Rum Doodle (MAX PARRISH & CO.)

The expedition planned for only three thousand porters but ended up with thirty thousand, because the local word for "three" and "thirty" was the same, "except for a snort," which was impossible to convey by telegram.[8]

To top it all off, the main party climbed the wrong mountain, only to turn and see the porters, who'd been left with Prone to move base camp, climbing to the true summit instead. Why? Because the local word for "mountain base" and "summit" was also the same, "except for a grunt." As for Prone, as you might expect, one of the porters carried him all the way up.⁹

Yes, it was British humor, but, you know, sometimes you just have to go along with it. The book was a tremendous success, and begot the bar and restaurant. And it is a great bar. Take a look.

Rum Doodle Restaurant (RUM DOODLE RESTAURANT)

We saw hundreds of large footprints, yeti footprints we were told, hanging from the ceiling, with names and expedition dates written on them. The beer on tap? Everest Premium Lager.¹⁰ And, on a wall behind the bar, are footprints signed by Everest climbers, including a very special one.

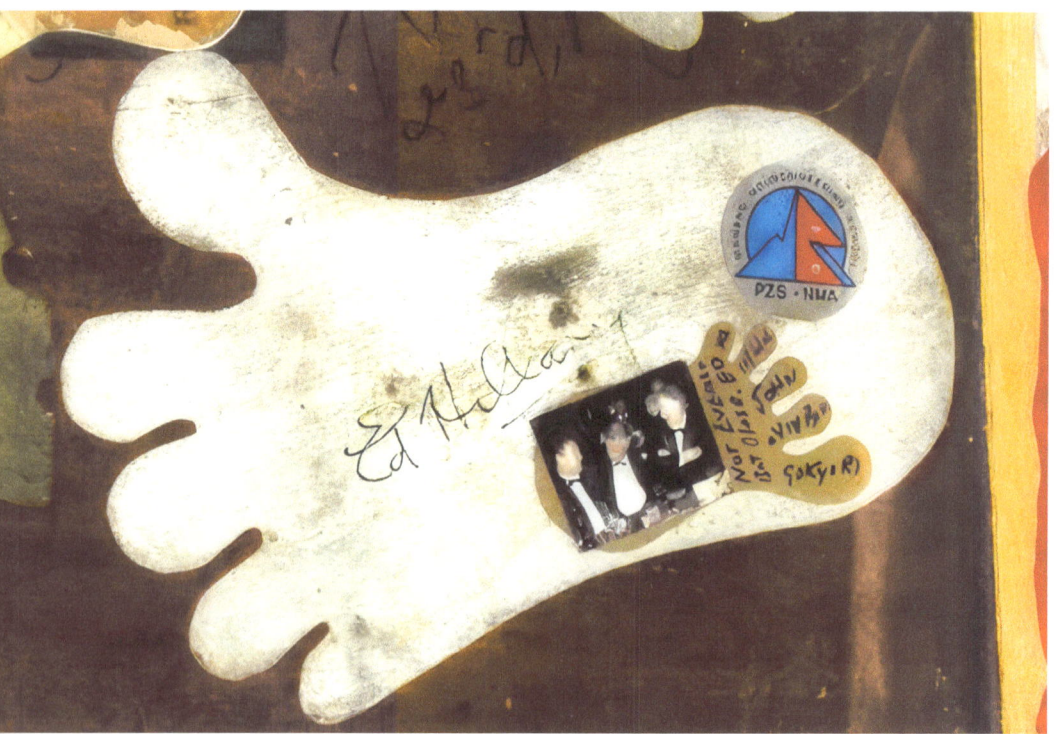

Hillary on a Yeti Footprint (BETULA 103/TRIPADVISOR)

Yes, "climb Mount Everest and you can eat here free for the rest of your life."

When Rum Doodle opened in 1979, the timing for this offer was perfect. Only 104 people had climbed to the top and over 80 percent of them were foreigners. They came, climbed, partied for a night or two, and *most importantly*, they left. The only problem was verifying if they really had climbed Mount Everest.

That was easy; all the bar had to do was call one person: Elizabeth Hawley. From 1963 until her death in 2018, Elizabeth recorded every Himalayan mountain climb, from both the Tibet and Nepal sides. She knew who had and had not climbed Everest.[11]

Let's tell you a little about her. Elizabeth was an American, born in the Midwest. During the 1950s, she worked in New York City as a researcher for *Fortune* magazine (in the days when women researched and men wrote). Finally, she couldn't take it anymore: it was a dead-end job, so she quit. She then spent two years on her own, traveling the world, ending up in Kathmandu in 1960.

> I came to Nepal. I never planned to stay. I just never left.[12]

She was the right person in the right place at the right time. It was the early days, things were happening, and, as a disciplined, Western-educated reporter and administrator, she was good to have around.

She began as a news correspondent. In 1960, when Edmund Hillary (by then Sir Edmund Hillary) created the Himalayan Trust to "give back" to the country (building schools, hospitals, and bridges, among other projects), she became its operating executive, dispensing the funds he raised. In time, she became New Zealand's Honorary Consul to Nepal.[13]

Hawley was also there at the birth of Nepalese tourism. In the mid-1960s, two Texans built Tiger Tops Jungle Lodge in a former royal hunting reserve. It was a pioneer in wildlife viewing: visitors rode on elephants to see rhinos, deer, boar, monkeys, birds, and, of course, the occasional tiger. Elizabeth managed the administration and accounts.

So, too, with the start of trekking. When a retired British officer set up Mountain Travel, Elizabeth was there to help. When it joined forces with Tiger Tops to create Tiger

Mountain, Elizabeth helped them both. And, in 1988, when they asked Elizabeth to keep them informed of the ever-changing political landscape, she was pleased to do so. From November of that year through May 2007, Elizabeth sent them monthly reports about the Nepal scene.[14]

Pretty impressive, but these were all sidelines. After Hillary and Norgay climbed Mount Everest, the rush was on. Mountaineering was in the news: explorations, expeditions, and first ascents. Elizabeth kept track of them all.

> I've never climbed a mountain or even done much trekking.[15]

Elizabeth Hawley (TONE SKARJA AND GORE-LJUDJE)

Still, she was the one who climbers met before and after their attempts. Her interviews were grueling and thorough, but she kept the mountaineers honest. And the climbing community knew:

> It doesn't matter who you are, your summit never happened unless Elizabeth Hawley says it did.[16]

As the years passed, the number of people who climbed Mount Everest increased. From eight ascents in 1980, the total reached 72 in 1990, 145 in 2000, and 544 in 2010.[17] These climbers were less and less experienced, and needed more and more help from the Sherpas—the Nepali guides and porters. They set the routes through the icefall, placed the ladders and protective ropes, transported the supplies between camps and, in some cases did, *literally*, carry their clients to the top.

Elizabeth recorded everything, and her expedition archives became the source material for the Himalayan Database, where you can find almost anything you want about any of the climbs.[18] Please see Appendix VII for the list of successful Mount Everest climbs through 2022. And if you go to the database's website, you can find the names of each and every climber.

Of course, in order to get their customers to the top, more Sherpas were themselves completing the climb. By 2015, the country with the most Everest summiteers was Nepal.[19] The difference between them and their clients, however, was that, after the climb, *they didn't leave*.

Rum Doodle saw the writing on the footprints on the wall, and quietly abandoned its "eat free for life" campaign. Who can blame them?

Then came the devastating 2015 earthquake. In Kathmandu, buildings collapsed everywhere, particularly in the part of town where climbers stayed. Rum Doodle was severely damaged and forced to move. It reopened in another location and resumed its place as the premier climber's and traveler's bar. It's an absolute must when you're in town.

The earthquake also damaged Mount Everest. The Hillary Step was gone. It was no longer a wall; it was a slope. Once the last test before the top, it became a ramp to the top.[20] Hillary would be disappointed: you can't be a pathfinder on a highway. But such a trip, after confirmation, would be duly noted in Hawley's records.

The Real Danger on Mount Everest (SUBIN THAKURI / 14 SUMMITS EXPEDITION)

SUMMIT FEVER

Since 2015, a swarm of climbers has overwhelmed Mount Everest. The Hillary Step, once virgin territory, has become a bottleneck, with long lines and traffic jams. People who have come for their once-in-a-lifetime climb must either wait for hours, dying on their feet from lack of oxygen, or force their way up, stepping over dead bodies, and preventing others from descending.[21]

For many, many people, too many perhaps, climbing Mount Everest has been their dream. Sometimes, however, the last thing you may really want is for your dream to come true.

But, but, there's always a but. Some people can just not, NOT climb.

Witness Number One: Nimsdai ("Nims") Purja. Born in Nepal, he served in the country's elite military as a Gurkha. Bitten by the climbing bug, he loved being in the "Death Zone," the area above 8,000 meters. In 2018, he announced "Project Possible," declaring that he would break the world record for summitting all fourteen Eight-Thousanders in the least amount of time.

It was an easy target. No climbers had ever taken less than seven years to climb all fourteen. Indeed, they were usually Westerners, who went to Nepal, climbed one or two peaks, celebrated at Rum Doodle, and then went home... to plan their next year's attempts. Little wonder it took them so long.

For Nims, he already *was* home and, with proper planning and daring, in 2019, he "bagged" all fourteen in less than seven months.

Witness Number Two: Kristin Harila, a woman from Norway. In the summer of 2023, she absolutely crushed Nims' record, climbing all fourteen in three months and one day.

Yes, the King of the Mountains is now a Queen.

MANAUS, BRAZIL

I know every tree,
Every single tree
One can see from here.

—RICHARD EVANS SCHULTES, *VINE OF THE SOUL*

Schultes in the Field (RICHARD EVANS SCHULTES / GOVINDA GALLERY)

*C*actus, mushrooms, and seeds.

When Richard Evans Schultes was a child, his father gave him a book: *Notes of a Botanist on the Amazon and Andes* (1908).[1] Written by Richard Spruce, a famous nineteenth-century botanist, its tales of exploration, discovery, foreign lands, unknown plants, and strange people fired the boy's imagination. Spruce became his hero, and Schultes dreamed of being just like him when he grew up.

Schultes lived in Boston and was a particularly good student, entering Harvard in 1933. There, he took a botany course, "Plants and Human Affairs." Its subjects ranged from the edible to the drinkable (brewing beer, making wine, and distilling alcohol), and then from the medicinal to the hallucinogenic. He was hooked.

For his senior thesis, Schultes chose "peyote" (botanical name: *Lophophora williamsii*), a small, psychoactive cactus that grows in the Southwest United States and Mexico. At the time, it was relatively unknown, with little, if anything, written about it. His adviser agreed, provided that he study peyote in relation to the rituals of the Kiowa Indians, for whom it was, and is, a sacrament. In the summer of 1936, Schultes traveled to Oklahoma to begin what would be his life's work.[2]

Peyote is blue-green and grows in clumps, with most of its body below ground, like a carrot. It has a circular "crown" or "button" that varies in size, from a golf ball to a softball.

Peyote buttons can be eaten fresh or dried. When dried, they shrink, so they can easily be stored in a bag or bowl, just like popcorn or jelly beans.

Peyote in the Ground (CHARLIE EDWARD / SHUTTERSTOCK)

Taken as part of a religious ceremony, peyote *is* a sacrament:

> The White Man goes into his Church House and talks *about* Jesus; the Indian goes into his Teepee and talks *to* Jesus.[3]

Schultes visited fifteen tribes during that summer and was a celebrant two to three times a week. If he wanted to know, there was no other way.

> He took a peyote button in his hand. He shut his eyes and experienced warm flushing sensations . . . his jaw moving up and down . . . The taste in his mouth changed . . . If the desert itself had a flavor, this was it. Time turned into color. Every thought unleashed a sound, every gesture a rainbow of light.[4]

Schultes's research was just beginning. For his doctoral dissertation, he studied other, relatively unknown plants. First was "teonanacatl" (*Psilocybe mexicana*), Aztec for "Flesh of the Gods." They were said to be ceremonial mushrooms, used to foresee the future. However, no scientist had ever confirmed their existence. In 1938, Schultes went looking and found them, in the boggy highlands of Oaxaca, Mexico.

Magic Mushrooms (ALAN ROCKEFELLER / WIKIMEDIA COMMONS)

They were small. For the natives, they were *los ninos santos*, the sacred children. But they were potent. Eaten fresh or mashed into a drinkable, tea-like infusion, they produced visual and auditory hallucinations and a dream-like, otherworldly state. Schultes identified and collected the first botanical specimens of what would soon be called "magic mushrooms." In doing so, he turned ethnographic myth into scientific fact.[5]

It was only natural for Schultes to look for the other classic Aztec hallucinogen, "ololiuqui" (*Turbina corymbosa*), "the Vine of the Serpent." It was, indeed, a vine, a climbing vine, with green leaves and lovely white, Morning Glory flowers.

But it wasn't the flowers that were worshipped, it was the seeds.

Morning Glory Flower (ROMAN SHYRIN/ALAMY)

Morning Glory Seeds (THITIMON ROYAL/ALAMY)

These seeds contained the natural analogue to lysergic acid dietylamide-25 (LSD for short) and Schultes discovered them in the wild in 1939, four years before Albert Hofmann created it in a lab.[6]

Let's have a recap. In 1936, Richard Evans Schultes wrote his undergraduate thesis on a cactus (active ingredient: mescaline). In 1939, he wrote his doctoral dissertation on mushrooms (psilocybin) and morning glory seeds (LSD). That could have been enough for any career. However, his writings got little attention. They went unpublished, and were deposited in the basement of Harvard's Economic Botany Library, where they gathered dust.[7]

Schultes had done great research, but what was he going to do for a job? He got only two offers. One was to be a biology teacher at a Massachusetts private school. The other was to hunt for curare, the plant used to make arrow poisons, in the Amazon. Which would you take?

The Amazon is a river with veins more than tributaries, and these veins have many colors: white, black, blue, and brown.

White headwaters descend eastward from the Andes Mountains, melting snow becoming glaciers, becoming waterfalls, becoming clear mountain streams. As they flow and merge, they collect rock and other riverbank sediment, carrying them downstream. Mile by mile, for 4,300 miles, give or take, the rivers gradually turn brown.

From the north comes the slow-moving Rio Negro and its sources, almost as large as the Amazon itself. As the name implies, these are the black-water rivers, flowing through forests, collecting plant matter that fails to decompose and sits like tea leaves darkening a pot.

THE AMAZON: RIVER AND RAINFOREST

From the southern highlands come the blue waters. They are filtered through white sand and flow slowly enough for their sediment to settle.

All these tributaries, more than a thousand of them (and of them, twelve more than a thousand miles long) flow to the brown river, the Amazon. Their combined current is so strong that the river carries nearly one billion tons of sediment a year into the Atlantic Ocean. And the river's fresh water can still be found a hundred miles out at sea.[8]

The Amazon is the largest river (by volume) in the world, but is it the longest? Some would argue for Egypt's Nile River, but we think the answer lies in a definition. What is the "source" of a river — is it the furthest upstream source? Is it the most distant uninterrupted upstream source? Or is it the source with the largest volume? We don't really care how you answer these questions — they're academic. No other river in the world dominates a continent like the Amazon dominates South America. Isn't that enough?

The Amazon Rainforest is also huge. It covers one-third of South America and is nearly as large as the United States or the European Union. And so you have it:

> the largest river in the world runs through the largest forest.[9]

Schultes spent twelve years (1941–53) in the Amazon, mostly in the northwest, in Colombia. He suffered twenty-one bouts of malaria, crippling beriberi, and near-death infections. Over and over, he risked the unknown, whether uncharted rivers, perilous rapids, or the very plants he went to study.

He returned with almost thirty thousand botanical specimens, including three hundred species new to science. Over one hundred plants are named for him: for example, *Schultesiophytum palmata* becomes Panama hats; *Marasimius schultesii* treats ear infections; *Justicia schultesii* cures sores; *Pourouma schultesii* heals ulcers and wounds.[10]

Oh, and a cockroach. Schultes once led a group of entomologists, including the world's foremost cockroach expert, up the Rio Negro. The expert had been disappointed not to discover anything new on the trip, so Schultes found a guide and a dugout canoe and took him into the flooded forest. There, feasting in nests hanging over the river, were so many distinct species of cockroach that the expert, a happy, happy man, named one of them *Schultesia*.[11]

Vines, vines, and vines.

In September 1941, Schultes arrived in Bogota, Colombia to study the basin of the Putumayo River, which flowed from Colombia into the Solimões (as the upper Amazon is called in Brazil). He was looking for sources of curare, the poison used by Indians when hunting.

Let's explain how "curare" (*Strychnos toxifera*) works. Its active ingredient is d-tubocurarine, a muscle relaxant. As a poison, it paralyzes the muscles around the respiratory system, leading to suffocation and death. However, with a lower dose, it relaxes a patient, enabling surgery with much less, and thus safer, anesthesia. Hospitals were just beginning to experiment with curare, and the medical community wanted to know more. The indigenous tribes, however, had been dipping their arrows in it for hundreds of years.[12]

Curare Leaves (SALLY WEIGAND/ALAMY)

Schultes identified and documented fourteen sources of curare. Inevitably, these sources were vines, and the active principle came from their bark. You must admit, though, that their leaves look very innocent.

While studying curare, Schultes watched the Indians prepare and partake of their most sacred plant: "ayahuasca" (*Banisteriopsis caapi*), the "Vine of the Soul" (also known as *caapi* or *yage*). Again, the key component was bark and its group of alkaloids featuring the beta-carbolines harmine and harmaline. It had first been scientifically identified and collected in the mid-nineteenth century by Richard Spruce (yes, *that* Richard Spruce) who, unfortunately, was not able to sample his discovery. Instead, he sent it to London, where it sat untouched for one hundred years, waiting to be tested.[13]

Ayahuasca is prepared in many different ways. After the bark is scraped off the vine, it can be served raw, simply squeezed in cold water to make a drink, or it can be boiled in water, with the resulting mixture being consumed. Or, it can be boiled with its leaves and stems, as shown below.[14]

Cooking Ayahuasca (BRIAN VAN TIGHEM / ALAMY)

Schultes learned that other plants, particularly "chagropanga" (*Diplopterys cabrerana*) and "chacruna" (*Psychotria viridis*) could be added to the pot to create different hallucinogenic effects, lasting for different periods of time, depending on the mixture. Eventually, he came up with over twenty "recipes."[15]

He attributed his drinking all the various concoctions to simple, good manners.

> I have tried several of the Indian hallucinogens, in part because the Indians consider them sacred plants, and it would have been an unpardonable rudeness to refuse them when the Indians were kind enough to offer them to me during a ceremony.[16]

In the spring of 1942, Schultes found another hallucinogenic plant, "ya-kee" (*Virola calophylla*), the "Semen of the Sun." He noted it, but just in passing, as "red resin in bark — intoxicating." Nine years later, in June 1951, while in the forest just north of the Apaporis River, he came upon it again.

His guide, the son of a local shaman, identified the vine-like tree and taught Schultes how to make snuff from it. Again, the key ingredient was bark, this time the inner, red layer. The boy sliced it from the tree, soaked it in a pot, and then shaved it. He put the cuttings into another pot and added hot water. He squeezed the mixture together and filtered it through a cloth towel into a smaller, third pot. He set it over a low fire to dry the bark. Finally, he pulverized it with a mortar and pestle.

Schultes brought out his camera. When the snuff was ready, the shaman's son put it into a long tube and blew it up a compatriot's nose. Click.[17]

Boys with Snuff (RICHARD EVANS SCHULTES / GOVINDA GALLERY)

Rubber.

At the end of 1942, the American government interrupted Schultes' work with curare. It needed him for a more important plant: "rubber" (*Hevea brasiliensis*).

First, a little background. During the late nineteenth century, Brazil had a complete monopoly on rubber. The Amazon was its *only* source. When a U.S. scientist invented a way for rubber to be used in both hot and cold weather, demand for it exploded. At the same time, the auto industry went from selling five hundred to fifteen million cars a year, each one requiring four tires and a spare. America needed all the rubber it could get.[18]

That rubber was shipped from one place: Manaus, a deep-water port nine hundred miles upriver from the Atlantic Ocean. It is located in the heart of the rain forest, where the main branches of the Amazon come together.

From Manaus, there are three classic water experiences. The first is Ilha de Anavilhanas, a biological reserve of almost four hundred uninhabited islands, up the Rio Negro. During the rainy season, many of the islands can't be seen. The river rises fifty feet and submerges them. For the others, canoeing through their flooded forests is surreal.

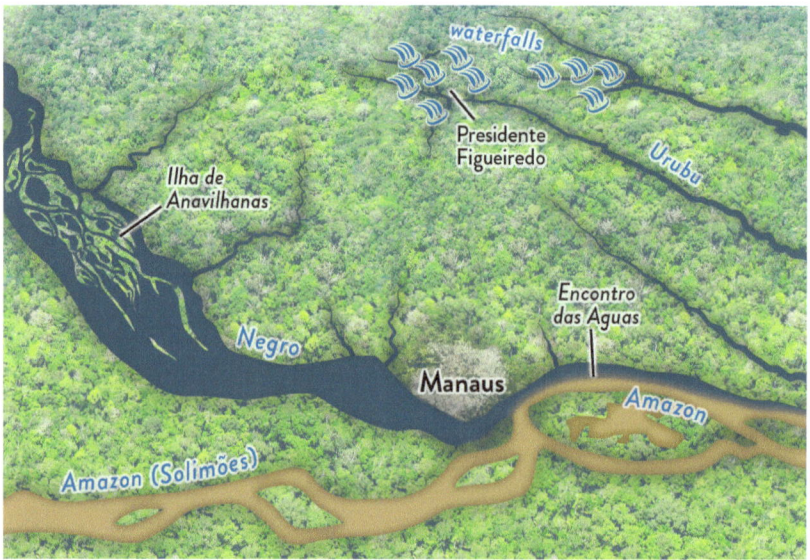

MANAUS: THREE WATER EXPERIENCES

Downstream is the Encontro das Aguas, the meeting of the black Rio Negro and the brown Amazon (aka Solimões). It takes almost four miles for them to merge and watching them flow, side by side, two rivers in one, is a remarkable sight.

And to the north, the little town of Presidente Figueiredo is blessed with more than one hundred waterfalls.

In the late 1800s, fed by the rubber boom, Manaus went "from seedy, riverside village to thriving city" almost overnight. The wealth was new, it was spectacular, and it was obscene. Men lit cigars with one-hundred-dollar bills, horses drank champagne, prostitutes charged ten thousand dollars a night, and housewives, rather than wash their undergarments in the dirty black or brown rivers, sent them to Portugal to be cleaned.[19]

There was, however, one problem with Brazil's rubber industry (besides the cruel, torturous, forced labor of the natives, of course). The trees only grew in the wild, and far apart from each other, the forest's way of combating the South American leaf blight. Indeed, all attempts to create an organized plantation system failed, and failed badly, defeated by the blight.

The British weren't any help. They had exported (some say stolen) rubber seeds from the Amazon and planted them in neat, orderly rows in Southeast Asia (no blight there).

Flash forward to 1940 and the world monopoly in rubber had moved. And by the time the Japanese attacked Pearl Harbor (December 7, 1941), they had already taken control of it.[20]

The United States was in a bind. It reduced rubber demand by prohibiting its use in any product not essential to the war effort. It tried to increase supply, either by creating synthetics or developing new, natural sources.

This is where Schultes came in. Beginning in 1943, he spent ten years on the rubber effort. He began as a plant explorer, mapping the Apaporis River and counting the rubber trees along the way. He then became a plant breeder, hoping to create hybrids of high-yielding and blight-resistant trees. Finally, he served as a plant grower, spending three tapping seasons (1944, 1945, and 1946), monitoring their production.[21]

When the war ended, so did the rubber crisis. Schultes still worked for the government, but it didn't know what to do with him, so it let him wander. He learned more about plants, and more about the Indians. Later, when asked how he was able to deal with all the "dangerous tribes," his answer was straightforward:

> I do not believe in hostile Indians. All that is required to bring out their gentle manliness is reciprocal gentle manliness.[22]

Schultes's rubber work did not receive the attention it deserved. Synthetic rubber had been a huge success, and it won the war. As a result, the government saw synthetics, alone, as the future. It was a mistake. Schultes knew that he and his fellow botanists had solved the technical problems of establishing high-yielding, blight-resistant rubber plantations. But the government wouldn't fund a final report documenting the results. Gradually, the forest closed in, and all his plantings disappeared.[23]

So, in 1953, after twelve years in the Amazon, Schultes returned to the Harvard Botanical Museum. He continued his research on hallucinogenic plants, producing almost five hundred scientific papers and ten books, including our favorite, *Plants of the Gods* (1979).[24]

What a book. It provides an overview of the plants and their usage, a lexicon with basic descriptions (including preparation and chemical components) of ninety-one plants, and a detailed discussion of the fourteen culturally, botanically, or historically most interesting ones. Please remember, though, as Schultes and his co-author Albert Hofmann (again, the inventor of LSD) cautioned, "the book is *not* intended as a guide to the use of hallucinogenic plants."[25]

Plants of the Gods (HUTCHINSON / AKG-IMAGES / WERNER FORMAN)

Schultes finally took a look at Richard Spruce's long-ignored sample of ayahuasca. He analyzed it and determined that, after one hundred years in storage, it was still potent.[26]

Schultes's office became a campus curiosity, with blow guns, spears, dance masks and, for a while, a bucket of peyote buttons available to any student looking for an extra credit project. He was considered the "Father of Ethnobotany," the greatest plant explorer of the twentieth century, the world's expert on hallucinogenic plants, and the mentor to countless students who dreamed of being just like him when they grew up.[27]

Then, his dusty old research found an audience. It began with teonanácatl. A New York banker/scientist read Schultes's paper on the mushrooms. Using it as guide, he went to Mexico and, in 1955, became the first outsider ever to eat them. He published a story about his "soul shattering experience" with "magic mushrooms" in *Life* magazine in May 1957. The "psychedelic era" was on its way.[28]

The reaction of new readers to his article on morning glory seeds was even better. They mobbed florists, hoping to get their hands on the most potent varieties, particularly, they thought, "Pearly Gates" and "Heavenly Blue." Schultes, who knew these commercial seeds were inert, was amused:

> Of course, you must keep in mind that people in Berkeley, California, can hallucinate on distilled water.[29]

Schultes disdained his Harvard colleague Timothy Leary, familiar for his mantra: "tune in, turn on, and drop out." As far as Schultes was concerned, Leary was a shameless showman, who turned religious devotions into recreational drugs. Worse yet, Leary had deliberately mistranslated the

Greek word "psych<u>o</u>delics" into the playful but incorrect "psych<u>e</u>delics." [30]

Schultes was very much a libertarian, and enjoyed helping students in trouble, particularly those who had been arrested for marijuana possession. Inevitably, they were accused, under the words of the relevant statute, of possessing *Cannabis sativa*.

The staid, respectable Dr. Richard Evans Schultes made a wonderful witness. He testified time and time again that there were three species of *Cannabis*: *sativa*, *indica*, and *ruderalis*. Only sativa was outlawed. Therefore, in order for a judge or jury to find the arrested student guilty, prosecutors had to prove, beyond a reasonable doubt, that the marijuana involved was sativa and not the others. They couldn't, so students were almost magically set free.[31]

The Three Species of *Cannabis,* Left to Right: *Sativa, Indica,* and *Ruderalis*

Still, nothing at Harvard could compare to the Amazon. In early 1952, Schultes traveled south along the Apaporis River to the Miriti Parana, the "River of Palms," and then upstream to its juncture with the Guacaya, where the Yukuna people lived.

Unknowingly, he had arrived just in time for a festival celebrating the harvesting of fruit from the peach palm. Delicious and nutritious, the fruit is a well-balanced dietary staple, and one tree can produce thousands of the orange or reddish delights each year.

The highlight of the festival was the *Kai-yah-ree*, the Dance of the Spirits. Participants wore brown shirts crafted from fig tree bark and full-length skirts made from Brazilian nut bark, dyed black halfway down by riverside clay. Their rattling anklets came from the fruit of a cucumber vine.

The ceremony began at midnight. The opening dancers wore masks representing tricksters, devils, satyrs, and other human monsters. They were followed, in turn, by villagers dressed as more than seventy different animal spirits. The "Boa People" wore snakeskin-decorated flat masks. The "Monkey Dance" featured little boys bouncing around. The "Jaguar Dancers" took careful half-steps, and then pounced.

There were tapirs, slow and lumbering, anteaters with long snouts, deer darting around, and wild bees, wasps, and bats, all buzzing and squeaking.

The ceremony lasted three nights and two days, a total of fifty-six hours. On the final morning, the "humans" met with the "animal chiefs" to mark the end of their temporary truce, reverting back to their normal relationship as hunter and prey.[32]

The Dance of the Spirits had a tremendous impact on Schultes. He had experienced the worldview of the Yukuna people, as they celebrated the origin and evolution of life. He was the first Western scientist ever to do so. He treasured his photos of the event, hanging them in his office at the Harvard Botanical Museum.

And he always displayed one particular photo during the opening lecture of his Economic Botany Class:

His comments were, invariably, short and sweet:

> Here you see three Indians of the Yukuna tribe, doing the sacred *Kai-yah-ree* dance to keep away the forces of darkness. The one on the right has a Harvard degree. Next slide please.[33]

Ka-ya-ree Dance (RICHARD EVANS SCHULTES / GOVINDA GALLERY)

AT THE END: TSODILO HILLS, BOTSWANA

Xnee ghom's e a Kurue, Kama ta se ta e, Kama se ta Xhong o.
We are made the same as the sand so this is our land,
because we were born here.

Bushman Family in Bush (TEMISTOCLE LUCARELLI / ALAMY)

A father and his sons were walking in the Kalahari. It could be a dream, something about to happen. It could be a memory, something that just did. We were in Botswana, looking for both.

Ah, words. What is the "correct" word for the Indigenous people of Southern Africa? Some would argue for "Khoisan," a compound of *khoi* (meaning person) and *san* (meaning hunter-gatherer or vagabond). Others would note that the khoi were cattle-herders and shepherds who looked down upon the wandering san.

The Dutch term *boschjesman* refers, as you might think, to people who live in the bush. It seems harmless, except that, historically, it also described orangutans in Malaysia.[1]

Nevertheless, anglicized, it became "Bushman," the word most used today. It implies the status of a "first people" and carries with it a certain romance. Some politicians and community organizers, however, might prefer san and some scholars would avoid anything to do with the suffix "man." [2]

We like Bushman, and we would like to think that most of them would worry less about what they are called or why they are studied and more about how they are treated.

———

DREAMS.

If the period of human existence were a clock where one hour represents the entire time span of humanity, fifty-nine minutes would be the time that people have lived by hunting and gathering. Only during the last minute have we produced food for ourselves.[3]

Indeed, once upon a time, and then, for thousands and thousands of years, the Bushmen, the first people of Africa, arguably the first people anywhere, lived off the land.

Their lives *were* a dream. The men hunted. The women gathered. Animals walked right into the hunters' paths and nuts and fruits fell from the trees.[4]

It was a perfectly balanced diet, protein from the meat, vitamins and minerals from the bush. And water, they got their water from plant roots, underground pools, or their favorite tsamma melons.[5]

In this earthly heaven, men and women only needed to work part-time to fulfill all their material needs.

They were egalitarian. Meat from a successful hunt was too much for one hunter and his family, so it was shared before it spoiled. And possessions were a nuisance when one must migrate to follow the game.

Isn't having enough and being equal the dream of economists? John Maynard Keynes certainly thought so. In his famous essay, "The Economic Possibilities for Our Grand-Children," he foresaw a promised land where, like the Bushmen, his descendants would have plenty of leisure time to explore the more important things in life.

Isn't this also the dream of anthropologists? Richard B. Lee at the famous 1966 University of Chicago Symposium on "Man the Hunter" thought so. In his paper "What Hunters Do for a Living, or, How to Make Out on Scarce Resources," he was quite clear that, for the Bushmen, "life in a state of nature was neither nasty nor brutish and short." And for Marshall Sahlins, another symposium participant, hunter-gatherers were "the original affluent society."[6]

Soon, all too soon, the dream was over. First came the Boers, Dutch settlers who moved inland from Cape Town to establish farms. Then came the British, looking for a port (Cape Town), that was halfway between London and its great colony, India. They, too, lusted for the interior. Finally, there were the Bantu, other native Africans who were always looking to expand their territory.

The Bushmen were continually moved along by *both* White *and* Black invaders who all believed, in the European sense of the word:

> He owned nothing, and therefore was owed nothing.[7]

Of course they resisted, but it was wiser and safer to retreat. Besides, they knew how to live off the land, even as it was reduced in size and quality. In time, though, they were left with only the desert, the Kalahari Desert.

And still they survived, for the Kalahari is not a normal desert. True, its name is derived from "Kgalagadi," meaning a "Great Thirst," but that's only because there is almost no *surface* water. The sand is porous: what rain that does fall seeps right through and vanishes. But it's still there if you know how to find it.

Spanning 350,000 square miles, seven times the size of England, the Kalahari supports the Bushmen by supporting the wildlife. All sorts of animals live here: the famous black-maned lion, many types of tasty antelopes — the gemsbok, the kudu, the springbok, the eland — and don't forget the honey badger. All sorts of plants and bushes thrive as well, offering up berries, melons, and nuts.

AT THE END: TSODILO HILLS, BOTSWANA | 316

THE KALAHARI DESERT

In short, the Kalahari enabled Bushmen to live "modern, prehistoric lives," to be "living fossils," to be our "contemporary stone age ancestors." Up until the 1950s, it also enabled them to live in "splendid isolation." It was unexplored, unmarked, and inaccessible. There were no roads, no signposts, nothing. Out of sight was out of mind.[8]

And then, into this lost world, came Sir Laurens van der Post.

Sir Laurens van der Post (ROBERT ESTALL PHOTO AGENCY / ALAMY)

Sir Laurens was born in 1906 and raised on a farm in South Africa, the thirteenth of fifteen children. When he was growing up, most of the Kalahari was still a vast unknown — so unknown that his father, a lawyer, once formed a syndicate to buy a huge amount of land, sight unseen, at its southwestern fringe, for a penny an acre.

His father visited the property only once, in 1913, just before he died, and seven-year-old Laurens went with him. They slept outside, beneath the stars. It was the boy's first time in the desert, a vast expanse of empty red sand. But after even the faintest amount of rain, flowers appeared from nowhere — and were suddenly everywhere. In such moments are mystics made.[9]

Flowers Appear from Nowhere. (ARTERRA PICTURE LIBRARY / ALAMY)

Later, van der Post learned of his ancestors' role in the expulsion of the Bushmen. They had been settlers who simply wanted more land, and took it. They never talked about how and who was killed in the process, and didn't answer any questions about it either. But Laurens sensed that something wrong had been done.[10]

In response, he dreamed of finding the Bushmen and bringing their plight to the world's attention. During the 1950s, he got his chance. Commissioned by the British Broadcasting Corporation, he went to see if Bushmen still existed, and, if so, to document their lives.

He looked for them first in the Okavango Delta, among the rivers, swamps, and marshes. Located on the northern frontier of the Kalahari, the delta offered both water and isolation. But it was too much water. Heavy flooding blocked the way. Van der Post and his men retreated through an attack of tsetse flies, bearers of the deadly sleeping sickness.

Where next?

Their guide suggested a grove of hills to the west. The Tsodilo Hills were said to be home not only to Bushmen but also to many ancient spirits. The hills even bore human names: "Male Hill" for the largest and "Female Hill" for the nearby circular group *(see next photo)*.

The Hills, however, were occupied by more than Bushmen and spirits. Sir Laurens had "discovered" more than four hundred sites, with more than four thousand individual rock paintings, representing more than one hundred thousand years of work. While he just missed the Bushmen, who had moved on before his arrival, he had, instead, found

> A great fortress of once-living Bushman culture,
> a Louvre of the desert filled with treasure.[11]

AT THE END: TSODILO HILLS, BOTSWANA | *320*

The Tsodilo Hills: Male Hill *(in front)* and Female Hill (COURTESY OF DESERT AND DELTA SAFARIS)

Eland on Rock (JUERGEN RITTERBACH / ALAMY)

He wrote of it. He wrote particularly of this eland, proud, majestic, high up on a rock.

He wrote of promising his guide that no one would kill an animal in the Hills, that no one would have blood on his hands.

But he forgot to tell his compatriots. Shots rang out and shortly thereafter two of them walked into camp with a warthog and a steenbok hung over their shoulders, dinner.

The spirits were disturbed. Soon the cameras would not work. Then the listening devices went dead. They could not take a picture or record a sound. What would happen next? Would their Land Rovers not start?

Van der Post was beside himself. He wrote a letter of apology to the spirits, had everyone sign it, placed it in a lime-juice bottle, and buried it on the ledge just below the painting of the eland.[12]

As they departed, van der Post asked his guide if the spirits would forgive them. "All is well" came the response:

> The spirits of the Hills are not what they were, Master. They are losing their power. Ten years ago, they would have killed you all . . .[13]

Van der Post kept looking, making slow progress through sand and scrub and brush. At last, in the middle of the Kalahari, he made contact. It was a dream come true.

He was there to learn. How to make fire, how to get food and water from a tsamma melon, how to find the secret sip wells so necessary in drought.

He was there to watch. To see them hunt, yes, to see them gather, to see them play (the tsamma melon made a good ball) to see them kill, not for sport, but only in order to live. And last, to see them sing, to see them dance. For the eland, for the fire, for the rain.

Though his visit was short, only a fortnight, it was long enough to introduce the rest of the planet to *The Lost World of the Kalahari* (1958).[14]

The Bushman lived.

———

MEMORIES.

Van der Post found something else in the dunes, something we could sense as well. He found the "Great Memory," the memory of all lives that have ever been, imparted to us through our natural instincts and feelings, the source of all meaning, the memory that knows our origin and destination are the same.

It is a memory we have as a child, lose as we are educated into the here and now, and then regain as we reach our final seasons. Even if forgotten, it is not forgotten. It comes down to us from before the word, beginning in a measureless, primordial past. It is an overarching memory, which does not belong to man but to life itself.[15]

For van der Post, there also was the "Little Memory." It maps the time and place in which we live our individual lives.

For him, the Kalahari brought the Great and Little Memories together, enabling him to live in and out of time, at the same time.[16]

———

The Bushmen needed help. They got it, at least for a while. In response to van der Post's reporting, the British — Bechuanaland, now Botswana, was, in the 1960s, still a colony — established the Central Kalahari Game Reserve in order to protect *both* the wildlife *and* the Bushmen.

> It was not intended to preserve the Bushmen of the Reserve as museum curiosities and pristine primitives, but to allow them the right to choose the life they wish to lead.[17]

That lasted for a generation. Independence came. Diamonds were discovered just outside the reserve, the world's largest find. Then they were found inside.

With a new government came a new scourge — regulation. The Bushmen, poor, illiterate, uninformed, but incredibly skilled, were required to apply in writing for . . . hunting licenses.[18]

The latest threat: tourists, i.e., us. Safari camps now dot the Reserve, complete with Bushmen hired to be Bushmen. If you like, you may take a walk with one.[19]

We did. We walked. We talked. He asked why we had come. "We were Looking for Legends," we said, and recounted the places we had been and the people we had seen.

"No," he laughed, "you may think that, but you were really Looking for Yourselves."

He had a point, so we talked some more. We relived the past. We foresaw the future. And then he asked us another question. It was the same question we asked you at the beginning, have been asking ourselves all along, and now, Dear Reader, ask you one more time: WHICH WOULD YOU RATHER HAVE, DREAMS OR MEMORIES?

EPILOGUE

THE ANSWER TO OUR QUESTION

DREAMS. We'd rather have dreams than memories.

Road Sign at Zagora, in the Draa Valley, Morocco (HEMIS / ALAMY)

We'd rather look forward than back. We prefer tomorrow to yesterday. And our favorite trip has always been the next one. And why not? You can't look forward unless you have a forward to look forward to.

Will we meet new friends along the way? We hope so. When we started traveling, we didn't have any . . . and look at us now.

Yes, this book is all about memories and we are pleased to share them. But don't you think we'd rather go back and make them all over again than just remember and share? And don't you think we know that someday, like everyone, all we will have is our memories, until we don't even have them?

Still, there is only one way in life: forward. Memories can hold you back. Memories can hold you down. Dreams, they get you up in the morning. Books to read. Maps to study. Places to go. People to see.

ACKNOWLEDGMENTS

Twenty-five years of travel and twenty-five years of writing, two people helped us every step of the way. A big THANK YOU to:

Pam Meyerson, of Omega World Travel, who organized itineraries, flights, hotels, and rescues: the adventure doesn't begin until something goes wrong.

And Cynthia Newton, who touched every word and every sentence and every paragraph, not complaining, understanding, forgiving, and correcting us over and over and over again.

Starting out, we didn't know how to travel and many times we learned the hard way. But we had teachers and protectors and we say THANK YOU to:

- Andrew, Robin, and Simon Shelley, Howard Harding, and the Ladies from WISPA (The Women's International Squash Players Association), especially Michelle, Sarah, Rachael, and Nicol.
- In Princeton, the University's Admissions Office and Stewart Country Day.
- In Wadi Rum, Susie Shinaco at Bait Ali.
- In San Antonio de Areco, Lucia Tore Deymonnaz and La Bamba de Areco.
- In Luxor, Tarek el Soultan and Yalla Tours.
- In Ilulissat, two Danish Guides and Bob Felch at Iceland Saga Travel.
- In Badaling, Ding Ding and Howard Smith of China Smith.

In Zermatt, Christina and Dr. Andreas Rickenbach, and Alpine Photo.
In Riobamba, Macarena Iturralde of Sanderos Naturales.
In El Chalten, and so many other places, Alejandro Luis Solares Frango.
In Abiquiu, Robert Cafazzo and Holly Sievers.
In Takanawa, Noriko Horai.
In Villnoss, Petra Überbacher and Edwin Domenegg.
In Al-Ain, Mohamed of Dubai Private Tour/Milan Tours.
In Lhasa, Jane from Lhasa China Travel and, again, Howard Smith.
On the Bygdoy Peninsula and in Tromso, Bernard Siebert.
In Isla Negra, Hebe Cafaretta of Wanderlust Expediciones de Trails SRL, Carolina Briones Méndez of the Fundación Pablo Neruda, Andrea De Las Nieves Duran of the Archivo Central Andres Bello at the University of Chile, and Cristina McDowell.
In St. Petersburg, Natalya Moshkina and the Belmond Grand Hotel Europe.
On Stavros Beach, Stavroula Stratigi.
For Kaladhungi, Katie Weiland of ATJ Travel and Jim's Jungle Retreat.
In Marrakech, the Hotel Mamounia.
In Bangkok, the Mandarin Oriental Hotel, Chatchawin Tangjaitrong, and Christopher Gadsden.
In Kathmandu, Amar Simha, and the Nepal Squash Rackets Association.
For Manaus, Chris Murray, the Cowfinder.
In the Kalahari and Tsodillo Hills, Wilderness Safaris and Wilderness Air.

When it came to the writing, we needed reviewers, critics, and the occasional supporter. That's what family and friends are for.

THANK YOU to Diane M. T. North and Franklyn L. Rogers. And also to Annis Lee Reeves, Diana Oppenlander, Cintra Rogers, Ru and David Scott, Maureen McCaffrey and James Lillie, Cintra Scott and Ian Mount, and—we saved the best for last—Lydia Hall and Guillaume Tranie.

Another THANK YOU to Wendy and Laurent Chaix, and Bill and Rosemary Weaver. And also to Bill McDowell, Warren Schmidt, Nat Taylor, Kirk Heilbrun, and John Madzin (okay, Lisa, too); Jerry and Pam Kearney, Bill and Glenda Ramsay, Summer Schachter and Michele Diamond, and Jack and Pam (her again) Meyerson; Ward Hinkle, and Will Dawkins; Julieanne Harris and Bill Lane; Bob Izzo; Bill Colehower, Bob Connor, Murray Pitkowski, and Lou Schwartz; Jerry Kretmar, LaToya Miller, Henry Wilcots, and Helen Marter; Eddie and Gloria Breznitz, Dan Keating and John Schellenberg; Jessie Hill and Ming Fang; Kate O'Neill; Hitch Blackburn, Al Beal, Bob Markowski, and Rhonda Jones; Peter Lundberg and John Clement; John Jeka and Cheryl Springfels; Kat and Alan Grant; Alex Cauterucci and John Lisko; Bill Casey, Roger Jones, Jim Mazzarelli, Zandy Nalle, Charlie Tyson, and Clay von Seldeneck; Margaret Gerety, George Felippi, Jeff Idler, John Nimick, Sandy Tilney, Joe Torsella, and Jim Zug; Mark Bernstein, Hugh Gilmore, Jim Gorman, and, last but not least, Janet Fries.

Of course, the proof is in the pudding. What you are holding in your hands has been crafted by the Meryl Moss Media Group: JeriAnn Geller, Raven Atkinson, John Lotte, and Jeffrey Michelson. If you like it, they get all the credit. If you don't, we get all the blame. And yes, a final THANK YOU to Maurice Possley and Meryl Moss.

APPENDIX I

Knud Rasmussen's Thule Expeditions

First   1912   Proved that Robert Peary Land was not an island separate from Greenland as he claimed. Journeyed 600 miles across inland ice.

Second   1916–1918   Mapped Northwest Coast of Greenland

Third   1919   Depot-laying for Roald Amundsen's polar drift the Maud

Fourth   1919–1920   Explored East Greenland around Angmagssalik

Fifth   1921–1924   Explored origins of Eskimo race: dogsled across Artic Canada from Greenland to Siberia

Sixth   1931   Worked to consolidate Denmark's claim to Eastern Greenland

Seventh   1933   To continue work of the previous expedition, but death intervened

APPENDIX II

Edward Whymper's 1880 Climbs Along the Avenue of Volcanoes

4 January
  VOLCANO: **Chimborazo**
  FACT: First ascent; tallest
  NOTE: Planted flagpole on top to prove ascent

2 February
  VOLCANO: **Corazon**
  FACT: Means "heart"
  NOTE: First climbed by La Condamine and Bouger

18 February
  VOLCANO: **Cotopaxi**
  FACT: Second tallest
  NOTE: Spent night on summit; peered down into crater; measured ground temperature in tent

23 February
  VOLCANO: **Sincholagua**
  FACT: First ascent
  NOTE: Climbed and returned in nine hours

10 March
  VOLCANO: **Antisana**
  FACT: First ascent
  NOTE: Hunted for condors on horseback

23 March
  VOLCANO: **Pichincha**
  FACT: Above Quito
  NOTE: Two peaks: Guagua and Rucu ("young" and "old")

4 April
    VOLCANO: **Cayambe**
    FACT: First ascent; third tallest
    NOTE: Located on equator

17 April
    VOLCANO: **Sara-Urcu**
    FACT: First ascent
    NOTE: Very foggy; used 4-foot reeds to mark return trail

24 April
    VOLCANO: **Cotocachi**
    FACT: First ascent
    NOTE: North of Otavalo; found Stars in Stone and other "antiquities"

4 May
    VOLCANO: **Illiniza**
    FACT: First ascent, Carrels only
    NOTE: Two peaks: Norte and Sur ("north" and "south")

29 June
    VOLCANO: **Carihuairazo**
    FACT: First ascent
    NOTE: Snow-blinded; descended to Abraspungo

3 July
    VOLCANO: **Chimborazo**
    FACT: Second ascent to prove first
    NOTE: Had native witnesses; found pole from first ascent; Cotopaxi erupted and covered them with ash

APPENDIX III

The Forty-Seven Ronin

	AGE		AGE
Horibe-Yahydye	76	Akabane-Genzo	34
Hazama-Kihyoye	68	Horibe-Yasubyoye	33
Yoshida-Chuzayemon	62	Fuwa-Kazuyemon	33
Mase-Kyudaiyu	62	Chikamatsu-Kanroku	33
Muramatsu-Kihyoye	61	Tominomori-Sukeyemon	33
Onodera-Junai	60	Kurahashi-Densuke	33
Okuda-Magodayu	56	Takebayashi-Tadashichi	32
Hara-Soyemon	55	Otaka-Gengo	31
Kaiga-Yazayemon	53	Yoshida-Sawayemon	28
Chiba-Saburobyoye	50	Yada-Goroyemon	28
Kimura-Okayemon	45	Onodera-Koyemon	27
Oishi-Kuranosuke	44	Sugino-Juheiji	27
Nakamura-Kansuke	44	Oishi-Sezayemon	26
Suganoya-Hannojo	43	Muramatsu-Sandiyu	26
Hayami-Tozayemon	39	Okuda-Sadayemon	25
Maebara-Isuke	39	Hazama-Jujiro	25
Terasaka-Kichiyemon	38	Isogai-Jurozayemon	24
Okajima-Ysoyemon	37	Okano-Kinyemon	23
Kanzaki-Yogoro	37	Hazama-Shinroku	23
Kayano-Wasuke	36	Katsuta-Shinzayemon	23
Kataoka-Gengoyemon	36	Mase-Magokuro	22
Yokogawa-Kampei	36	Yato-Yemonshichi	17
Mimura-Jirozayemon	36	Oishi-Chikara	15
Ushioda-Matanojo	34		

Source: Sakae Shioya, *Chushingura, An Exposition* (Toyko: Hokuseido Press, 1956), 72.

APPENDIX IV

First Ascents of the 8,000 Meter Mountains

3 June 1950
    MTN: **Annapurna**
    CLIMBERS: Maurice Herzog and Louis Lachenal
    EXPEDITION: French
    BOOK: *Annapurna* by Maurice Herzog

29 May 1953
    MTN: **Everest**
    CLIMBERS: Edmund Hillary and Tenzing Norgay
    EXPEDITION: British
    BOOK: *The Ascent of Everest* by John Hunt

3 July 1953
    MTN: **Nanga Parbat**
    CLIMBER: Hermann Buhl
    EXPEDITION: German / Austrian
    BOOK: *Nanga Parbat* by Karl Herrlighoffer

31 July 1954
    MTN: **K-2**
    CLIMBERS: L. Lacedelli and A. Compagnini
    EXPEDITION: Italian
    BOOK: *Ascent of K-2* by Ardito Desio

19 October 1954
    MTN: **Cho Oyu**
    CLIMBER: Herbert Tichy
    EXPEDITION: Austrian
    BOOK: *Cho Oyu* by Herbert Tichy

—*more*—

—*continued from previous page*—

15 May 1955
    MTN: **Makalu**
    CLIMBER: Jean Franco
    EXPEDITION: French
    BOOK: *Makalu* by Jean Franco

25 May 1955
    MTN: **Kangchenjunga**
    CLIMBERS: George Band and Joe Brown
    EXPEDITION: British
    BOOK: *Kangchenjunga, The Untrodden Peak* by Charles Evans

9 May 1956
    MTN: **Manaslu**
    CLIMBER: Y. Maki
    EXPEDITION: Japanese
    BOOK: *Manaslu 1954-1956* by Japanese Alpine Club

18 May 1956
    MTN: **Lhotse**
    CLIMBERS: F. Luchsinger and E. Reiss
    EXPEDITION: Swiss
    BOOK: *The Everest-Lhotse Adventure* by Albert Eggler

7 July 1956
    MTN: **Gasherbrum II**
    CLIMBER: S. Larch
    EXPEDITION: Austrian
    BOOK: *Weisse Berge - Schwarze Menschen* by Fritz Moravec

9 June 1957
> MTN: **Broad Peak**
> CLIMBERS: Marcus Schmuck, Fritz Wintersteller, Hermann Buhl and Kurt Diemberger
> EXPEDITION: Austrian
> BOOK: *Broad Peak* by Marcus Schmuck

4 July 1958
> MTN: **Gasherbrum I**
> CLIMBERS: P. Schoening and Nicholas Clinch
> EXPEDITION: American
> BOOK: *A Walk in the Sky* by Nicholas Clinch

15 May 1960
> MTN: **Dhaulagiri**
> CLIMBER: Max Eiselin
> EXPEDITION: Swiss
> BOOK: *The Ascent of Dhaulagiri* by Max Eiselin

2 May 1964
> MTN: **Shisha Pangma**
> CLIMBERS: Six Chinese / Four Tibetan
> EXPEDITION: Chinese / Tibetan
> BOOK: *Footprints on the Peaks* by Zhou Zheng

APPENDIX V

First Ascents of the Seven Summits

NORTH AMERICA
  MTN: **Denali** AKA **Mt. Mckinley**
  FIRST ASCENT: 7 June 1913
  CLIMBERS: Hudson Stuck, Harry Karstens, Walter Harper and Rubert Tatum
  BOOK: *The Ascent of Denali: A Narrative of the First Complete Ascent of the Highest Peak in North America* by Hudson Stuck

SOUTH AMERICA
  MTN: **Mt. Aconcagua**
  FIRST ASCENT: 14 January 1897
  CLIMBER: Mathias Zurbriggen
  BOOK: *The Highest Andes: A Record of the First Ascent of Aconcagua and Tupungato* by E. A. Fitzgerald

ANTARCTICA
  MTN: **Mt. Vinson**
  FIRST ASCENT: 17 December 1966
  CLIMBER: Nicholas B. Clinch
  BOOK: *First Conquest of Antarctica's Highest Peaks* by Nicholas B. Clinch

EUROPE
  MTN: **Mt. Elbrus** — East Summit
  FIRST ASCENT: 1828
  CLIMBER: Khillar Khachirov

EUROPE, continued

MTN: **Mt. Elbrus** — West Summit
FIRST ASCENT: 1874
CLIMBER: F. Crawford Grove

MTN: **Mt. Blanc**
FIRST ASCENT: 8 August 1786
CLIMBERS: Dr. Michel Paccard and Jacques Balmat
BOOK: *The Story of Mt. Blanc* by Albert Smith

AFRICA

MTN: **Mt. Kilamanjaro**
FIRST ASCENT: 1889
CLIMBERS: Hans Meyer and L. Purtscheller
BOOK: *Across East African Glaciers: An Account of the First Ascent of Kilamanjaro* by Hans Meyer

ASIA

MTN: **Mt. Everest**
FIRST ASCENT: 1953
CLIMBERS: Edmund Hillary and Tenzing Norgay
BOOK: *The Ascent of Everest* by John Hunt

AUSTRALIA

MTN: **Mt. Kosciuszko**
FIRST ASCENT: Date unknown
CLIMBER: Unknown

MTN: **Carstensz Pyramid**
FIRST ASCENT: 1962
CLIMBER: Heinrich Harrer
BOOK: *I Come From the Stone Age* by Heinrich Harrer

APPENDIX VI

Jim Corbett Hunts the Man-Eaters of Kumaon

Champawat Man-Eater (tigress)*

YEAR SHOT: 1907

HUMAN KILLS: 436

THE HUNT: Driven out of Nepal after 200 kills. Jim follows her from village to village. He conducts a "beat," drives her into a river gorge, shoots her twice but runs out of bullets. He grabs another rifle and shoots her at twenty feet as she approaches from an overhanging rock. She became a man-eater after losing half of her upper right tooth and all of her lower one.

Muktesar Man-Eater (tigress)**

YEAR SHOT: 1910

HUMAN KILLS: 24

THE HUNT: Jim "sits up" at night in a tree over a kill. He takes a "sound shot" in the dark but misses and she escapes into a ravine. A beat in dense brushwood fails but Jim sees her, takes a hurried shot and, again, misses. She turns and charges but Jim kills her at six feet. She had lost an eye in a battle with a porcupine and had fifty quills in her right arm and under the pad of her right foreleg.

Panar Man-Eater (male leopard)**

YEAR SHOT: 1910

HUMAN KILLS: 400

THE HUNT: He operated in a remote area and thus got little publicity. Jim makes two attempts: first in April of 1910, second in September. Jim uses two goats as bait. The leopard gets the first one and hides in a patch of dense brushwood. Jim "night sits" on an oak tree branch overlooking the second goat. He carries a double-barreled shot gun instead of a rifle, better chance of hitting the mark that way. The leopard tries to shake Jim off the tree but fails. He then goes for the second goat and gets it. Jim takes a shot in the dark and wounds the leopard. Jim and his men follow him with torches and Jim kills him when he turns to attack.

Rudraprayag Man-Eater (male leopard)***

YEAR SHOT: 1926

HUMAN KILLS: 125

THE HUNT: He terrorized the pilgrim trail to Kedarnath and Badrinath for eight years. He was headline news in India and became world famous. Jim hunts him for ten weeks in late 1925 using bait, traps, poison, to no avail. Jim returns in spring of 1926, sits up in a "machan" (a hunting platform) in a mango tree 100 yards from a pilgrim shelter for ten nights with no luck. He was going to quit but he spends one more night and, at long last, shoots him. The leopard was old, with a bullet wound in his left hind paw.

Talla Des Man-Eater (tigress and two cubs)**

YEAR SHOT: 1929

HUMAN KILLS: 150

THE HUNT: Jim tracks, then shoots them all in a row. The cubs die but the wounded tigress slides into a tree, dangles and then falls over the edge of a small cliff. Though lame, she escapes across the valley up a hill and Jim misses her twice, running out of bullets. He hunts her, picking up her blood trail but rain washes it out. He tries again and finds her pug marks. He follows her through water channels, game tracks and cattle paths. Finally, he shoots her again but must shoot her two more times to finish her. Tigress had twenty porcupine quills in her right shoulder and leg.

Chowgarh Man-Eater (tigress and cub)*

YEAR SHOT: 1930

HUMAN KILLS: 64

THE HUNT: Their first kill was in 1925, their last one in 1930. It was a reign of terror that covered 1,500 square miles. Jim follows the "drag marks" of a kill, and shoots the cub. He returns in February 1930, and shoots a leopard and two other tigers. On his third visit, in March, he kills two leopards, then spends almost a month tracking the tigress. Finally, he comes face to face with her, eight feet apart. He looks into her eyes and slowly, slowly, brings his rifle around and shoots her. She was very old and her and teeth were broken and worn. She had depended on her cub to kill.

Mohan Man-Eater (tiger)*

YEAR SHOT: 1931

HUMAN KILLS: –

THE HUNT: It roamed in the Kosi River valley for several years. Jim uses two buffalos as bait. He can't sit up or conduct a beat: he's sick and the area is too large. So, he stalks. He looks for scratch marks on trees and "pug" (paw) marks on the roads. Finally, he follows the drag marks of one buffalo and shoots the tiger sleeping after his meal. Jim regrets not waking the tiger and giving him a sporting chance. The tiger was wounded by twenty-five to thirty porcupine quills in his left leg.

Kanda Man-Eater (tiger)*

YEAR SHOT: 1932

HUMAN KILLS: –

THE HUNT: Jim sits up on a tree branch only eight feet above the ground at the edge of a river bank. He tries to call up the tiger, who answers but doesn't come close. However, as night falls, the tiger sneaks up to the tree and then goes off to his kill. Jim shoots him, but, upon being hit, the tiger turns and charges. Jim shoots him again just as he roars and springs for the tree. The tiger hits the tree and rolls down the river bank.

Chuka Man-Eater (tiger)**

YEAR SHOT: 1938

HUMAN KILLS: 3

THE HUNT: Jim has six buffalo to use as bait. The tiger gets two of them. Jim follows the blood trail and finds the second one, but the tiger later moves it. A third buffalo is set out and also killed and carried away. Jim follows the drag and locates it. He then sits up in a ficus tree over it. The tiger comes and sleeps under the tree. Jim leans out and over, and, with his rifle upside down, shoots him. He fires a second time, just to be sure. The tiger's right tooth was broken and there was buckshot in his body.

Thak Man-Eater (tigress)*

YEAR SHOT: 1938

HUMAN KILLS: 4

THE HUNT: Forest Department needed her killed in order to cut down the forest. Jim stalks her after a kill, follows the blood trail and sits up in a tree over the kill. No luck. He sits up over another kill — still no luck. He uses three buffalos as bait — tigress kills and eats one, but gets away. He sets out goats — not interested. Finally, he "calls up" the tigress by cupping his hands around his mouth and giving the mating cry. She answers — love is in the air… after all, it was mating season. He sits on a ledge behind a rock and shoots her at point blank range.

*See *Man Eaters of Kumaon* (New York, Oxford University Press, 1946)

**See *The Temple Tiger and More Man Eaters* (New York, Oxford University Press, 1955)

***See *The Man Eating Leopard of Rudraprayag* (New York, Oxford University Press, 1948)

APPENDIX VII

Successful Ascents of Mount Everest

Number of successful Everest climbs yearly

Year	Count	Year	Count
1950	0	1970	4
1951	0	1971	0
1952	0	1972	0
1953	2	1973	10
1954	0	1974	0
1955	0	1975	15
1956	4	1976	4
1957	0	1977	2
1958	0	1978	25
1959	0	1979	20
	SUB: 6		SUB: 80
1960	3	1980	8
1961	0	1981	5
1962	0	1982	18
1963	6	1983	23
1964	0	1984	16
1965	9	1985	30
1966	0	1986	4
1967	0	1987	2
1968	0	1988	50
1969	0	1989	24
	SUB: 18		SUB: 180

Year	Climbs	Year	Climbs
1990	72	2010	544
1991	38	2011	553
1992	90	2012	580
1993	129	2013	683
1994	51	2014	134
1995	83	2015	0
1996	98	2016	681
1997	85	2017	692
1998	121	2018	817
1999	118	2019	878
	SUB: 885		SUB: 5,562
2000	145	2020	28
2001	182	2021	472
2002	159	2022	683
2003	267		SUB: 1,183
2004	337		
2005	307		
2006	494		
2007	634		
2008	432		
2009	468		
	SUB: 3,425		

1950-2022 Total Successful Climbs: 11,339

Source: www.himalayandatabase.com

NOTES

The world exists to end up in a book.

—STÉPHANE MALLARMÉ

PRINCETON, NEW JERSEY

Epigraph: Richard Halliburton, *The Royal Road to Romance* (Indianapolis: Bobbs-Merrill Co., 1925), 1.

1. We give a special thank you to Lawrence Biemiller at www.iceandcoal.org. See "Where the Only Station Stop is Princeton," *The Chronicle of Higher Education*, May 16, 2003. Lawrence, we sure tried to use your photo.

2. And it *is* the first sentence in Richard Halliburton, *The Royal Road to Romance*.

3. Richard Halliburton, *The Royal Road to Romance*, 4.

    Richard Halliburton's parents donated the Halliburton Tower to Rhodes College in Memphis, Tennessee, as a memorial to their son. It bears a plaque inscribed with this quote.

4. Alfred Lord Tennyson, "Ulysses," as quoted in Richard Halliburton, *The Glorious Adventure* (Indianapolis: Bobbs-Merrill Co., 1927), 17.

5. Richard Halliburton, *New Worlds to Conquer* (Indianapolis: Bobbs-Merrill Co., 1929).

6. Richard Halliburton, *The Flying Carpet* (Indianapolis: Bobbs-Merrill Co., 1932).

7. Richard Halliburton, *The Flying Carpet*, 99. Pinard is dirt-cheap red wine and what is the only cure for a bad glass of it? Another one.

8. Richard Halliburton, *The Flying Carpet*, 290, quoting George Mallory.

9. Richard Halliburton, *Seven League Boots* (Indianapolis: Bobbs-Merrill Co., 1935), 14.

10. Richard Halliburton, *Richard Halliburton: His Story of His Life's Adventures as Told in Letters to his Mother and Father* (Indianapolis: Bobbs-Merrill Co., 1940).

    As Halliburton described it (at page 420):

    > "The *Sea Dragon's* stern is my special pride and joy ... the central section is brilliant, with a huge painting of a phoenix, the Chinese good-luck bird. The brightness of his feathers makes up, perhaps, for the fact that the native painter gave him only one leg."

11. Richard Halliburton, *His Story of His Life's Adventures as Told in Letters to his Mother and Father*, 433.

WADI RUM, JORDAN

Epigraph: T. E. Lawrence, *Seven Pillars of Wisdom: A Triumph* (New York: Doubleday, 1935), 375, 414.

1. *Wadi* means "valley" in Arabic. Archeologists suggest that the word *rum* is derived from the Aramaic word *iram*, which means "high place" or "pillar." Thus, *Wadi Rum* may mean a "valley of pillars," and as we all know, one man's "pillar" is another man's "mountain."

2. It is ironic that Wadi Rum is so identified with Lawrence. While he wrote of it in glowing terms, his diary records that during the two-year wartime period of 1917 and 1918, he spent a total of eleven nights here. See Appendix II, T. E. Lawrence, *Seven Pillars of Wisdom: A Triumph*.

3. T. E. Lawrence, "Suppressed Introductory Chapter for Seven Pillars of Wisdom: A Triumph" in *Oriental Assembly* (London: Williams and Norgate, 1939), 143.

4. T. E. Lawrence, *Oriental Assembly*, 144–45.

5. Jeremy Wilson, *T. E. Lawrence* (London: National Portrait Gallery Press, 1988), 142–81 as updated by Wikipedia at February 21, 2018.

6. Jeremy Wilson, *T. E. Lawrence*, 146, as priced at Abebooks.com in May 2023.

7. Jeremy Wilson, *T. E. Lawrence*, 148.
8. See the movie *Lawrence of Arabia*, directed by David Lean (Horizon Pictures, 1962), 3 hr., 47 min.
9. You are looking south from Jebel Rum with Jebel Um Ishrin on the left and Jebel Khazali on the right.
10. T. E. Lawrence, *Seven Pillars of Wisdom: A Triumph*, 351.
11. Tony Howard and Di Taylor, *Treks and Climbs in Wadi Rum, Jordan*. 4th ed. (Milnthorpe, England: Cicerone Press, 2007), 21.
12. Tony Howard and Di Taylor, *Treks and Climbs in Wadi Rum, Jordan*. 4th ed., 88.
13. E-mail interview with Tony Howard, December 30, 2009.
14. Tony and Di run N.O.M.A.D.S. (New Opportunities for Mountaineering, Adventure and Desert Sports), an adventure travel consultancy. They climb and trek worldwide and, besides Jordan, have written or contributed to guides to the United Kingdom, Norway, Oman, and Palestine. For more information, see www.nomadstravel.co.uk.

SAN ANTONIO DE ARECO, ARGENTINA

Epigraph: Ricardo Güiraldes, *Don Segundo Sombra*, as quoted in Alex Decotte, *Gauchos* (Buenos Aires: Librerias B.C., 1978), 80.

1. La Portena dates back to the year 1800 when its first owner was Manuel Jose Guerrico. He was the president of the Argentine Railroad Company, and he named the estate after its famous locomotive "La Portena." One of his daughters married José Antonio Güiraldes, and the Estancia has been linked to the Güiraldes family ever since. Manuel J. Güiraldes, Ricardo's father, was the mayor of Buenos Aires.
2. See Denis Boyles, *Everything Explained That Is Explainable* (New York: Alfred A. Knopf, 2016).
3. Dennis Boyles, *Everything Explained That Is Explainable*, 280. Oxford University had been offered 10 percent, but passed.
4. See Bonifacio Del Carril, *El Gaucho* (Buenos Aires: Emecé Editores, 1993).

This seems like the right place, even if not the right time, to include the only "poem" we have ever found on the inside of a bathroom stall door (it was in a restaurant in Santiago, Chile, consider the source) that is worth remembering:

> Said an Argentine Gaucho named Bruno
> Of one thing I definitely do know,
> Women are fine,
> Sheep are divine,
> But the Llama is numero uno.

5. Of many translations, see Ricardo Güiraldes, *Don Segundo Sombra* (New York: Farrar & Rinehart, 1935).

    The link between Güiraldes and San Antonio de Areco cannot be overstated. After his death, the town created the Ricardo Güiraldes Museum in his honor. A National Historic Monument, it is the country's largest gaucho museum.

6. Simon Collier, Artemis Cooper, Maria Susanna Azzi, et al.., *Tango: The Dance, the Song, the Story* (London: Thames & Hudson, 1995), 76.

    Indeed, as one Parisian comtesse remarked upon seeing her first tango, "Is one supposed to dance it standing up?"

7. Horacio Salas, *Tango: The Poetry of Buenos Aires* (Buenas Aires: Manrique Zago Ediciones, 1998), 18. This description is attributed to the tango musician and writer Enrique Santos Discépolo.

8. Men and women share the same experience differently. To the men, the wait was eternal, to the women, the line was infinite. Who was right?

9. Which bred the great definition: An Argentine is an Italian who speaks Spanish, dresses as if he were British, and acts as if he were French.

    For a variation of this, see Simon Collier, Artemis Cooper, Maria Susanna Azzi, et al., *Tango: The Dance, the Song, the Story*, 95.

10. Horacio Salas, *Tango: Poetry of Buenos Aires*, 129. This characterization is attributed to the Argentine writer and poet Leopoldo Lugones.

11. Simon Collier, Artemis Cooper, Maria Susanna Azzi, et al., *Tango: The Dance, the Song, the Story*, 67–76, 145.

12. Horacio Salas, *Tango: The Poetry of Buenos Aires*, 104.

13. Simon Collier, Artemis Cooper, Maria Susanna Azzi, et al., *Tango: The Dance, the Song, the Story*, 72.

   Others report the year as 1910. See Horacio Ferrer, *Inventario del Tango, Toma I (1849–1939)* (Argentina, Fondo Nacional de las Artes, 1949) 98.

14. Simon Collier, Artemis Cooper, Maria Susanna Azzi, et al., *Tango: The Dance, the Song, the Story*, 76.

LUXOR, EGYPT

Epigraph: as cited in Daniel Meyerson, *The Linguist and the Emperor* (New York: Random House, 2005), 205.

1. Richard Parkinson, *Cracking Codes: The Rosetta Stone and Decipherment* (Berkeley, CA: University of California Press, 1999), 12, 19, and 20.

2. Franco Serino, *Déscription de L'Egypte: Napoleon's Expedition and the Rediscovery of Ancient Egypt* (Cairo: The American University in Cairo Press, 2003), 5.

3. Lesley Adkins and Roy Adkins, *The Keys of Egypt* (New York: HarperCollins, 2000), 23.

4. Richard Parkinson, *Cracking Codes: The Rosetta Stone and Decipherment*, 200.

5. Richard Parkinson, *Cracking Codes: The Rosetta Stone and Decipherment*, 23.

   Two inscriptions can be seen on the side of the stone, written in clear English: "Captured in Egypt by the British Army 1801" and "Presented to King George III."

6. See Daniel Meyerson, *The Linguist and The Emperor* for a rendering of the interconnected lives of Champollion and Napoleon.

NOTES | *352*

7. The house on rue de la Boudousquerie in Figeac (now rue des Freres Champollion) where both brothers were born is now a museum, featuring a giant replica of the Rosetta Stone in its courtyard. See Richard Parkinson, *Cracking Codes: The Rosetta Stone and Decipherment*, 43.

8. Belzoni's feats in transporting the obelisk from Philae to the Mediterranean coast for shipment (it was so heavy it collapsed a pier and was nearly lost in the Nile) and digging out the Temple of Abu Simbel (he was the first person to enter it in centuries) were heroic.

    However, they pale in comparison to the efforts of the Egyptian government in the mid-1960s. While constructing the High Aswan Dam, the buildings on the island of Philae were disassembled piece by piece and then put back together on the nearby but higher Agilika Island. Similarly, the Temple of Abu Simbel honoring Ramses II and the adjacent Temple of Hathor honoring Queen Nefertari were relocated on an artificial cliff seven hundred feet back from and two hundred feet above their original positions. In each instance, these great monuments were saved from drowning by the new dam. *Egypt, Eyewitness Travel Guide* (London: Dorling Kindersley Ltd., 2007), 212–14.

9. Lesley Adkins and Roy Adkins, *The Keys of Egypt*, 194.

10. Lesley Adkins and Roy Adkins, *The Keys of Egypt*, 171.

11. Lesley Adkins and Roy Adkins, *The Keys of Egypt*, 173.

12. Lesley Adkins and Roy Adkins, *The Keys of Egypt*, 180, 181, 182.

13. Lesley Adkins and Roy Adkins, *The Keys of Egypt*, 207.

14. Lesley Adkins and Roy Adkins, *The Keys of Egypt*, 250, 251.

15. Lesley Adkins and Roy Adkins, *The Keys of Egypt*, 260.

16. See Joyce Tyldesley, *Egypt: How a Lost Civilization Was Rediscovered* (Berkeley, CA: University of California Press, 2005), 87

17. Lesley Adkins and Roy Adkins, *The Keys of Egypt*, 272–73

ILULISSAT, GREENLAND

Epigraph: Knud Rasmussen, as cited in Gretel Ehrlich, *This Cold Heaven: Seven Seasons in Greenland* (New York: Random House, 2001), 9.

1. More than you might think. Life in northwestern Greenland has historically been based on consensual toleration. If a man wished to bestow that ultimate form of affection upon his dog, it was allowed with certain conditions. "First, out of respect for the dog, she had to be in heat … Second … you had to do it out on the ice in front of the whole village." Gretel Ehrlich, *This Cold Heaven: Seven Seasons in Greenland*, 178.
2. Gretel Ehrlich, *This Cold Heaven: Seven Seasons in Greenland*, 142.
3. On the other hand, climate change may bring Greenland economic independence, as the retreating ice opens up underground mining prospects and underwater oil and gas deposits.
4. The Danes colonized Greenland in 1721, establishing a trading post and a church. As of 2022, it remains a Danish protectorate, getting more than 40 percent of its gross domestic product from Danish assistance.
5. See Joanna Kavenna, *The Ice Museum: In Search of the Lost Land of Thule* (New York: Viking Penguin, 2006).
6. Knud Rasmussen, *The People of the Polar North: A Record* (London: Kegan, Paul, Trench, Trübner & Co., 1908), Author's Preface.
7. Jean Malaurie, *The Last Kings of Thule* (New York: E. P. Dutton, 1982), 93.
8. Knud Rasmussen, *The People of the Polar North: A Record*, 159.
9. Knud Rasmussen, *The New People* was published in London in 1908 as *The People of the Polar North*.
10. Jean Malaurie, *The Last Kings of Thule*, 448, Footnote 64.
11. Knud knew his real estate, even if he didn't know that he knew it. His humble trading post turned out to be equidistant between Washington, D.C. and Moscow. So, in due time, this center of Inuit life became a U.S. military base. Between 1950 and 1952, in the name of "preventive deterrence," the United States invested

$800 million here, moving the Inuit sixty-five miles north to a new Thule, now called "Qaanaaq" in the Greenlandic language.

12. Knud Rasmussen, *Greenland by the Polar Sea: The Story of the Thule Expedition from Melville Bay to Cape Morris Jessup* (London: Heinemann, 1921), xxii.

13. In Greenland, war only takes a day. People still remember the Great Massacre of Inuarfissuaq:

> "Two boys were fighting on the shore of the island ... They were fighting pretty roughly, the way many children do. One boy was thrown down by the other. He cried out, and to make him be quiet, the other kicked and punched him.
>
> "By chance, the grandfather of the boy on the ground saw what was happening. He ran over to them and intervened, as was right. There was a fight. The man was very angry, and struck the other child so hard that he fell down on the rocks, quite dead.
>
> "The other grandfather was furious, and he intervened in turn, and then the fathers, the shrieking mothers, the mothers-in-law, uncles, aunts, cousins, nephews, and nieces. The whole camp was embroiled. There were insults and curses — horrifying scenes.
>
> "Everyone was in a state of indescribable violence. People hurled rocks and bones at one another's heads, flung themselves on one another savagely. One man chased a woman, grasping a bloody harpoon. In the end, they all efficiently finished each other off. Not a living person was left."

See Jean Malaurie, *The Last Kings of Thule*, 320.

14. See also, Knud Rasmussen, *Across Arctic America: Narrative of the Fifth Thule Expedition* (New York: G. P. Putnam's Sons, 1927).

15. Gretel Ehrlich, *This Cold Heaven: Seven Seasons in Greenland*, 47.

BADALING, CHINA

Epigraph: William Edgar Geil, *The Great Wall of China* (London: John Murray, 1909), 3, and William Lindsay, *Alone on the Great Wall* (London: Hodder & Stoughton, 1989), 17.

1. William Lindsay, *The Great Wall Revisited* (Cambridge, MA: Harvard University Press, 2008), 278.
2. William Lindsay, *The Great Wall Revisited*, 21–22.
3. William Lindsay, *The Great Wall Revisited*, 48.
4. We thank the Doylestown, PA Historical Society for its many contributions. See also *The Philadelphia Inquirer*, June 29, 2009, A1, A8.
5. William Lindsay, *The Great Wall Revisited*, 216.
6. William Lindsay, *The Great Wall Revisited*, 201.
7. From left to right: James, William, Thomas, and Qi Lindsay.

    Lindsay is the world's leading non-Chinese expert in Great Wall studies. Besides the books cited here, he has produced documentaries and curated exhibits regarding the Great Wall and its history.

    He and his family operate Wild Wall Experiences. They provide an opportunity for travelers to experience the "Wild Wall," i.e., the parts of the Great Wall that have not been renovated. For more information, see www.wildwall.com or contact Lindsay at william@wildwall.com.

ZERMATT, SWITZERLAND

Epigraph: Edward Whymper, *Scrambles Amongst the Alps* (London: John Murray, 1871), 321.

1. George Band, *Summit: 150 Years of the Alpine Club* (London: HarperCollins, 2006), 24. 26–27.
2. The mountain takes its name from German words: *matte* meaning "meadow" and *horn* meaning "peak." The Italian ("Monte Cervino") and French ("Mont Cervin") names have a Latin derivation.

3. See Edward Whymper, *The Valley of Zermatt and the Matterhorn: A Guide*, Reprint ed. (Reading, England: Gaston's Alpine Books Publisher, 1978).

4. Sella's nephew, Vittoria Sella, would climb the Matterhorn in 1882 and take twelve panoramic photographs from its summit. These would help establish him as the first great mountain photographer.

5. Edward Whymper, *Scrambles Amongst the Alps* (Salt Lake City: Peregrine Smith books, 1986), 311.

6. Edward Whymper, *Scrambles Amongst the Alps*, 316.

7. And quite a view it was. See Edward Whymper, *Scrambles Amongst the Alps*, 320.

> Not one of the principal peaks of the Alps was hidden. I see them clearly now — the great inner circles of giants, backed by the ranges, chains, and massifs. Then Monte Rosa … Behind were the Bernese Oberland. Towards the south we looked … The Viso — one hundred miles away — seemed close upon us. The Maritime Alps — one hundred and thirty miles distant — were free from haze. Then came my first love — the Pelvoux; and lastly, in the west, gorgeous in the full sunlight, rose the monarch of all — Mont Blanc.

8. The Monte Rosa Hotel was "the Club Room of Zermatt" for the Alpine Club during the "Golden Age." It was from here that Edward Whymper set out on his fateful climb. And the hotel won't let you forget it. There is a large plaque on the building dedicated to Whymper, its bar is named "Edward's Bar" and, in its basement is the "Whymper-Stube," a restaurant that features fondue, raclette and a fantastic meringue dessert.

9. The First Ascent of the Matterhorn was not the end but the beginning. On July 17, 1865, only three days later, Jean-Antoine Carrel made his ascent — and the first ascent — from the Italian side. On July 25, 1868, John Tyndall made the First Traverse, crossing the mountain from Italy to Switzerland.

Remember — it's always better to be the first than to be the best — there will always be another best, but there will never be another first … until, of course, there's a different one.

On July 22, 1871, Lucy Walker became the first woman to climb the Matterhorn. On March 17, 1882, Vittorio Sella, guided by Carrel, made the First Winter Ascent. The following July, Sella returned, carried his heavy photographic equipment to the summit, and took the twelve-plate panorama, which became one of the highlights of his great photographic career.

And on and on. Can you top this? First solo climb, first winter solo climb, first climb on the North Face, first winter solo climb on the North Face.

And, never, never forget Ulrich Inderbinen, who climbed the Matterhorn a mere 370 times, the last time in 1990, at age 90.

10. For books, see Edward Whymper, *Scrambles Amongst the Alps*.

    For lithographs, see Gustave Doré, *The Ascent of the Matterhorn: Arrival at the Summit* and *The Ascent of the Matterhorn: The Fall*, the two lithographs shown here. Originally produced in black and white, we present versions colored by Matthias Taugwalder, a descendant of one of Whymper's guides.

    For paintings, see Ferdinand Hodler and his two monumental, twenty-five-foot-tall works, *Aufstieg* and *Absturz*, which were commissioned for the 1894 World Exhibition in Antwerp. They were later cut into sections, only to be partially reassembled in the Alpine Museum in Bern, Switzerland.

    Finally, for a movie, see *The Challenge* (1939), in which it is Carrel who finds the broken rope in order to prove that Whymper did not cut it.

11. Edward Whymper, *Scrambles Amongst the Alps*, 334.

RIOBAMBA, ECUADOR

Epigraph: Edward Whymper, *Travels Amongst the Great Andes of the Equator* (London: John Murray, 1892), 23.

1. Larrie D. Ferreiro, *Measure of the Earth* (New York: Basic Books, 2011), 29.

2. The first thing to do in studying the effects of high altitude is to measure the altitude. Whymper took with him two mountain mercurial barometers of the Fortin pattern, boiling point

thermometers in two series (150°–1855° and 180°–215°) and seven aneroids. For a listing of his measurements, barometer ranges, comparison of aneroid and mercurial barometers, various boiling point observations, and external and body temperature comparisons, we refer you to appendices A through F in Edward Whymper, *Travels Amongst the Great Andes of the Equator*.

3. People generally agree that there are three types of volcanoes: active, dormant, and extinct. What they disagree about is the relevant measuring time. For example, active usually refers to a volcano that erupts regularly. However, since volcanoes have a life span of millions of years, "regularly" can mean once every thousand years. Thus, an active volcano may be dormant during our lifetimes and extinct over several generations.

4. *The Heart of the Andes* is more than five feet tall and nearly ten feet wide.

   When unveiled to the New York City public in 1859, people waited hours in line to see it. When sold, it realized the highest price ever for the work of a living American artist. It is now part of the permanent collection of the Metropolitan Museum in New York City and can be found in Gallery 760.

5. Of note is the method used to capture condors. Set out a dead horse and let it decay. In time, the condors will come and eat their fill. Afterward, they will be too sated to fly away quickly and can easily be lassoed from horseback.

6. Edward Whymper, *Travels Amongst the Great Andes of the Equator*, 50.

7. Edward Whymper, *Travels Amongst the Great Andes of the Equator*, 327. Whymper made this etching from a photograph taken on July 3, 1880. From left to right are David Beltram, Jean-Antoine Carrel, the First Ascent flagpole and Javier Campana.

   Among other things, Whymper measured the amount of volcanic dust on the ground in three locations and from that calculated the number of millions of tons ejected by Cotopaxi's eruption.

8. See, for example, Yossi Brain, *Ecuador: A Climbing Guide* (Seattle: Mountaineers Books, 2000).

9. See Marco Cruz, *Mountains of Ecuador* (Quito: Dinediciones, 1992) and his website www.expediciones-andinas.com.

EL CHALTÉN, PATAGONIA

Epigraph: Douglas R. Tompkins, "Fitz Roy, 1968" in the *American Alpine Journal 1969*, pages 263–69, as found in Yvon Chouinard, Dick Dorworth, Chris Jones, et al., *Climbing Fitz Roy 1968: Reflections on the Lost Photos of the Third Ascent* (Ventura, CA: Patagonia Inc., 2013), 22–28.

1. See Gregory Crouch, *Enduring Patagonia* (New York: Random House, 2001), 50 and 60, where Crouch relates finding a story about Patagonia in *Climbing Ice* by Yvon Chouinard. He read it over and over until he knew every detail and resolved to go there and climb.
2. See Alberto Maria de Agostini, *Andes Patagónicos* (Santiago, Chile: Pontifical Catholic University of Chile, 2010).
3. See Charles Darwin, *The Voyage of the Beagle* (London: The Amalgamated Press, 1905).
4. Lionel Terray, *Conquistadors of the Useless* (London: Victor Gollanz Ltd., 1963), 317.
5. Doug Tompkins, "Fitz Roy, 1968" as found in *Climbing Fitz Roy 1968: Reflections on the Lost Photos of the Third Ascent*.
6. Yvon Chouinard, Jeff Johnson, and Chris Mallory. *180° South: Conquerors of the Useless* (Ventura, CA: Patagonia Inc., 2013).
7. See Werner Herzog, *Scream of Stone* (1991), available in English on a Korean produced and subtitled DVD. To get rid of the subtitles, click on "Subtitle," click on "None," and then click on "Resume."
8. See Rolando Garibotti, "A Mountain Unveiled" in *American Alpine Journal 2004*.

    Garibotti has climbed in and written about the Chalten Massif since 1986, when he was fifteen years old. His book with Dörte Pietron, *Patagonia Vertical: Climbing Guide* (Ljubljana, Slovenia: Sidharta, 2012) is the best guidebook we have ever read.
9. See Ken Wilson, "A Mountain Desecrated" and "Interview with Cesare Maestri," *Mountain* (no. 23, September 1972). Then see Reinhold Messner, "The Murder of the Impossible," *Mountain* (no. 15).

10. See Stefano Louison, "Taliban on Cerro Torre" in PlanetMountain.com, September 2, 2012.
11. David Gelles, "Billionaire Gives Away His Company to Fight Climate Change," *The New York Times*, September 15, 2022, A1, B6.
12. For a tribute to Doug Tompkins, see Jonathan Franklin, *A Wild Idea* (New York: HarperOne, 2021). For more details, see https://tompkinsconservation.org.
13. See Kalan Robb Photography, www.kalanrobb.com, for a January 14, 2017, blog on "El Chaltén and the Secret Fitz Roy Cascades."

See also www.atlasandboots.com, for a January 13, 2016, blog on "Six Outstanding El Chaltén Hiking Trails."

ABIQUIU, NEW MEXICO

Epigraph: Rev. James Hall, as quoted in Lesley Poling-Kempes, *Ghost Ranch* (Tucson, AZ: University of Arizona Press, 2005), 247.

1. See Lesley Poling-Kempes, *Ghost Ranch*, 3–16.
2. Lesley Poling-Kempes, *Ghost Ranch*, 16–36.
3. Lesley Poling-Kempes, *Ghost Ranch*, 36–65.
4. Lesley Poling-Kempes, *Ghost Ranch*, 65–84. Quote at 83.
5. Painting: *Part of the Cliffs* by Georgia O'Keeffe, 1937, as shown in Barbara Buhler Lynes, Lesley Poling-Kempes, and Frederick W. Turner, *Georgia O'Keeffe and New Mexico: A Sense of Place*. (Princeton, NJ: Princeton University Press, 2004), 26.

   This book was the catalogue of an exhibition of the same name that compared Georgia O'Keeffe paintings to photographs of the subjects she painted, most of them at the Ghost Ranch. It has become the basis for a very popular trail walk or ride at the ranch.

6. Lesley Poling-Kempes, *Ghost Ranch*, 154.
7. Lesley Poling-Kemps, *Ghost Ranch*, 180–93. Quote on page 183.
8. Lesley Poling-Kempes, *Ghost Ranch*, 199.

9. Arthur Newton Pack, *We Called It Ghost Ranch* (Abiquiu, NM: Ghost Ranch Conference Center, 1965), 137. See also Lesley Poling-Kempes, *Ghost Ranch*, 204.

10. You can start by visiting the ranch's website: www.ghostranch.org. It is very thorough, discussing the ranch's history, its relationship with Georgia O'Keeffe, its lodging and spiritual retreat offerings, and its outdoor adventure activities.

TAKANAWA, JAPAN

Epigraph: Death Poem of Asano Takuminokami Naganori. See Hiroaki Sato, *Legends of the Samurai* (Old Saybrook, CT: Konecky and Konecky, 1995), 319.

1. Hiroaki Sato, *Legends of the Samurai*, 305, 307–12.

2. Hiroaki Sato, *Legends of the Samurai*, 322, as edited.

3. Hiroaki Sato, *Legends of the Samurai*, 321.

4. For the first English telling of this story see A. B. Mitford, *Tales of Old Japan* (London: Macmillan, 1871), Volume 1, 1–34.

5. Hiroaki Sato, *Legends of the Samurai*. Footnote 24 on page 332. Official records indicate that only forty-six ronin attacked Lord Kira. One had previously committed suicide because his family prevented him from joining the others. He was later granted the honor of inclusion.

6. What became of Lord Kira's head? His retainers beseeched Oishi and the ronin for its return: without a head, the family could not bury the body. Oishi accommodated them because, after all, there was no personal animosity toward Kira. The Forty-Seven had simply upheld their duty to their own lord. One of the more curious artifacts you will find at Sengaku-Ji is the receipt for the head. See A. B. Mitford, *Tales of Old Japan*, 30.

7. See Donald Keene, *Chushingura — The Treasury of Loyal Retainers* (New York: Columbia University Press, 1971), 29.

   The opening lines expound on the theme:

   > The sweetest food, if left untasted, remains unknown,
   > its savor wasted. The same holds true of a country at peace:

the loyalty and courage of its fine soldiers remain hidden, but the stars, though invisible by day, at night reveal themselves, scattered over the firmament.

8. To an outsider, the number forty-seven seems quite propitious. There are forty-seven symbols in the *kana* (the Japanese alphabet) and forty-seven prefectures (states) in Japan. See Donald Keene, *Chushingura*, ix.

9. For a collection of the portraits, see David R. Weinberg, *Kuniyoshi: The Faithful Samurai* (Leiden, Netherlands: Hotei Publishing, 2000).

   Hokusai claimed a special relationship with his subject matter, being a descendant of one of the ronin. Others say that he really was a descendant of Lord Kira. See David Bell, *Chushingura and the Floating World* (United Kingdom: Japan Library, 2001) 56, footnote 16.

10. For a more complete list, see the Bibliography.

11. If you count the number of headstones set in the rectangular area, you will find that there are forty-nine. One is ceremonial, which leaves forty-eight graves. Why the extra one? Do you remember the Satsuma man who spat in Oishi's face as he lay in the street? After the Forty-Seven had been buried, he visited their graves and, to atone for having misjudged Oishi, he, himself, committed *seppuku*. Seeing this, the temple monks believed that he deserved to be buried alongside the others.

12. Jorge Luis Borges, "The Insulting Master of Etiquette Kotsuke no Suke," *A Universal History of Infamy* (New York: Dutton, 1972) 69–74.

    Borges was more elegant but less gracious in his summation:
    > This is the end of the story of the forty-seven loyal men — except that it has no end — for the rest of us, who are not loyal, perhaps, but who will never wholly give up the hope of being so, will go on honoring them with words.

VILLNÖSS, SOUTH TYROL

Epigraph: Joke told by Petra Überbacher, South Tyrol, July, 2012.

1. Reinhold Messner, *Free Spirit: A Climber's Life* (Seattle: The Mountaineers Books, 1991), 16.

2. In German, *drei zinnen* means "Three Merlons." In Italian, *tre cime di Lavaredo* means "the Three Peaks of Lavaredo." These photos view the group from the north. From left to right (east to west), their names are, in German, Kleine Zinne, Gross Zinne, and Westliche Zinne, or, in Italian, Cima Piccola, Cima Grande, and Cima Ovest. In English, however, they lose all their mystery: they are Little Peak, Big Peak, and Western Peak. The North Face of Gross Zinne (Cima Grande) is considered one of the six great north face climbs in all of Europe.

3. In addition to his physical efforts, Messner has contributed to the philosophy of mountain climbing. For example, in 1966, he wrote an essay entitled *The Murder of the Impossible*. In it, he argued that, with the use of bolts and other mechanical climbing aids, there was no such thing as "impossible" anymore, and, if "impossible" no longer existed, "adventures" were unthinkable. As he continued:

    > I only experience real adventure when I don't know what the outcome will be. Adventure means stepping into the unknown, or maybe the impossible. It's like being on another planet. If I do everything right I come back safe, if not then maybe I won't.

    Reinhold Messner, *My Life at the Limit* (Seattle: The Mountaineers Books, 2014), 42.

    Others say that it is Messner, himself, who has killed the "impossible." According to one fellow climber: "After Messner, the mystery of possibility was gone: there remained only the mystery of whether *you* could do it."

4. Reinhold Messner, *Free Spirit: A Climber's Life*, 121.

5. Reinhold Messner, *Free Spirit: A Climber's Life*, 121–33.

    Of course, Gunther and Reinhold knew the risks:

    > Naturally, I had no idea that things would turn out as badly as they did. We just pushed all the hassles to the back of our

> minds, took a deep breath, and got on with it. We wanted to go to Nanga Parbat. My brother Gunther was right when he said, "We would have gone to Nanga Parbat with the Devil himself."

See Reinhold Messner, *My Life at the Limit*, 55.

Reinhold was accused of abandoning Gunther near the top of the Rupal Face so he could finish a first-ever traverse (up one side, down another) of an eight-thousander. Reinhold contended that Gunther had become too tired to descend the way they had climbed and they were making an emergency descent of the gentler, western Diamir side when Gunther was overcome by an avalanche.

It took thirty-five years for Reinhold to be vindicated. In 2005, two climbers on the Diamir side found Gunther's remains exposed in the melting snow and ice.

6. See Reinhold Messner, *All 14 Eight-Thousanders* (Seattle: Cloudcap, 1988), for an in-depth discussion of each of his climbs.

7. Messner, *Free Spirit: A Climber's Life*, 154–60.

8. You gotta love America. Where else would two fifty-year-old, inexperienced climbers "decide" to climb the Seven Summits … and then actually do it. See, Richard Bass, *Seven Summits* (New York: Warner Books, 1986).

9. The debate over which mountains are the "true" Seven Summits was not just academic. Bragging rights were involved. Dick Bass was the first to climb them all *if* Mount Elbrus and Mount Kosciuszko are part of the Seven (on April 30, 1985). Patrick Morrow was the first to climb *if* Mount Elbus and Carstensz are (August 5, 1986). And Reinhold Messner? He was the first *if* Mont Blanc and Carstensz are the appropriate ones (December 3, 1986).

10. See Reinhold Messner, *My Quest for the Yeti* (London: Macmillan, 2000), 165.

    > During my last expedition, an old nomad came to my tent. He aped my voice, then threw stones at me when I tried to get him to leave. "Yeti!" he shouted, making derogatory gestures and waving his hands at me, as if to shoo me away.

11. We send a special "Thank You" to Ruth Ennemoser of Messner's office for her review of, and assistance with, this chapter.

AL AIN, UNITED ARAB EMIRATES

Epigraph: Wilfred Thesiger, *Arabian Sands* (New York: E. P. Dutton & Co., 1959), 23.

1. "Mubarak bin London" means "The Blessed One from London."
2. Wilfred Thesiger, *Arabian Sands*, 25.
3. See Bertram Thomas, *Arabia Felix* (London: Jonathan Cape, 1932).

   It was here (in a footnote on page 257) that we learned of camel nomenclature. Owners may give them individual names but disinterested parties name them after their stage in life: *Huwar* (suckling), *Inferid* (fending for self), *Madhriba* (may be covered by a bull), *Yadha* (able to calve), etc.

4. See H. St. John Philby, *The Empty Quarter* (New York: Henry Holt and Co., 1933).

   From page 276, we learned the cure (?) for camel flatulence. One plasters over the anal orifice with a dough of camel-dung and then ties the tail between the legs and under the stomach, thus preventing the emission of wind. Philby's guide swore by it.

5. Wilfred Thesiger, *Arabian Sands*, 27–28.
6. Wilfred Thesiger, *Arabian Sands*, 49.
7. Wilfred Thesiger, *Arabian Sands*, 42–45, 50–51.
8. Wilfred Thesiger, *Arabian Sands*, 186–204.
9. Wilfred Thesiger, *Arabian Sands*, 224–25.
10. Wilfred Thesiger, *Arabian Sands*, 244.
11. Wilfred Thesiger, *Arabian Sands*, 251, 269–75.
12. The Arabs are excellent falconers. See Wilfred Thesiger, *Arabian Sands*, 269.

    > I have been told that in England it takes fifty days to train a wild falcon, but here the Arabs had them ready in a fortnight to three weeks. This is because they were never separated from them. A man who was training a falcon carried it about everywhere with him. He even fed with it sitting on his left wrist, and slept with it perched on its block beside his head. Always he was stroking it, speaking to it, hooding and unhooding it.

To learn more, see Sheikh Zayed, *Falconry as a Sport: Our Arab Heritage* (Kent, England: Westerham Press, Ltd, 1977), in which he discusses training and hunting techniques, training equipment, and falcon diseases and treatment.

13. All of these were European "Firsts," as any explorer would proudly say. See Wilfred Thesiger, *Arabian Sands*, 260.

> I would not myself have wished to cross the Empty Quarter in a car. Luckily this was impossible when I did my journeys, for to have done the journey on a camel when I could have done it in a car would have turned the venture into a stunt.

In 2002, 2004, and 2008, George Steinmetz flew over parts of the Empty Quarter in a motorized paraglider taking photographs that were later featured in his book *Empty Quarter* (New York: Abrams, 2009).

In 2011, Adrian Hayes celebrated the fortieth anniversary of the founding of the UAE by retracing — on camel-back — Thesiger's first crossing and depicted it in his book *Footsteps of Thesiger* (Dubai: Motivate Publishing, 2012).

And pretty much every weekend these days, wealthy Emiratis and tourists visit the Liwa Oasis ... where they can drag race up the giant Moreeb Sand Dune in souped-up jeeps and dune-buggies.

So much for "stunts."

14. In 2004, after Thesiger died, his collection of thirty-eight thousand photo negatives and seventy-one personal albums were accepted by the British Government in lieu of inheritance taxes and placed in the Pitt Rivers Museum at Oxford University.

LHASA, TIBET

Epigraph: Heinrich Harrer, *Seven Years in Tibet* (New York: E. P. Dutton & Co., 1953), 314. Heinrich Harrer, *Return to Tibet* (New York: Schocken Books, 1985), 174.

1. Heinrich Harrer, *The White Spider* (New York: E. P. Dutton & Co, 1960), 25–27.
2. Heinrich Harrer, *The White Spider*, 31.
3. See Heinrich Harrer, *The White Spider*, 80–123.

4. See Heinrich Harrer, *Seven Years in Tibet*, for Harrer's complete narrative of his time in Tibet.

5. Compare page 37 in Heinrich Harrer, *Seven Years in Tibet* with page 37 in Heinrich Harrer, *Lost Lhasa* (New York: Harry N. Abrams, 1992).

6. Compare page 96 in Heinrich Harrer, *Return to Tibet* with pages 37 and 38 in Harrer, *Lost Lhasa*.

    We have a sneaking suspicion that this story got better and better the more he told it.

7. Martin Brauen, ed. *Peter Aufschnaiter's Eight Years in Tibet* (Bangkok: Orchid Press, 2002) 25, 26 and 27, 30 and 31, 60 and 61, 66 and 67.

8. Heinrich Harrer, *Lost Lhasa*, 86.

9. Knud Larsen and Amund Sinding-Larsen, *The Lhasa Atlas: Traditional Tibetan Architecture and Townscape* (Boston: Shambala Publications, Inc., 2001), 21.

10. Knud Larsen and Amund Sinding-Larsen, *The Lhasa Atlas: Traditional Tibetan Architecture and Townscape*, 43.

11. Heinrich Harrer, *Beyond Seven Years in Tibet*, 169.

12. Heinrich Harrer, *Beyond Seven Years in Tibet*, 483.

13. For Harrer's own discussion of these and related events, see Heinrich Harrer, *Beyond Seven Years in Tibet*, 39–45.

14. See H. G. Bissinger, "The Last Explorer," *Vanity Fair*, October 1997, 332–338, 369–371.

    See also Jean-Jacques Annaud, Becky Johnston, and Laurence B. Chollet, *The Seven Years in Tibet: Screenplay and Story Behind the Film* (New York: Newmarket Press, 1997).

BYGDØY PENINSULA, NORWAY

Epigraph: See Fridtjof Nansen, *Farthest North: Volumes I and II* (New York: Harper & Brothers Publishers, 1897).

1. Fridtjof Nansen, *Farthest North: Volume I*, s16.

2. Fridtjof Nansen, *The First Crossing of Greenland* (London: Longmans, Green & Co., 1890), 5.

3. Fridtjof Nansen, *The First Crossing of Greenland*. See 72–114, where Nansen provides a history of the "two pieces of wood" and their effect on transportation over snow and ice.
4. For a technical discussion of the *Fram*, See Fridtjof Nansen, *Farthest North, Volume I*, 57–72 and Roald Amundsen, *The South Pole, Volume II* (New York: John Murray, 1913), Appendix I at 356.
5. Fridtjof Nansen, *Farthest North, Volume II*, 170.
6. See Roald Amundsen, *The Northwest Passage* (London: Archibald Constable & Co., 1908), two volumes.
7. For a deeper discussion of the race, see also Ross D. E. MacPhee, *Race to the End: Amundsen, Scott, and the Attainment of the South Pole* (New York: American Museum of Natural History and Sterling Publishing Co., 2010). See also Roald Amundsen, *The South Pole, Volumes I and II*.
8. Roald Amundsen, *The South Pole, Volume II*, 132.
9. Amundsen met a hero's death on June 18, 1928, trying to save Umberto Nobile, an Arctic aviator whose plane the *Italia* had crashed on the ice.

ISLA NEGRA, CHILE

Epigraph: "Tonight I Can Write" from *Viente Poemas de Amor y Una Canción Desesperada: Edición end Dos Idiomas* by Pablo Neruda, translated by W. S. Merwin, Translated from the Spanish *20 Poemas de Amor y Una Cancion Desesperada*, first published in Santiago de Chile 1924. English translation copyright © 1969 by W. S. Merwin. Used by permission of Viking Books, an imprint of Penguin Publishing Group, a division of Penguin Random House LLC. All rights reserved.

1. See Adam Feinstein, *Pablo Neruda: A Passion for Life* (New York: Bloomsbury, 2004).

   See also Pablo Neruda, *Memoirs (I Confess That I Have Lived)*, Hardie St. Martin, translator (New York: Farrar, Straus and Giroux, 1977).

2. "Tonight I Can Write" from *Viente Poemas de Amor y Una Canción Desesperada: Edición end Dos Idiomas* by Pablo Neruda, translated by W. S. Merwin, Translated from the Spanish *20 Poemas de Amor y*

Una Cancion Desesperada, first published in Santiago de Chile 1924. English translation copyright © 1969 by W. S. Merwin. Used by permission of Viking Books, an imprint of Penguin Publishing Group, a division of Penguin Random House LLC. All rights reserved.

3. See Adam Feinstein, *Pablo Neruda: A Passion for Life*.

As if having three wives wasn't complicated enough.

Neruda married his first, Maria Antonieta Haagenar Vogelzang (aka "Maruca") on December 6, 1930, in Batavia, Java. (77). He wasn't happy with or faithful to her and, by 1936, they had separated.

That year, he took up with Delia del Carril Iraeta, with whom he spent the next eighteen years.

However, divorce was not permitted under Chilean law. So when Neruda was posted to Mexico, which did allow it, he divorced Maruca on February 8, 1943 (164) ... and, five months later, married Delia on July 2 (167).

These events would have quite ironic consequences. First, in 1952, Neruda's political enemy, President González Videla, summoned Maruca to Chile to sue Neruda for the crime of bigamy, claiming that he couldn't be married to Delia because he was still married to her. Videla wanted to put Neruda in jail for the crime. Maruca only wanted money and, when she got it, she left the country and the case collapsed (283–86).

No matter, because Neruda had already found another woman, Matilde Urrutia, with whom he would spend the rest of his life.

On March 27, 1965, Maruca died and, in the eyes of Chile, Neruda was a widower, free to officially remarry. (287)

However, in the eyes of Delia, now back in Chile, Neruda needed a divorce, which she would not grant. Neruda petitioned the Chilean court, arguing, as Maruca had before, that he could never have legally married Delia because he had still been married to Maruca. On June 16, 1966, a Santiago court ruled in Neruda's favor and declared his marriage to Delia annulled. (342). On October, 28 1966, Neruda married Matilde at Isla Negra (348).

Oh, and we haven't even mentioned that Pablo and Matilde were really "married by the moon" in Capri on May 3, 1952 (276) ... or that he later had an affair with Matilde's niece (371). Ah, women.

4. See Adam Feinstein, *Pablo Neruda: A Passion for Life*, 81–103.

5. See Adam Feinstein, *Pablo Neruda: A Passion for Life*, 105–19.

6. See Pablo Neruda, as translated by Donald D. Walsh, "I Explain a Few Things" from "Spain in Our Hearts," in *Residence on Earth* (New York: New Directions, 1973), 255–61. Copyright © 1973 by Pablo Neruda and Donald D. Walsh. Reprinted by permission of New Directions Publishing Corp.

   See also Adam Feinstein, *Pablo Neruda: A Passion for Life*, 139.

7. Adam Feinstein, *Pablo Neruda: A Passion for Life*, 132.

8. Adam Feinstein, *Pablo Neruda: A Passion for Life*, 144–45.

9. Adam Feinstein, *Pablo Neruda: A Passion for Life*, 148.

   > We live twice on the road to Isla Negra —
   > once in our dreams and once in our shoes.

   See William O'Daly, *The Road to Isla Negra* (Meredith, NH: Folded Word, 2015).

10. And the water *is* freezing cold, being part of the Humboldt Current which flows from Antarctica up the Pacific coast of South America.

11. Adam Feinstein, *Pablo Neruda: A Passion for Life*, 175.

12. Adam Feinstein, *Pablo Neruda: A Passion for Life*, 178.

13. Adam Feinstein, *Pablo Neruda: A Passion for Life*, 179–81.

14. Adam Feinstein, *Pablo Neruda: A Passion for Life*, 189–90.

15. Adam Feinstein, *Pablo Neruda: A Passion for Life*, 194.

16. Adam Feinstein, *Pablo Neruda: A Passion for Life*, 196–97.

17. Adam Feinstein, *Pablo Neruda: A Passion for Life*, 199.

18. Adam Feinstein, *Pablo Neruda: A Passion for Life*, 202–35.

19. Today the road between San Martín de Los Andes and San Carlos de Bariloche provides a memorable tour through the Lake District of Argentina. Often referred to as the *Ruta de Los Siete Lagos* (the Route of the Seven Lakes), one can count twice as many along the way.

    However, you can't fly there directly from Chile. You have to go from Santiago to Buenos Aires and then back to either town. Still, it's worth it, for there are some great places along the way, especially Llao Llao, one of the best hotels in the world.

20. Adam Feinstein, *Pablo Neruda: A Passion for Life*, 231.

21. Adam Feinstein, *Pablo Neruda: A Passion for Life*, 234, as slightly modified.

    Years later, in his Nobel Prize acceptance speech, Neruda would refer to his daring escape over the mountains. He would then discuss the need for "burning patience" in order to achieve "light, justice and dignity" for all. See Pablo Neruda, *Toward the Splendid City* (New York: Farrar, Straus and Giroux, 1974).

    This phrase was adopted as the title of a book in which Neruda helps an Isla Negra mailman use poetry to win his love. See Antonio Skármeta, *Burning Patience* (New York: Pantheon Books, 1987).

    In time, the book became a movie. The title was changed to *Il Postino* (The Postman), and it was set in Italy during Neruda's political exile. In 1995, it received five Academy Award nominations, including Best Picture.

22. Adam Feinstein, *Pablo Neruda: A Passion for Life*, 236–82.
23. See Stephen Dobyns, foreword to *Twenty Love Poems and a Song of Despair* (San Francisco: Chronicle Books, 1993).
24. Adam Feinstein, *Pablo Neruda: A Passion for Life*, 373.
25. Adam Feinstein, *Pablo Neruda: A Passion for Life*, 359–90.
26. Adam Feinstein, *Pablo Neruda: A Passion for Life*, 410.
27. Adam Feinstein, *Pablo Neruda: A Passion for Life*, 413.

ST. PETERSBURG, RUSSIA

Epigraph: Anna Akhmatova, excerpt from *Requiem*, in *Complete Poems of Anna Akhmatova, Volume Two*, translated by Judith Hemschemeyer, edited and introduced by Roberta Reader, 95. Copyright © 1989, 1992, 1997 by Judith Hemschemeyer. Reprinted with the permission of The Permissions Company, LLC on behalf of Zephyr Press, zephyrpress.org.

1. See Paul Schmidt, *The Stray Dog Cabaret: A Book of Russian Poems*, first published in English by *The New York Review of Books*, translation © 2006 by the estate of Paul Schmidt, vii.

   See also Nancy K. Anderson, *The Word that Causes Death's Defeat: Poems of Memory* (New Haven, CT: Yale University Press, 2004), 16–17.

2. Anna's grandmother probably *was* a descendant of Genghis Khan, as are a lot of people. See Tatiana Zerjal et al., "The Genetic Legacy of the Mongols," *American Journal of Human Genetics*, 72, (March 2003); 717–21.

   For a poet, Anna's was a name well-chosen. As noted by Joseph Brodsky, one of "Anna's Boys" who would later win the Nobel Prize for literature, "The five open "a's" of Anna Akhmatova had a hypnotic effect and put this name's carrier firmly at the top of the alphabet of Russian poetry. In a sense, her name was her first successful line …" See Ronald Meyer, translator and editor, *Anna Akhmatova, My Half Century: Selected Prose* (Ann Arbor, MI: Ardis Publishers, 1992), xxii.

3. Nancy K. Anderson, *The Word that Causes Death's Defeat: Poems of Memory*, 18.

4. See Amanda Haight, *Anna Akhmatova: A Poetic Pilgrimage* (New York and London: Oxford University Press, 1976), 30.

5. Anna Akhmatova, from *Rosary* as translated by Paul Schmidt in *The Stray Dog Cabaret: A Book of Russian Poems.*

   May we have a quick word about translation? What do you translate? The words or the meaning? How do you translate? Literally or figuratively? For Schmidt, the translator was an actor and the translation a performance. Fantastic.

6. Just take a look at www.necrometrics.com. It is a website created by Matthew White. He has collected different body counts for all the major atrocities of the 20th century. He compares the various historical sources, trying to achieve a consensus. He understands both the uncertainty and the politics of atrocity statistics. His day job — he's a librarian.

7. See *Military Casualties — World War-Estimated* (Statistics Branch, GS United States, War Department: February 25, 1924: cited in *World War I: People, Politics, and Power*, published by Britannica Educational Publishing: 2010), 219. See also Wikipedia: *World War I Casualties.*

8. See Boris Urlanis, *Wars and Population* (Moscow: 1971), 266–68, as cited in www.necrometrics.com.

9. Again, see Urlanis as cited in www.necrometrics.com.

10. See Robert Conquest, "Victims of Stalinism: A Comment" in *Europe — Asia Studies* (Volume 49, No. 7, 1997), 1317–19. Also cited in Wikipedia: *Excess Mortality in the Soviet Union Under Joseph Stalin*.

11. Based on official records from Soviet archives released after the Soviet Union dissolved. See Seumas Milne, "The Battle for History" (*The Guardian*: 12 September 2002). See Michael Haynes, *A Century of State Murder?: Death and Policy in Twentieth Century Russia* (Pluto Press, 2003), 214–15.

    See Anne Applebaum, *Gulag: A History* (New York: Doubleday, 2003), 582–83. See J. Otto Pohl, *The Stalinist Penal System* (Jefferson, NC: McFarland & Co., 1997) 58, 148. All cited in Wikipedia, *Excess Morality in the Soviet Union Under Joseph Stalin*.

12. See G. F. Krivosheev, *Soviet Casualties and Combat Losses* (London: Greenhill Books, 1997) 85–87. As cited in Wikipedia, *World War II Casualties*.

13. See Michael Clodfelter, *Warfare and Armed Conflicts — A Statistical Reference to Casualty and Other Figures* (Jefferson, NC: McFarland & Co., 2015) 465. See also Maureen Perrie, *The Cambridge History of Russia: The Twentieth Century* (Boston: Cambridge University Press, 2006), 226. Both cited in Wikipedia, *World War II Casualties*.

14. Nancy K. Anderson, *The Word that Causes Death's Defeat: Poems of Memory*, 46.

15. See Nina Popova, Tatiana Pozdnyakova and Leonid Kopylov, *Beneath the Roof of Fountain House: A Short Guide to the Anna Akhmatova Museum at Fountain House* (St. Petersburg, The Anna Akhmatova Museum at Fountain House, 2012).

16. Nancy K. Anderson, *The Word that Causes Death's Defeat: Poems of Memory*, 34–35.

17. Nina Popova, et al.ia, *Beneath the Roof of Fountain House*, 4.

18. Russian reference cited in "Kresty Prison" article in Wikipedia.

NOTES | 374

19. See, again, Anna Akhmatova, excerpt from *Requiem*, in *Complete Poems of Anna Akhmatova, Volume Two*, translated by Judith Hemschemeyer, edited and introduced by Roberta Reader, 95. Copyright © 1989, 1992, 1997 by Judith Hemschemeyer. Reprinted with the permission of The Permissions Company, LLC on behalf of Zephyr Press, zephyrpress.org.

    What would you do for a poet? In 1973, Hemschemeyer read a few of Akhmatova's poems and was so inspired that she spent three years learning Russian so she could spend ten years more understanding and translating her poems.

    See her "Translator's Preface" in *The Complete Poems, Volume One*, 1–19.

20. Nancy K. Anderson, *The Word that Causes Death's Defeat: Poems of Memory*, 83.

21. And so, a word can, indeed, cause death's defeat.

22. Nancy K. Anderson, *The Word that Causes Death's Defeat: Poems of Memory*, 93.

23. See Anna Akhmatova's poem "Courage" quoted in Anderson, *The Word that Causes Death's Defeat: Poems of Memory*, 96.

    Another word on translation. Most of the early English translations of Anna's work were in free verse, based on the English version of Anna's Russian word. Anderson decided to strengthen the stanza structure by making the ending words rhyme, even if the words she used differed from Anna's. And why not, they *are* poems.

24. Nancy K. Anderson, *The Word that Causes Death's Defeat: Poems of Memory*, 108–13.

25. See Elaine Feinstein, *Anna of All the Russians* (New York: Knopf, 2006) 146–47.

26. See Roberta Reeder, "Miracles and Masks: The Life and Poetic Works of Anna Akhmatova." See Hemshemeyer, *The Complete Poems of Anna Akhmatova, Volume I*, 147, wherein she quotes Raisa Orlova and Lev Kopelev, "Anna Vseya Rus," *Literaturnoe Oboz Renie*, No. 5 (1989), p. 103.

27. It is as if Anna had personally requisitioned the site.

> And if ever in Russia I have such acclaim
> That a monument's set up to honor my name,
>
> My consent to a statue I only would grant
> With a condition on where it should stand.
>
> Not down by the southern sea where I was born—
> My last tie to the seacoast has long been torn—
>
> Nor in the Tsar's park by the stump of that tree
> Where an unconsoled ghost is still looking for me,
>
> But here, where I stood while three hundred hours passed,
> And the gates never budged, and the bolts remained fast.
>
> —*Requiem*, translated by Nancy K. Anderson, *The Word that Causes Death's Defeat: Poems of Memory*, 142.

The monument was created by sculptor Galina Dodonova and architect Vladimir Reppo.

STAVROS BEACH, CRETE

Epigraph: Nikos Kazantzakis, *Zorba the Greek*, translated by Carl Wildman (New York: Simon and Schuster, 1952), 300; as modified by Anthony Quinn in the movie *Zorba the Greek*, 20th Century Fox, now part of Walt Disney Studios.

1. Katerina Tsouchtidi, *The Most Beautiful Beaches and Gorges of Crete* (Attica, Greece: Michalis Toubis Editions S. A., 2008) 5.
2. Katerina Tsouchtidi, *The Most Beautiful Beaches and Gorges of Crete*, 56 and 96.
3. Katerina Tsouchtidi, *The Most Beautiful Beaches and Gorges of Crete*, 31, 50, and 126.
4. See Nikos Kazantzakis, *Zorba the Greek*.
5. Thank you, Stavroula Stratigi, for being our guide and translator. Her email address is: stavroti@gmail.com. If you ever need a guide when you're in Crete, we recommend her highly.

6. Litsa Chatzopoulou, *Kazantzakis: Through the Museum Collections*, translated by Ben Petre (Heraklion, Crete: Nikos Kazantzakis Museum, 2008) 29.
7. See George I. Panagiotakis, *The Life and Works of Nikos Kazantzakis* (Heraklion, Crete: Typokreta G. Kazanakis S. A., 2002).
8. Nikos Kazantzakis, *Zorba the Greek*, 174–75.
9. See Nikos Kazantzakis, *The Odyssey; A Modern Sequel*, translated by Kimon Friar (New York: Simon and Schuster, 1958).
10. See Nikos Kazantzakis, *The Saviors of God*, translated by Kimon Friar (New York: Simon and Schuster, 1960).
11. See George I. Panagiotakis, *The Life and Works of Nikos Kazantzakis*, 274–81.
12. Nikos Kazantzakis, *Zorba the Greek*, 222.
13. See Nikos Kazantzakis, *The Last Temptation of Christ*, translated by P. A. Bien (New York: Simon and Schuster, 1960).
14. Nikos Kazantzakis, *Report to Greco*, translated by P. A. Bien (New York: Simon and Schuster, 1965) 445–59. When Georgios Zorbas died in 1941, Kazantzakis sat down and wrote *Zorba the Greek*, not just to honor, but also to *resurrect* him.
15. Nikos Kazantzakis, *Zorba the Greek*, 35.

KALADHUNGI, INDIA

Epigraph: Jim Corbett, *Man-Eaters of Kumaon* (New York: Oxford University Press, 1946), xviii. and Jim Corbett, *The Man-Eating Leopard of Rudraprayag* (New York: Oxford University Press, 1948), 28.

1. Martin Booth, *Carpet Sahib: A Life of Jim Corbett* (London, Constable, 1986), 37–38.
2. Martin Booth, *Carpet Sahib: A Life of Jim Corbett*, 64.
3. Jim Corbett, *Jungle Lore* (New York: Oxford University Press, 1953), 52–53.
4. Jim Corbett, *Jungle Lore*, 64–65.
5. Martin Booth, *Carpet Sahib: The Life of Jim Corbett*, 49, 172. See also Corbett, *Man-Eaters of Kumaon*, 225.

6. Jim Corbett, *Jungle Lore*, 58–59.
7. Jim Corbett, *Jungle Lore*, 150. See also Corbett, *Man-Eaters of Kumaon*, 131, 168.
8. Jim Corbett, *Jungle Lore*, 88.
9. Jim Corbett, *Jungle Lore*, 33.
10. Jim Corbett, *Man-Eaters of Kumaon*, 51.
11. Jim Corbett, *Man-Eaters of Kumaon*, 91, 160. See also Corbett, *Jungle Lore*, 165–72.
12. Jim Corbett, *Man-Eaters of Kumaon*, 131, 139.
13. Jim Corbett, *Man-Eaters of Kumaon*, 135.
14. Jim Corbett, *Man-Eaters of Kumaon*, 225.
15. Jim Corbett, *Man-Eaters of Kumaon*, 135, see also 23–26.
16. Dane Huckelbridge, *No Beast So Fierce* (New York: William Morrow, 2019), 15–18.
17. Dane Huckelbridge, *No Beast So Fierce*, 40, 200.
18. Jim Corbett, *Man-Eaters of Kumaon*, xiii.
19. Dane Huckelbridge, *No Beast So Fierce*, 33.
20. Jim Corbett, *Man-Eaters of Kumaon*, 29.
21. Jim Corbett, *Man-Eaters of Kumaon*, 4, 13. See also Jim Corbett, *The Temple Tiger and More Man-Eaters of Kumaon* (New York: Oxford University Press, 1955), 69.
22. Jim Corbett, *Man-Eaters of Kumaon*, 13.
23. Jim Corbett, *Man-Eaters of Kumaon*, 21, 22.
24. Jim Corbett, *Man-Eaters of Kumaon*, 24–32.
25. Jim Corbett, *The Man-Eating Leopard of Rudraprayag*, 3–7.
26. Jim Corbett, *The Man-Eating Leopard of Rudraprayag*, 8.
27. Jim Corbett, *The Man-Eating Leopard of Rudraprayag*, 9, 11.
28. Jim Corbett, *The Man-Eating Leopard of Rudraprayag*, 28.
29. Jim Corbett, *The Man-Eating Leopard of Rudraprayag*, 31–85.
30. Jim Corbett, *The Man-Eating Leopard of Rudraprayag*, 86–146.

31. Jim Corbett, *The Man-Eating Leopard of Rudraprayag*, 155, 168–182.
32. Jim Corbett, *The Man-Eating Leopard of Rudraprayag*, 180.
33. Martin Booth, *Carpet Sahib: A Life of Jim Corbett*, 128.
34. Martin Booth, *Carpet Sahib: A Life of Jim Corbett*, 183.
35. R.E. Hawkins, ed., *Jim Corbett's India* (Oxford: Oxford University Press, 1978), 241. See also Booth, *Carpet Sahib: A Life of Jim Corbett*, 170.
36. Reeta Dutta, Gupta, *Jim Corbett, The Hunter-Conservationist* (New Delhi: Rupa & Co., 2006), 40.

    It is an odd and slightly disturbing fact that, as of 2019, there were more tigers in captivity in the United States than there were in the wild in Asia. See Sharon Guynup, "The Tigers Next Door" in *National Geographic,* November 14, 2019.

    On the other hand, tigers are the mascots of twenty-three American universities, including LSU, Clemson, Auburn and, best of them all, Princeton.

37. Jim Corbett, *Man-Eaters of Kumaon*, xviii.
38. Martin Booth, *Carpet Sahib: A Life of Jim Corbett*, 214–15.
39. Ashima Kumar, and Dushyant Parasher, *Corbett National Park: Domain of the Wild* (New Delhi and Seattle, Konark Publishers, 2017), 55–57.
40. Ashima Kumar, *Corbett National Park: Domain of the Wild*, 70, 75–95.

MARRAKESH, MOROCCO

Epigraph: Gavin Maxwell, *Lords of the Atlas* (London: Cassell & Co., 2000), 231.

1. Gavin Maxwell, *Lords of the Atlas*, 117, 135, 141, 151.
2. Gavin Maxwell, *Lords of the Atlas*, 144, 155, 157, 252–53.
3. Gavin Maxwell, *Lords of the Atlas*, 143.
4. Gavin Maxwell, *Lords of the Atlas*, 151, 168.
5. Gavin Maxwell, *Lords of the Atlas*, 87, 97.
6. Gavin Maxwell, *Lords of the Atlas*, 10.

7. Gavin Maxwell, *Lords of the Atlas*, 31.

   See also, Walter B. Harris, *Morocco That Was* (London: William Blackwood & Sons, 1921), 2.

8. Gavin Maxwell, *Lords of the Atlas*, 36. Harris, *Morocco That Was*, 11.

9. Gavin Maxwell, *Lords of the Atlas*, 38–42.

10. Gavin Maxwell, *Lords of the Atlas*, 43, 44, 53.

11. Lady Agnes Grove. *Seventy-One Days Camping in Morocco* (London: Longmans, Green, and Co., 1902), 6 and 7.

12. Lady Agnes Grove. *Seventy-One Days Camping in Morocco*, 33–35.

13. Lady Agnes Grove. *Seventy-One Days Camping in Morocco*, 110.

14. Lady Agnes Grove. *Seventy-One Days Camping in Morocco*, 116.

15. Paula Da Silva. "Tbourida Today," in *Untacked* (July/August 2019), 25–33.

16. Gavin Maxwell, *Lords of the Atlas*, 63–115.

17. Gavin Maxwell, *Lords of the Atlas*, 127.

18. Gavin Maxwell, *Lords of the Atlas*, 159.

19. Gavin Maxwell, *Lords of the Atlas*, 147–50.

20. Renovated and reopened in 2017, Dar El Bacha now hosts the Museum of Confluences. It celebrates the harmonious coexistence of the Jewish, Christian, and Muslim faiths in Morocco. And, it has a wonderful coffee shop.

21. Gavin Maxwell, *Lords of the Atlas*, 164–65.

22. Touria El Glaoui, ed. *Meetings in Marrakesh: The Paintings of Hassan El Glaoui and Winston Churchill* (Marrakesh: Skira, 2014), 13.

23. Gavin Maxwell, *Lords of the Atlas*, 174–75.

24. Gavin Maxwell, *Lords of the Atlas*, 180–202.

    The French treatment of T'hami El Glaoui inspired the creation of a new word in its political lexicon: *glaouise*. It was an adjective that meant, in no uncertain terms, "betrayed." See pages 26 and 224.

25. Gavin Maxwell, *Lords of the Atlas*, 230.

26. Hassan El Glaoui, *Fantasia Sur Fond Bleu*, 1990.

The Estate of Hassan El Glaoui (www.hassanelglaoui.com) has kindly authorized the use of this work. In particular, we thank Brian Bexter for his patience and goodwill.

See also Touria El Glaoui, ed. *Le Sel De Ma Terre* (Rabat, Morocco: Malika Editions, 2019), 91.

Touria El Glaoui, Hassan's daughter, has contributed to the art world in her own way. After co-curating an exhibition of paintings by Winston Churchill and her father, she founded the 1-54 Contemporary Africa Art Fair. Held annually in London, New York and Marrakesh, its purpose is to present contemporary art from the continent's 54 independent countries.

BANGKOK, THAILAND

Epigraph: Jim Thompson, as cited in Joshua Kurlantzick, *The Ideal Man: The Tragedy of Jim Thompson and the American Way of War* (Hoboken, NJ: John Wiley & Sons, 2011), 4.

1. See Joshua Kurlantzick, *The Ideal Man: The Tragedy of Jim Thompson and the American Way of War*, at 219. "The food really wasn't so great. Really, it was just street food."
2. William Warren, *Jim Thompson, The Legendary American of Thailand* (Boston, Houghton Mifflin Co., 1970) 32–34. Please note that Jim's very first architectural project was designing a public lavatory in the summer resort of Rehoboth, Delaware.
3. William Warren, *Jim Thompson, The Legendary American of Thailand*, 36–46.
4. William Warren, *Jim Thompson, The Legendary American of Thailand*, 48–51, 57–58, 60–62.
5. William Warren, *Jim Thompson, The Legendary American of Thailand*, 73–77.
6. William Warren, *Jim Thompson, The Legendary American of Thailand*, 89–91, 118–119.
7. See William Warren, text and Brian Brake, photographs, *The House on the Khlong* (New York, Tokyo: Walker/Weatherhill, 1968).

See also William Warren, *Jim Thompson: The House on the Khlong* (Singapore: Archipelago Press, 1999).

8. William Warren, *Jim Thompson, The Legendary American of Thailand*, 103–05.

9. William Warren, *Jim Thompson, The Legendary American of Thailand*, 108–14.

10. William Warren, *Jim Thompson, The Legendary American of Thailand*, 111–14.

11. Indeed, the great Ethel Merman once visited Jim and belted out "Hello Cocky" in the bird's honor. See Warren, *Jim Thompson: The House on the Khlong*, 51.

12. See also William Warren, *Jim Thompson, The Legendary American of Thailand*, x.

13. See Joshua Kurlantzick, *The Ideal Man: The Tragedy of Jim Thompson and the American Way of War*, 145. American planes dropped more bombs on Laos during the Cold War than they had on all of Europe during World War II.

14. See Joshua Kurlantzick, *The Ideal Man: The Tragedy of Jim Thompson and the American Way of War*, 122 and 179. In 1953, J. Edgar Hoover personally approved an FBI investigation of Thompson's potential "un-American activities." By 1967, even the CIA thought Jim was a communist, but he wasn't.

15. William Warren, *Jim Thompson, The Legendary American of Thailand*, 139.

16. William Warren, *Jim Thompson, The Legendary American of Thailand*, 3–5.

17. William Warren, *Jim Thompson, The Legendary American of Thailand*, 23.

18. William Warren, *Jim Thompson, The Legendary American of Thailand*, 20.

19. William Warren, *Jim Thompson, The Legendary American of Thailand*, 165. See also Matthews, Francine, *The Secret Agent* (New York: Bantam Books, 2002).

20. See Edward Roy De Souza, *Solved!: The Mysterious Disappearance of Jim Thompson, The Legendary Thai Silk King* (Tarentum, PA: Word Association Publishers, 2010), 106.

21. See Shannon Gilligan, *The Case of The Silk King* (Waitsfield, VT: Chooseco, 2005).
22. William Warren, *Jim Thompson, The Legendary American of Thailand*, 65–72, quote at 69.
23. William Warren, *Jim Thompson, The Legendary American of Thailand*, 124.
24. William Warren, *Jim Thompson, The Legendary American of Thailand*, 127.
25. William Warren, *Jim Thompson, The Legendary American of Thailand*, 127.
26. William Warren, *Jim Thompson, The Legendary American of Thailand*, 127.
27. William Warren, *Jim Thompson, The Legendary American of Thailand*, 129.
28. William Warren, *Jim Thompson, The Legendary American of Thailand*, 237.
29. William Warren, *Jim Thompson, The Legendary American of Thailand*, 242.
30. Based on a private conversation with that bright young lawyer, now retired.
31. Both the Jim Thompson House (www.jimthompsonhouse.com) and the Jim Thompson Thai Silk Company (www.jimthompson.com) have quite informative websites. If that's not enough for you, try the Jim Thompson Art Center, Jim Thompson Fabrics, Jim Thompson Restaurants, and the Jim Thompson Farm.

KATHMANDU, NEPAL

Epigraph: Judith Schalansky, *Atlas of Remote Islands* (New York: Penguin, 2010), 20.

1. Lieutenant colonel E.F. Norton, D.S.O. *The Fight For Everest: 1924* (New York: Longman's Green & Co, 1925), 130.
2. *The New York Times*, March 18, 1923.
3. Brigadier Sir John Hunt, C.B.E., D.S.O., *The Ascent of Everest* (London: Hodder & Stoughton, 1953). Appendix I, Diary of the Expedition, 235–38, at 236.

4. Brigadier Sir John Hunt, *The Ascent of Everest*, 203. See also Edmund Hillary, *High Adventure* (London: Hodder & Stoughton, 1955), 205. See also Tenzing Norgay with James Ramsay Ullma, *Tiger of the Snows* (New York: G. P. Putnam's Sons, 1955), 243.

5. Brigadier Sir John Hunt, *The Ascent of Everest*, 204. See also Hillary, *High Adventure*, 206–07. See also Norgay, *Tiger of the Snows*, 247.

    After Hillary and Norgay returned from Everest, politicians immediately wanted to know which one of them reached the top first. In Nepal and India, they demanded that it be Norgay. In Great Britain, they thought otherwise. Makes you hate politicians, doesn't it?

6. W. E. Bowman, *The Ascent of Rum Doodle* (London: Max Parrish & Co, Ltd, 1956), Cover Illustration, 32.

    This book is so beloved in England that Hatchards Books sponsored an exclusive Limited Edition in 2019.

7. W. E. Bowman, *The Ascent of Rum Doodle*, 14.

8. W. E. Bowman, *The Ascent of Rum Doodle*, 25.

9. W. E. Bowman, *The Ascent of Rum Doodle*, 127.

10. Everest Premium Lager was introduced in 2003 to commemorate the Golden Jubilee Anniversary of the first ascent of Mount Everest by Norgay and Hillary.

11. For example, see Bernadette McDonald, *I'll Call You in Kathmandu* (Seattle: The Mountaineers Books, 2005) at 209–10. One time, Rum Doodle called Elizabeth for verification of three people who claimed to have been to the summit and wanted to eat for free. "Don't let them" she said. "The three did reach the summit, but one of them died on the way down."

12. See Lisa Choegyal and Mike Dunham, Eds., *The Nepal Scene: Chronicles of Elizabeth Hawley: 1988–2007, Volume One* (Kathmandu: Vajra Publishing, 2015), xii.

13. Lisa Choegyal and Mike Dunham, Eds., *The Nepal Scene: Chronicles of Elizabeth Hawley: 1988–2007, Volume One*, xii.

14. Lisa Choegyal and Mike Dunham, Eds., *The Nepal Scene: Chronicles of Elizabeth Hawley: 1988–2007, Volume One*, xiv and xv.

15. Lisa Choegyal and Mike Dunham, Eds., *The Nepal Scene: Chronicles of Elizabeth Hawley: 1988–2007, Volume One*, xii.

16. Lisa Choegyal and Mike Dunham, Eds., *The Nepal Scene: Chronicles of Elizabeth Hawley: 1988–2007, Volume One*, xiii.

17. Go to www.himalayandatabase.com, click on "Himalayan Database online," then click on "Peak Ascents Report." In Peak ID box, type "Ever" and then click on "Submit." Have fun.

18. See www.himalayandatabase.com.

19. See www.himalayandatabase.com.

20. See "Everest 2017: What Really Happened to the Hillary Step," May 22, 2017, at www.alanarnette.com.

21. See Jeffrey Gettleman, et al., *The New York Times*, May 26, 2019.

MANAUS, BRAZIL

Epigraph: As cited by Wade Davis in Richard Evans Schultes and Robert T. Raffauf, *Vine of the Soul: Medicine Men, Their Plants and Rituals in the Colombian Amazonia* (Santa Fe, NM: Synergetic Press, 1992, 2004), v.

See also Wade Davis, *One River: Explorations and Discoveries in the Amazon Rain Forest* (New York: Simon & Schuster, 1996), 482.

1. See Richard Spruce, *Notes of a Botanist on the Amazon and Andes* (London: MacMillan & Co, 2018).

2. Wade Davis, *One River*, 68–71.

3. Richard Evans Schultes and Albert Hoffman, *Plants of the Gods: Origins of Hallucinogenic Use* (London: Hutchinson, 1980), 143, quoting J. S. Slotkin.

4. Wade Davis, *One River: Explorations and Discoveries in the Amazon Rain Forest*, 88.

5. Wade Davis, *One River: Explorations and Discoveries in the Amazon Rain Forest*, 104–11.

6. Wade Davis, *One River: Explorations and Discoveries in the Amazon Rain Forest*, 112–17, 120–22.

7. Wade Davis, *One River: Explorations and Discoveries in the Amazon Rain Forest*, 497–98.

8. Loren McIntyre, *Amazonia* (San Francisco: Sierra Club Books, 1991), 1.

9. Wade Davis, *One River: Explorations and Discoveries in the Amazon Rain Forest*, quoting Richard Spruce, 378. See also Spruce, *Notes of a Botanist on the Amazon and Andes*, Volume I, 256.

10. Wade Davis, *The Lost Amazon: The Photographic Journey of Richard Evans Schultes* (San Francisco: Chronicle Books, 2004), 1, 20.

11. Wade Davis, *One River: Explorations and Discoveries in the Amazon Rain Forest*, 162.

12. Wade Davis, *One River: Explorations and Discoveries in the Amazon Rain Forest*, 215.

13. Wade Davis, *One River: Explorations and Discoveries in the Amazon Rain Forest*, 392–93.

14. Wade Davis, *One River: Explorations and Discoveries in the Amazon Rain Forest*, 215–17.

15. Wade Davis, *One River: Explorations and Discoveries in the Amazon Rain Forest*, 215–17.

16. Brian Hettler and Mark Plotkin, *Amazonian Travels of Richard Evans Schultes, Chapter I — Sacred Plants of the Putumayo* (www.amazonteam.org), 15.

17. Wade Davis, *One River: Explorations and Discoveries in the Amazon Rain Forest*, 471–77.

18. Wade Davis, *One River: Explorations and Discoveries in the Amazon Rain Forest*, 233.

19. Wade Davis, *One River: Explorations and Discoveries in the Amazon Rain Forest*, 234.

20. Wade Davis, *One River: Explorations and Discoveries in the Amazon Rain Forest*, 235, 302–07.

21. Wade Davis, *One River: Explorations and Discoveries in the Amazon Rain Forest*, 335–50.

22. See www.schultescenter.org. It is the website for the Richard Evans Schultes Center for Amazonian Ethnobotanical Research. Click on "Richard Evans Schultes."
23. Wade Davis, *One River: Explorations and Discoveries in the Amazon Rain Forest*, 359–69.
24. Wade Davis, *One River: Explorations and Discoveries in the Amazon Rain Forest*, 495.
25. Schultes and Hoffman, *Plants of the Gods*, 4.
26. Wade Davis, *One River: Explorations and Discoveries in the Amazon Rain Forest*, 393.
27. Wade Davis, *One River: Explorations and Discoveries in the Amazon Rain Forest*, 22–23. Schultes understood that the student is as important as the teacher. He had two particular ones who have guided us in our travels: Wade Davis and Mark Plotkin. Wade's two books, please see the Bibliography, and Mark's book and website production, Bibliography again, are inspiring for the love, respect, and gratitude they give to Dr. Schultes.
28. Wade Davis, *One River: Explorations and Discoveries in the Amazon Rain Forest*, 117–20.
29. Richard Evans Schultes, as quoted in Hettler and Plotkin, *The Amazonian Travels of Richard Evans Schultes*, Introduction: Early Life and Explorations (www.amazonteam.org) 13.
30. Wade Davis, *One River: Explorations and Discoveries in the Amazon Rain Forest*, 120.
31. Wade Davis, *One River: Explorations and Discoveries in the Amazon Rain Forest*, 24.
32. Wade Davis, *One River: Explorations and Discoveries in the Amazon Rain Forest*, 479–80.
33. As quoted in Hettler and Plotkin, *The Amazonian Travels of Richard Evans Schultes*, Chapter IV, Dance of the Spirits (www.amazonteam.org), 11.

TSODILO HILLS, BOTSWANA

Epigraph: See Sandy Gall, *The Bushmen of Southern Africa: Slaughter of the Innocent* (London: Chatto & Windus, 2001), 11.

1. See James Suzman, *Affluence Without Abundance* (London: Bloomsbury, 2017), ix–xi.
2. See Ilisa Barbash, *Where the Roads All End: Photography and Anthropology in the Kalahari* (Cambridge, MA: Peabody Museum Press: Harvard University, 2016), xvii and xviii.
3. Alec Campbell, Larry Robbins, and Michael Taylor, editors, *Tsodilo Hills, Copper Bracelet of the Kalahari* (Lansing, MI: Michigan State University Press, 2010), 52.
4. For the Bushmen, hunting was a matter of skill rather than violence. For example, they used the lion as a hunting dog. They would drive game into the lion's way, let the lion kill and eat enough to end its hunger, scare the lion off with smoke and fire and then move in and eat the rest of the kill. In time, the lion learned that the Bushmen made good partners. See Laurens van der Post, *The Lost World of the Kalahari* (New York: William Morrow and Co., 1988) 17.
5. Sandy Gall, *The Bushmen of Southern Africa*, 14.
6. James Suzman, *Affluence Without Abundance*, 6–11.

    Isn't having enough and being equal also the dream of filmmakers? How else to describe a movie, *The Gods Must Be Crazy*, which depicts the trials and tribulations of a Bushman who seeks to remove from the world a Coca-Cola bottle discarded from an airplane that has caused ownership conflict in his tribe. The movie, starring N!xau Toma, a Namibian Bushman, lead to one official sequel, *The Gods Must Be Crazy II* and three unofficial ones: *Crazy Safari*, *Crazy Hong Kong*, and *The Gods Must Be Funny in China*.

7. Sir Laurens van der Post, *The Lost World of the Kalahari*, 33.
8. James Suzman, *Affluence Without Abundance*, 8–13.

    Prior to the 1950s, there was almost no international interest in the Bushmen. Then came the Marshall family from America—

father, mother, son and daughter. They made eight expeditions to Nyae Nyae, located in the western Kalahari, where they lived with and studied the Bushmen. See Barbash, *Where the Roads All End: Photography and Anthropology in the Kalahari*. They have been followed by an army of anthropologists. Indeed, as of 2022, there have probably been more academic articles and books written *about* the Bushmen than there *are* Bushmen (Suzman, *Affluence Without Abundance*, 262).

9. See Sir Laurens van der Post, *The Voice of the Thunder* (New York: William Morrow & Co., 1993), 91–96.
10. Sir Laurens van der Post, *The Lost World of the Kalahari*, 9–53.
11. Sir Laurens van der Post, *The Lost World of the Kalahari*, 162–64.
12. Sir Laurens van der Post, *The Lost World of the Kalahari*, 169.

Written on paper from the Victoria Falls Hotel, van der Post's note took on a life of its own. So many tourists found the bottle and extracted his message that the paper began to crumble. As a result, Alec Campbell (see Campbell et alia, *Tsodilo Hills: Copper Bracelet of the Kalahari*) placed it in the local museum. He then put a copy of the note in the bottle and set it back below the Eland. Shortly thereafter, both message and bottle disappeared. (See Gall, *The Bushmen of Southern Africa*, footnote at 21.)

13. Sir Laurens van der Post, *The Lost World of the Kalahari*, 169.
14. Sir Laurens would make a career out of his two-week stay with the Bushmen. See his Bibliography attached.
15. Sir Laurens van der Post, *The Lost World of the Kalahari*, 224–25.
16. Sir Laurens van der Post, *The Lost World of the Kalahari*, 225.
17. Sandy Gall, *The Bushmen of Southern Africa*, 10 (with slight edit).
18. Sandy Gall, *The Bushmen of Southern Africa*, 243.
19. Google "Kalahari Plains Camp." Click on the "And Beyond" link, then scroll down to "Bushman Nature Walk in Central Kalahari."

BIBLIOGRAPHY

What we become depends on what we read after all our professors have finished with us. The greatest university of all is the collection of books.

—THOMAS CARLYLE

PRINCETON, NEW JERSEY

Books by Richard Halliburton

Halliburton, Richard. *The Royal Road to Romance*. Indianapolis: Bobbs-Merrill Co., 1925.

Halliburton, Richard. *The Glorious Adventure*. Indianapolis: Bobbs-Merrill Co., 1927.

Halliburton, Richard. *New Worlds to Conquer*. Indianapolis: Bobbs-Merrill Co., 1929.

Halliburton, Richard. *The Flying Carpet*. Indianapolis: Bobbs-Merrill Co., 1932.

Halliburton, Richard. *Seven League Boots*. Indianapolis: Bobbs-Merrill Co., 1935.

Halliburton, Richard. *Richard Halliburton's Book of Marvels: The Occident*. Indianapolis: Bobbs-Merrill Co., 1937.

Halliburton, Richard. *Richard Halliburton's Second Book of Marvels: The Orient*. Indianapolis: Bobbs-Merrill Co., 1938.

Books Published Post-Mortem

Halliburton, Richard. *Richard Halliburton: His Story of His Life's Adventures as Told in Letters to his Mother and Father*. Indianapolis: Bobbs-Merrill Co., 1940.

Halliburton, Richard. *Richard Halliburton's Complete Book of Marvels*. Indianapolis: Bobbs-Merrill Co., 1941.

Halliburton, Richard. *The Romantic World of Richard Halliburton*. Indianapolis: Bobbs-Merrill Co., 1961.

One Book about Halliburton

Prince, Cathryn J. *American Daredevil: The Extraordinary Life of Richard Halliburton, The World's First Celebrity Travel Writer*. Chicago: Chicago Review Press, 2016.

WADI RUM, JORDAN

Books by T. E. Lawrence

Lawrence, T. E. *Revolt in the Desert*. London: Jonathan Cape, 1927.

Lawrence, T. E. *Seven Pillars of Wisdom: A Triumph*. New York: Doubleday, 1935.

Lawrence, T. E. *Oriental Assembly*. London: Williams and Norgate, 1939.

Books about T. E. Lawrence

Becker, Boris. *Desert Images, Mapping Lawrence of Arabia*. Cologne, Germany: Wienand Verlag, 2011.

Brown, Malcolm. *Lawrence of Arabia: The Life, The Legend*. New York: Thames & Hudson, 2005.

Morris, L. Robert and Leonard Raskin. *Lawrence of Arabia: 30th Anniversary Pictorial History*. New York: Doubleday, 1992.

Wilson, Jeremy. *T. E. Lawrence: Lawrence of Arabia*. London: National Portrait Gallery Press, 1988.

Wilson, Jeremy. *Lawrence of Arabia: The Authorized Biography of T. E. Lawrence*. New York: Atheneum Books, 1989.

Books by Tony Howard and Di Taylor

Howard, Tony, and Di Taylor. *Treks and Climbs in Wadi Rum, Jordan*. 4th ed. Milnthorpe, England: Cicerone Press, 2007.

Howard, Tony, and Di Taylor. *Jordan, Walks, Treks, Caves, Climbs and Canyons*. 2nd ed. Milnthorpe, England: Cicerone Press, 2008.

Howard, Tony, and Di Taylor. *Walks, Treks, Climbs & Caves in Al Ayoun, Jordan*. Sheffield, England: Vertebrate Publishing, 2012.

Other Books by Tony Howard

Howard, Tony. *Troll Wall: The Untold Story of the British First Ascent of Europe's Tallest Rock Face*. Sheffield, England: Vertebrate Publishing, 2012.

Howard, Tony. *Adventures in the Northlands: The Yukon, Greenland, Iceland and Norway*. Sheffield, England: Vertebrate Publishing, 2012.

Howard, Tony. *Quest Into the Unknown*. Sheffield, England: Vertebrate Publishing, 2018.

Other Sources (Websites)

"Welcome to N.O.M.A.D.S." N.O.M.A.D.S. www.nomadstravel.co.uk/.

"Bedouinroads.Wadi Rum." BEDOUINROADS. www.bedouinroads.com/.

"Adventure Travels Worldwide." KE Adventure Travel. www.keadventure.com/.

SAN ANTONIO DE ARECO, ARGENTINA

Boyles, Denis. *Everything Explained That Is Explainable*. New York: Alfred A. Knopf, 2016.

Collier, Simon, Artemis Cooper, Maria Susanna Azzi and Martin Richard. *Tango: The Dance, the Song, the Story*. London: Thames & Hudson, 1995.

Decotte, Alex. *Gauchos*. Buenos Aires: Librerías A.B.C., 1978.

Del Carril, Bonifacio. *El Gaucho*. Buenos Aires: Emecé Editores, 1993.

Ferrer, Horacio. *The Golden Age of Tango*. Buenos Aires: Manrique Zago Ediciones, 1998.

Ferrer, Horacio and Oscar del Priore. *Inventario del Tango Tomo I (1849–1939)*. Buenos Aires: Fondo Nacional de las Artes, 1999.

Ferrer, Horacio and Oscar del Priore. *Inventario del Tango Tomo II (1940–1998)*. Buenos Aires: Fondo Nacional de las Artes, 1999.

Salas, Horacio. *Tango: The Poetry of Buenos Aires*. Buenos Aires: Manrique Zago Ediciones, 1998.

And, of course,

Encyclopedia Britannica. 11th ed. Edinburgh, Scotland: Encyclopedia Britannica, Inc., 1911.

Guiraldes, Ricardo. *Don Segundo Sombra: Shadows on the Pampas*. New York: Farrar & Rinehart, 1935.

LUXOR, EGYPT

Adkins, Lesley and Roy Adkins. *The Keys of Egypt*. New York: HarperCollins, 2000.

Meyerson, Daniel. *The Linguist and the Emperor*. New York: Random House, 2004.

Parkinson, Richard. *Cracking Codes: The Rosetta Stone and Decipherment*. Berkeley, CA: University of California Press, 1999.

Robinson, Andrew. *Cracking the Egyptian Code*, New York: Oxford University Press, 2012.

Serino, Franco. *Déscription de L'Egypte: Napoleon's Expedition and the Rediscovery of Ancient Egypt*. Cairo: The American University in Cairo Press, 2003.

Tyldesley, Joyce. *Egypt: How a Lost Civilization was Rediscovered*. Berkeley, CA: University of California Press, 2005.

ILULISSAT, GREENLAND

Books by Knud Rasmussen

Rasmussen, Knud. *The People of the Polar North: A Record*. London: Kegan, Paul, Trench, Trübner & Co., 1908.

Rasmussen, Knud. *Greenland by the Polar Sea: The Story of the Thule Expedition from Melville Bay to Cape Morris Jessup*. London: Heinemann, 1921.

Rasmussen, Knud. *Across Arctic America: Narrative of the Fifth Thule Expedition*. New York: G. P. Putnam's Sons, 1927.

Other Books about Rasmussen, Ilulissat and Greenland

Bown, Stephen R. *White Eskimo*. Cambridge, MA: Da Capo Press, 2015.

Ehrlich, Gretel. *This Cold Heaven: Seven Seasons in Greenland*. New York: Random House, 2001.

Kavenna, Joanna. *The Ice Museum: In Search of the Lost Land of Thule*. New York: Viking Penguin, 2006.

Malaurie, Jean. *The Last Kings of Thule*. New York: E. P. Dutton, 1982.

Malaurie, Jean. *Ultima Thule*. New York: W. W. Norton & Co., 2003.

O'Carroll, Etain, and Mark Elliott. *Greenland & the Arctic*. Fort Mill, SC: Lonely Planet, 2005.

BADALING, CHINA

Books by William Lindesay

Lindesay, William. *Alone on the Great Wall*. London: Hodder & Stoughton, 1989.

Lindesay, William. *The Great Wall Revisited*. Cambridge, MA: Harvard University Press, 2008.

Lindesay, William. *The Great Wall Explained*. Beijing: China Intercontinental Press, 2016.

Lindesay, William. *The Great Wall in 50 Objects*. Melbourne, Australia: Penguin Random House, 2015.

Lindesay, William. *Wild Wall: The Foundation Years*. Subscriber Limited Edition. Beijing: Wild Wall Books, 2022.

Lindesay, William. *Wild Wall: The Jiankou Years*. Subscriber Limited Edition. Beijing: Wild Wall Books, 2022.

Books by William Edgar Geil

Geil, William Edgar. *The Great Wall of China*. London: John Murray, 1909.

Geil, William Edgar. *The Great Wall of China*. New York: Sturgis & Walton, 1909.

Photography Books about The Great Wall

Michaud, Roland, Sabrina Michaud and Michel Jan. *The Great Wall of China*. New York: Abbeville Press, 2001.

Schwartz, Daniel. *The Great Wall of China*. New York: Thames & Hudson, 1990.

Shaobai, Li. *The Invisible Great Wall*. Beijing: Foreign Language Press, 2007.

Yamashita, Michael and William Lindesay. *The Great Wall: From Beginning to End*. New York: Stirling Publishing, 2007.

Other Books

Wilson, Phillip Whitwell. *An Explorer of Changing Horizons: William Edgar Geil*. New York: George H. Doran Co., 1927.

Hayes, L. Newton. *The Great Wall of China*. Shanghai: Kelly & Walsh Ltd., 1929.

ZERMATT, SWITZERLAND

Books by Edward Whymper

Whymper, Edward. *Scrambles Amongst the Alps*. Salt Lake City: Peregrine Smith Books, 1986.

Whymper, Edward. *The Valley of Zermatt and the Matterhorn: A Guide*. Reprint ed. Reading, England: Gaston's Alpine Books Publisher, 1978.

Other Books on Zermatt and Mountain Climbers in the Alps

Band, George. *Summit: 150 Years of the Alpine Club*. London: HarperCollins, 2006.

Hodler, Ferdinand. *Aufstieg and Absturz*. Bern, Switzerland: Swiss Alpine Museum, 1999.

RIOBAMA, ECUADOR

General Books

Ferreiro, Larrie D. *Measure of the Earth*. New York: Basic Books, 2011.

Jacobs, Michael. *Andes*. London: Granta Publications, 2010.

Books by Jorge Juan Anhalzer

Anhalzer, Jorge Juan. *Ecuador: The Highlands*. Quito, Ecuador: Edición Mariscal, 1987.

Anhalzer, Jorge Juan. *Ecuador Panoramas*. Quito, Ecuador: Edición Mariscal, 2007.

Anhalzer, Jorge Juan. *The High Andes of Ecuador*. Quito, Ecuador: Edición Mariscal, 2008.

Book by Marco Cruz

Cruz, Marco. *Mountains of Ecuador*. Quito, Ecuador: Dinediciones, 1992

And Finally

Whymper, Edward. *Travels Amongst the Great Andes of the Equator*. New York: Charles Scribner's Sons, 1892.

EL CHALTÉN, PATAGONIA

Chouinard, Yvon, Jeff Johnson, and Chris Malloy. *180° South: Conquerors of the Useless*. Ventura, CA: Patagonia Books, 2010.

Chouinard, Yvon, Dick Dorworth, Chris Jones, Lito Tejada-Flores, and Doug Tompkins. *Climbing Fitz Roy, 1968: Reflections on the Lost Photos of the Third Ascent*. Ventura, CA: Patagonia Books, 2013.

Crouch, Gregory. *Enduring Patagonia*. New York: Random House, 2001.

De Agostini, Alberto M. *Andes Patagónicos*. Santiago, Chile: Pontifical Catholic University of Chile, 2010.

Ditsch, Helmut. *The Triumph of Painting*. Edited by Carl Aigner. Munich: Prestel Publishing, 2009.

Franklin, Jonathan. *A Wild Idea*. New York: HarperOne, 2021.

Garibotti, Rolando and Dörte Pietron. *Patagonia Vertical: Chaltén Massif and Climbing Guide*. Ljubljana, Slovenia: Sidarta D.O.O., 2012.

Neilson, David. *Patagonia: Images of a Wild Land*. Emerald, Australia: Snowgum Press, 1999.

Terray, Lionel. *Conquistadors of the Useless*. London: Victor Gollanz Ltd., 1963.

ABIQUIU, NEW MEXICO

Colbert, Edwin H. *The Little Dinosaurs of Ghost Ranch*. New York: Columbia University Press, 1995.

Lynes, Barbara Buhler, Lesley Poling-Kempes, and Frederick W. Turner. *Georgia O'Keeffe and New Mexico: A Sense of Place*. Princeton, NJ: Princeton University Press, 2004.

Pack, Arthur Newton. *We Called It Ghost Ranch*. Abiquiu, NM: Ghost Ranch Conference Center, 1965.

Poling-Kempes, Lesley. *Ghost Ranch*. Tucson, AZ: University of Arizona Press, 2005.

Poling-Kempes, Lesley. *Valley of Shining Stone: The Story of Abiquiu*. Tucson, AZ: University of Arizona Press, 1997.

Additional Reading

Leongard, John. *Georgia O'Keeffe at Ghost Ranch*. New York: Stuart, Tabor and Chang, 1995.

Scheinbaum, David, Janet Russek, and Edward T. Hall. *Ghost Ranch: Land of Light*. South Pasadena, CA: Balcony Press, 1998.

Varjabedian, Craig. *Ghost Ranch and the Faraway Nearby*. Albuquerque, NM: University of New Mexico Press, 2009.

TAKANAWA, JAPAN

Bell, David. *Chushingura and the Floating World*. Richmond, England: Japan Library, 2001.

Brandon, James R., ed. *Chushingura, Studies in Kabuki and the Puppet Theatre*. Honolulu: University of Hawaii Press, 1982.

Herwig, Arendie and Henk Herwig. *Heroes of the Kabuki Stage*. Leiden, Netherlands: Hotei Publishing, 2004.

Inouye, Jukichi, trans. *Chushingura, or the Forty-Seven Ronin*. Tokyo: Maruzen Company, Ltd., 1937.

Keene, Donald. *Chushingura—The Treasury of the Loyal Retainers)*. New York: Columbia University Press, 1971.

Mitford, A.B. *Tales of Old Japan (Two Volume Set)*. London: Macmillan, 1871.

Sato, Hiroaki. *Legends of the Samurai*. Old Saybrook, CT., Konecky & Konecky, 1995.

Shioya, Sakae. *Chushingura: An Exposition*. 2nd ed. Tokyo: Hokuseido Press, 1956.

Stewart, Basil. *A Guide to Japanese Prints and Their Subject Matter*. New York: Dover Publications, 1979.

Weinberg, David R. *Kuniyoshi: The Faithful Samurai*. Leiden, Netherlands: Hotei Publishing, 2000.

VILLNOSS, SOUTH TYROL

Books by Reinhold Messner

Messner, Reinhold. *All 14 Eight-Thousanders*. Seattle: Cloudcap, 1988.

Messner, Reinhold. *Free Spirit: A Climber's Life*. Seattle: The Mountaineers, 1991.

Messner, Reinhold. *My Quest for the Yeti*. London: Macmillan, 2000.

Messner, Reinhold. *My Life at the Limit*. Interviewed by Thomas Huetlin. Seattle: The Mountaineers Books, 2014.

Book on the Messner Museums

Hempel, Andreas Gottlieb. *Die Messner Mountain Museum: Architektur & Berge*. Munich: Callwey, 2011.

Other Books on the Eight Thousand Meter Mountains

Hinkes, Alan. *8,000 Meters: Climbing the World's Highest Mountains*. Milnthorpe, England: Cicerone Press, 2013.

Sale, Richard and John Cleare. *Climbing the World's 14 Highest Mountains: The History of the 8,000-Meter Peaks*. Seattle: The Mountaineers Books, 2000.

Sale, Richard, Eberhard Jurgalski and George Rodway. *On Top of the World: The New Millennium, The Continuing Quest to Climb the World's Highest Mountains*. Coberley, England: Snowfinch Publishing, 2012.

Books on the Seven Summits

Anderson, Robert. *Summits: Climbing the Seven Summits Solo*. New York: Clarkson Potter, 1995.

Bass, Dick and Frank Wells with Rick Ridgeway. *Seven Summits*. New York: Warner Books, 1986.

Bell, Steve. *Seven Summits: The Quest to Reach the Highest Point on Every Continent*. New York: Gramercy Books 2000.

Hamill, Mike. *Climbing the Seven Summits: A Comprehensive Guide to Each Continent's Highest Peak*. Seattle: The Mountaineers Books, 2012.

Morrow, Patrick. *Beyond Everest: Quest for the Seven Summits*. Columbia, SC: Camden House Publishing, 1986.

AL AIN, UNITED ARAB EMIRATES

Books about the Empty Quarter by Sir Wilfred Patrick Thesiger

Thesiger, Sir Wilfred Patrick. *Arabian Sands*. New York: E. P. Dutton, 1959.

Thesiger, Sir Wilfred Patrick. *Desert, Marsh and Mountain*. London: Collins, 1979

Thesiger, Sir Wilfred Patrick. *The Last Nomad*. New York: E. P. Dutton, 1980. An abridgement of *Desert, Mash and Mountain*, combined with other writings and even more photographs.

Thesiger, Sir Wilfred Patrick. *The Thesiger Collection*. Dubai, UAE: Motivate Media Group, 1992. A catalogue of unique photographs.

Thesiger, Sir Wilfred Patrick. *Crossing the Sands*. Dubai, UAE: Motivate Media Group, 1999. A slight abridgement of *Arabian Sands*, with more photographs.

Thesiger, Sir Wilfred Patrick. *Arabian Sands*. Centenary ed. Dubai, UAE: Motivate Media Group, 2012.

Books about Sir Wilfred Patrick Thesiger

Asher, Michael. *Thesiger*. London: Viking Penguin 1994.

Maitland, Alexander. *Wilfred Thesiger: The Life of the Great Explorer*. London: HarperCollins, 2006.

Maitland, Alexander. *Wilfred Thesiger: A Life in Pictures*. London: HarperCollins, 2004.

Other Books about the Empty Quarter

Thomas, Bertram. *Arabia Felix: Across the Empty Quarter of Arabia*. London: Jonathan Cape, 1932.

Philby, H. St. John. *The Empty Quarter*. New York: Henry Holt & Co., 1933.

Steinmetz, George. *Empty Quarter*. New York: Abrams Books, 2009.

Hayes, Adrian. *Footsteps of Thesiger*. Dubai, UAE: Motivate Media Group, 2012.

Books about Falconry

Al Nahayan, Zaid Bin Sultan, *Falconry as a Sport: Our Arab Heritage*. Kent, England: Westerham Press, 1977.

LHASA, TIBET

Books by Heinrich Harrer

Harrer, Heinrich. *Seven Years in Tibet*. New York: E. P. Dutton, 1954.

Harrer, Heinrich. *The White Spider: The Story of the North Face of the Eiger*. New York: E. P. Dutton, 1960.

Harrer, Heinrich. *Return to Tibet*. New York: Schocken Books, 1985.

Harrer, Heinrich. *Lost Lhasa*. New York: Harry N. Abrams Ltd., 1992.

Harrer, Heinrich. *Beyond Seven Years in Tibet: My Life Before, During, and After*. Bristol, England: Labyrinth Press, 2007.

Other Related Articles and Books

Annaud, Jean-Jacques, Becky Johnston and Laurence B. Chollet. *The Seven Years in Tibet: Screenplay and Story Behind the Film*. New York: Newmarket Press, 1997.

Bissinger, H. G. "The Last Explorer." *Vanity Fair*, October 1997.

Brauen, Martin, ed. *Peter Aufschnaiter's Eight Years in Tibet*. Bangkok: Orchid Press, 2002.

Larsen, Knud and Amund Sinding-Larsen. *The Lhasa Atlas: Traditional Tibetan Architecture and Townscape*. Boulder, CO: Shambhala Publications, 2001.

BYGDØY PENINSULA, NORWAY

About the North Pole

Nansen, Fridtjof. *The First Crossing of Greenland*. Vol. 1 & 2. London: Longmans, Green and Co., 1890.

Nansen, Fridtjof. *Farthest North*. Vol. 1 & 2. New York: Harper & Brothers, 1897.

Huntford, Roland. *Nansen: The Explorer as Hero*. London: Duckworth Books, 1997.

About the South Pole

Amundsen, Roald. *The Northwest Passage*. Vol. 1 & 2. London: Archibald Constable & Co., 1908.

Amundsen, Roald. *The South Pole*. Vol. 1 & 2. New York: L. Keedick Publisher, 1913.

Huntford, Roland. *Scott and Amundsen*. London: Hodder & Stoughton, 1979.

MacPhee, Ross D. E. *Race to the End: Amundsen, Scott and the Attainment of the South Pole*. New York: Sterling Publishing, 2010.

Other

Berg, Kare. *Heroes of the Polar Wastes: Pioneer Norwegian Explorers in the Arctic and Antarctic*. Skein, Norway: Andersen & Butenschon, 2003.

Sale, Richard, ed. *Polar Reaches: The History of Arctic and Antarctic Exploration*. Seattle: The Mountaineers Books, 2002.

Sverdrup, Otto. *New Land: Four Years in the Arctic Regions*. Vol. 1 & 2. London: Longmans, Green & Co., 1904.

ISLA NEGRA, CHILE

Selected Books by Pablo Neruda

Neruda, Pablo. *The Heights of Machu Picchu*. Translated by Nathaniel Tarn. New York: Farrar, Straus and Giroux, 1966.

Neruda, Pablo. *Twenty Love Poems and a Song of Despair*. Translated by W. S. Merwin. London: Jonathan Cape, 1969.

Neruda, Pablo. *The Captain's Verses*. Translated by Donald D. Walsh. New York: New Directions, 1972.

Neruda, Pablo. *Residence on Earth*. Translated by Donald D. Walsh. New York: New Directions, 1973.

Neruda, Pablo. *Extravagaria*. Translated by Alastair Reid. New York: Farrar, Straus and Giroux, 1974.

Neruda, Pablo. *Toward the Splendid City: Nobel Lecture*. Translated by Margaret Sayers Peden. New York: Farrar, Straus and Giroux, 1974.

Neruda, Pablo. *Memoirs (I Confess That I Have Lived)*. Translated by Hardie St. Martin. New York: Farrar, Straus and Giroux, 1977.

Neruda, Pablo. *Passions and Impressions*. Translated by Margaret Sayers Peden. New York: Farrar, Straus and Giroux, 1983.

Neruda, Pablo. *One Hundred Love Sonnets*. Translated by Stephen Tapscott. Austin, TX: University of Texas Press, 1986.

Neruda, Pablo. *Canto General*. Translated by Jack Schmitt. Berkeley, CA: University of California Press, 1991.

Neruda, Pablo. *The Poetry of Pablo Neruda*. Edited by Ilan Stavans. New York: Farrar, Straus and Giroux, 2003.

Neruda, Pablo. *All the Odes*. Edited by Ilan Stavans. New York: Farrar, Straus and Giroux, 2013.

Books about Pablo Neruda

De Costa, René. *The Poetry of Pablo Neruda*. Cambridge, MA: Harvard University Press, 1979.

Feinstein, Adam. *Pablo Neruda: A Passion for Life*. New York: Bloomsbury, 2004.

Teitelboim, Volodia. *Neruda: An Intimate Biography*. Austin, TX: University of Texas Press, 1991.

Urrutia, Matilde. *My Life with Pablo Neruda*. Stanford, CA: Stanford University Press, 2004.

Books about Isla Negra

Pablo Neruda's Houses: Isla Negra, La Sebastiana, La Chascona. Santiago, Chile: Fundación Pablo Neruda, 2018.

Facio, Sara. *Pablo Neruda en Isla Negra*. Buenos Aires: La Azotea Editorial Fotográfica, 2004.

Neruda, Pablo. *The House at Isla Negra*. Translated by Dennis Maloney and Clark M. Zlotchew. Fredonia, NY: White Pine Press, 1988.

Neruda, Pablo. *The House in the Sand: Prose Poems*. Translated by Dennis Maloney and Clark M. Zlotchew. Minneapolis: Milkweek Editions, 1990. Includes poems from *The House at Isla Negra*.

Neruda, Pablo. *Isla Negra: A Notebook*. Translated by Alastair Reid. New York: Farrar, Straus and Giroux, 1981.

Neruda, Pablo. *Neruda at Isla Negra*. Translated by Maria Jacketti, Dennis Maloney, and Clark Zlotchew. Fredonia, NY: White Pine Press, 1998.

Neruda, Pablo. *The Stones of Chile*. Translated by Dennis Maloney. Fredonia, NY: White Pine Press, 1986.

O'Daly, William. *The Road to Isla Negra*. Meredith, NH: Folded Word, 2015.

Other Books

Skármeta, Antonio. *Burning Patience*. Translated by Katherine Silver. New York: Pantheon Books, 1987.

Wheeler, Sara. *Travels in a Thin Country — A Journey Through Chile*. London: Little, Brown and Co., 1994.

Movies

Radford, Michael, director. *Il Postino: The Postman*. Cecchi Gori Group Tiger Cinematografica, 1994. 1 hr., 56 min.

Larraín, Pablo, director. *Neruda*. AZ Films, 2016. 1 hr., 47 min.

ST. PETERSBURG, RUSSIA

Books by Anna Akhmatova

Akhmatova, Anna. *The Complete Poems of Anna Akhmatova*. Vol 1 & 2. Edited and introduced by Roberta Reeder. Translated by Judith Hemschemeyer. Somerville, MA: Zephyr Press, 1990.

Akhmatova, Anna. *Anna Akhmatova Selected Poems*. Translated and edited by Walter Arndt. Ann Arbor, MI: Ardis Publishers, 1976.

Akhmatova, Anna. *My Half-Century: Selected Prose*. Translated and edited by Ronald Meyer. Ann Arbor, MI: Ardis Publishers, 1992.

Books With Poems by Anna Akhmatova

The Stray Dog Cabaret: A Book of Russian Poems. First published in English by *New York Review of Books*. Translation Copyright © 2006 by The Estate of Paul Schmidt.

Books about Anna Akhmatova

Akhmatova, Anna. *The Word that Causes Death's Defeat*. Translated by Nancy K. Anderson. New Haven, CT: Yale University Press, 2004.

Chukovskaya, Lydia. *The Akhmatova Journals (1938–1941)*. Translated by Milena Michalski, Sylva Rubashova, and Peter Norma. Vol. 1. New York: Havrill, 1994.

Feinstein, Elaine. *Anna of All the Russians*. New York: Alfred A. Knopf, 2006.

Figes, Orlando. *Natasha's Dance: A Cultural History of Russia*. New York: Metropolitan Books, 2002.

Haight, Amanda. *Anna Akhmatova: A Poetic Pilgrimage*. New York: Oxford University Press, 1976.

Polivanov, Konstantin. *Anna Akhmatova and Her Circle,* Translated by Patricia Beriozkina. Fayetteville, AR: University of Arkansas Press, 1994.

Reeder, Roberta. *Anna Akhmatova: Poet and Prophet*. New York: St. Martin's Press, 1994.

Books about the Anna Akhmatova Museum at Fountain House

Popova, N. I. and O. E. Rubinchik. *Anna Akhmatova in the Fountain House*. St. Petersburg: Museum of Anna Akhmatova at Fountain House, 2003.

Popova, Nina, Tatiana Pozdnyakova and Leonid Kopylov. *Beneath the Roof of Fountain House: A Short Guide to the Anna Akhmatova Museum at Fountain House*. St. Petersburg: The Anna Akhmatova Museum in Fountain House, 2012.

Pozdnyakova, Tatiana and Leonid Kopylov. *The Flight of Time: A Photographic Chronicle of Anna Akhmatova's Life*. St. Petersburg: The Anna Akhmatova Museum at Fountain House, 2012.

See Also

Oliver, Lois. *Boris Anrep: The National Gallery Mosaics*. London: National Gallery Company, 2004.

Mandelstam, Nadezhda. *Hope Against Hope: A Memoir*. New York: Atheneum Books, 1970.

STAVROS BEACH, CRETE

Books by Nikos Kazantzakis

Kazantzakis, Nikos. *Zorba the Greek*. Translated by Carl Wildman. New York: Simon & Schuster, 1952.

Kazantzakis, Nikos. *The Odyssey: A Modern Sequel*. Translated by Kimon Friar. New York: Simon & Schuster, 1958.

Kazantzakis, Nikos. *The Last Temptation of Christ*. Translated by P. A. Bien. New York: Simon & Schuster, 1960.

Kazantzakis, Nikos. *The Saviors of God: Spiritual Exercises*. Translated by Kimon Friar. New York: Simon & Schuster, 1960.

Kazantzakis, Nikos. *Report to Greco*. Translated by P. A. Bien. New York: Simon & Schuster, 1965.

Books about Nikos Kazantzakis

Chatzopoulou, Litsa. *Nikos Kazantzakis: Traveling by Light and Darkness*. Translated by Ben Petre. Heraklion, Greece: The Historical Museum of Crete, 2007.

Chatzopoulou, Litza. *Kazantzakis: Through the Museum Collections*. Translated by Ben Petre. Heraklion, Greece: Nikos Kazantzakis Museum, 2008.

Friar, Kimon. *The Spiritual Odyssey of Nikos Kazantzakis*. Minneapolis: The North Central Publishing Company, 1979.

Kazantzakis, Helen. *Nikos Kazantzakis: A Biography Based on His Letters*. Translated by Amy Mims. New York: Simon & Schuster, 1968.

Panagiotakis, George I. *The Life and Works of Nikos Kazantzakis*. Heraklion, Greece: George I Panagiotakis, 2002.

Beach Book

Tsouchtidi, Katerina. *The Most Beautiful Beaches and Gorges of Crete*. Attica, Greece: Michalis Toubis Editions S. A., 2008

KALADHUNGI, INDIA

Books by Jim Corbett

Corbett, Jim. *Man-Eaters of Kumaon*. New York: Oxford University Press, 1946.

Corbett, Jim. *The Man-Eating Leopard of Rudraprayag*. New York: Oxford University Press, 1948.

Corbett, Jim. *My India*. New York: Oxford University Press, 1952.

Corbett, Jim. *Jungle Lore*. New York: Oxford University Press, 1953.

Corbett, Jim. *The Temple Tiger and More Man-Eaters of Kumaon*. New York: Oxford University Press, 1955.

Corbett, Jim. *Jim Corbett's India*. Edited by R.E. Hawkins. Oxford, England: Oxford University Press, 1978.

Corbett, Jim. *My Kumaon: Uncollected Writings*. New Delhi: Oxford University Press, 2012.

Books about Jim Corbett

Alter, Stephen. *In the Jungles of the Night*. New Delhi: Aleph Book Company, 2016.

Booth, Martin. *Carpet Sahib: A Life of Jim Corbett*. London: Constable, 1986.

Byrne, Peter. *Gentleman Hunter*. Huntington Beach, CA: Safari Press, 2007.

Gadhvi, Priyurat, Preetum Gheerawo, Manfred Walti, Joseph Jordania, and Fernando Quevedo de Oliveira. *Behind Jim Corbett's Stories*. Tbilisi, Georgia: Logos Press Ltd., 2016.

Gupta, Reeta Dutta. *Jim Corbett The Hunter-Conservationist*. New Delhi: Rupa Publications India, 2006.

Huckelbridge, Dane. *No Beast So Fierce: The Terrifying True Story of the Champawat Tiger, The Deadliest Animal in History*. New York: William Morrow, 2019.

Jaleel, Jerry A. *Under the Shadows of the Man Eaters: The Life and Legend of Jim Corbett*. New Delhi: Orient Longman, 2001.

Kala, P. C. *Jim Corbett of Kumaon*. New Delhi: Ravi Dayal Publisher, 1999.

Singh, N. K. *Jim Corbett: Portrait of an Artist*. New Delhi: Classical Publishing, 1991.

Ward, Geoffrey C. and Diane Raines Ward. *Tiger Wallahs*. New York: HarperCollins, 1993.

Books about Corbett National Park

Bedi, Ramesh. *Corbett National Park*. New Delhi: Clarion Books, 1987.

Kumar, Ashima and Dushyant Parasher. *Corbett National Park: Domain of the Wild*. New Delhi: Konark Publishers, 2017.

Other Related Books

Champion, F. W. *With a Camera in Tiger-Land*. New York: Doubleday, Doran & Co., 1928.

Champion, F. W. *The Jungle in Sunlight and Shadow*. New York: Charles Scribner's Sons, 1934.

MARRAKESH, MOROCCO

Books about Morocco

Harris, Walter B. *Morocco That Was*. London: W. Blackwood and Sons, 1921.

Maxwell, Gavin. *Lords of the Atlas*. London: Cassell & Co., 2000.

Books about Travel in Morocco

Graham, R.B. Cunningham. *Mogreb-el-Acksa: A Journey in Morocco*. New York: Viking Press, 1930.

Grove, Lady Agnes. *Seventy-One Days' Camping in Morocco*. London: Longmans, Green & Co., 1902.

Wharton, Edith. *In Morocco*. New York: Charles Scribner's Sons, 1920.

Books about Marrakesh

Canetti, Elias. *The Voices of Marrakesh: A Record of a Visit*. New York: Seabury Press, 1978.

Hamilton, Richard. *The Last Storytellers: Tales From the Heart of Morocco*. London: I.B. Taurus & Co. Ltd., 2011.

Mayne, Peter. *The Alleys of Marrakesh*. New York: Little, Brown & Co., 1953.

Roy-Bhattacharya, Joydeep. *The Storyteller of Marrakesh*. New York: W. W. Norton & Co., 2011.

Books about Hassan El Glaoui

Ben Jelloun, Tahar. *Meetings in Marrakesh: The Paintings of Hassan El Glaoui and Winston Churchill*. Edited by Touria El Glaoui. Milan: Skira Editore, 2014.

Clement, Jean-François. *Hassan El Glaoui : L'Homme et L'Astiste*. Marrakesh, Morocco: Matisse Art Gallery, 2005.

El Glaoui, Touria, ed. *Hassan El Glaoui: Le Sel De Ma Terre*. Rabat, Morocco: Malika, 2019.

BANGKOK, THAILAND

Books about Jim Thompson

Galleher, Molly. *The Missing Thai Silk King: A Niece's Search for Jim Thompson*. N.P.: M. Galleher, 2007.

Kurlantzick, Joshua. *The Ideal Man: The Tragedy of Jim Thompson and the American Way of War*. Hoboken, NJ: John Wiley & Sons, 2011.

Warren, William. *The Legendary American: The Remarkable Career and Strange Disappearance of Jim Thompson*. Boston: Houghton Mifflin 1970.

Books about the Jim Thompson House

Thompson, James H. W. *6 Soi Kasemsan II, Bangkok: An Illustrated Survey of the Bangkok Home of James H.W. Thompson*. Photographs by Niphon Nimboonchai. Bangkok: Siva Phorn, 1962.

Warren, William. *The House on the Klong*. New York: Walker Weatherhill, 1968.

Warren, William and Jean-Michel Beurdeley. *Jim Thompson: The House on the Klong*. Singapore: Archipelago Press, 1999.

Warren, William. *Jim Thompson: The Thai Silk Sketchbook*. N.p,. Singapore: Archipelago Press, 1997.

Fiction about Jim Thompson

Gilligan, Shannon. *The Case of the Silk King*. Waitsfield, VT: Chooseco, LLC., 2005.

Matthews, Francine. *The Secret Agent*. New York: Bantam Books, 2002.

Tuck, Lily. *Siam, or the Woman Who Shot a Man*. Woodstock, NY: The Overlook Press, 1999.

KATHMANDU, NEPAL

Books about Mount Everest (in chronological order)

Howard-Bury, Lieutenant-Colonel Charles. *Mount Everest: The Reconnaissance, 1921*. New York: Longmans, Green & Co., 1922.

Bruce, Brigadier-General, Hon. Charles Granville. *The Assault on Mount Everest 1922*. New York: Longmans, Green & Co., 1923.

Norton, Lieutenant-Colonel E. F., *The Fight for Everest: 1924*. New York: Longmans, Green & Co., 1925.

Hunt, John. *The Assent of Everest*. London: Hodder & Stoughton, 1953.

Hillary, Edmund. *High Adventure*. London: Hodder & Stoughton, 1955.

Norgay, Tenzing, with James Ramsey Ullman, *Tiger of the Snows*. New York: G. P. Putnam's Sons, 1955.

Purja, Nimsdai. *Beyond Possible*. London: Hodder & Stoughton, 2020.

Books/Writings by or about Elizabeth Hawley

Hawley, Elizabeth and Richard Salisbury. *The Himalaya by the Numbers.* Kathmandu, Nepal: Vajra Publications, 2011.

Hawley, Elizabeth and Richard Salisbury. *The Himalayan Database: The Expedition Archives of Elizabeth Hawley.* Golden, CO: American Alpine Club, 2004.

Choegyal, Lisa and Mikel Dunham, ed. *The Nepal Scene, Chronicles of Elizabeth Hawley 1988–2007,* Vols. 1 & 2. Kathmandu, Nepal: Vajra Books, 2015.

Hawley, Elizabeth. *Seasonal Stories for the Nepalese Himalaya: 1985–2014.* Ann Arbor, MI: The Himalayan Database, 2014.

McDonald, Bernadette. *I'll Call You in Kathmandu: The Elizabeth Hawley Story.* Seattle: The Mountaineers Books, 2005.

Websites about Mount Everest

Alan Arnette, n.d. www.alanarnette.com/. It includes daily reports during the climbing seasons.

The Himalayan Database, The Expedition Archives of Elizabeth Hawley. Richard Salisbury, n.d. www.himalayandatabase.com/.

MANAUS, BRAZIL

Books by Richard Evans Schultes

Schultes, Richard Evans. *Hallucinogenic Plants.* New York: Golden Press, 1976.

Schultes, Richard Evans and Albert Hofmann. *Plants of the Gods: Origins of Hallucinogenic Use.* London: Hutchinson & Co., 1980.

Schultes, Richard Evans and Albert Hofmann. *The Botany and Chemistry of Hallucinogens.* Springfield, IL: Charles C. Thomas, 1980.

Schultes, Richard Evans. *Where the Gods Rein: Plants and People of the Colombian Amazon.* Oracle, AZ: Synergetic Press, 1988.

Schultes, Richard Evans and Robert F. Raffauf. *The Healing Forest: Medicine and Toxic Plants of the Northwest Amazon.* Portland, OR: Dioscorides Press, 1990.

Schultes, Richard Evans and Robert F. Raffauf. *Vine of the Soul: Medicine Men, Their Plants and Rituals in the Colombian Amazon.* Santa Fe, NM: Synergetic Press, 2004.

Schultes, Richard Evans and Siri von Reis. *Ethnobotany: Evolution of a Discipline.* Portland, OR: Dioscorides Press, 1995.

Books and Other Sources about Dr. Schultes

Davis, Wade. *One River: Explorations and Discoveries in the Amazon Rainforest.* New York: Simon & Schuster, 1996.

Davis, Wade. *The Lost Amazon.* San Francisco: Chronicle Books, 2004.

Plotkin, Mark, Brian Hettler, and the Amazon Conservation Team. *The Amazonian Travels of Richard Evans Schultes.* (See banrepcultural.org/schultes and www.amazonteam.org.)

"The Amazonian Travels of Richard Evans Schultes—Banrepcultural." The Amazonian Travels of Richard Evans Schultes. The Amazon Conservation Team, n.d. www.banrepcultural.org/schultes/. Amazon Conservation Team. The Amazon Conservation Team, n.d. www.amazonteam.org/.

"Richard Evans Schultes Center for Amazonian Ethnobotanical Research." The Schultes Center. Richard Evans Schultes Center, n.d. www.schultescenter.org/.

Books about the Amazon

Hemming, John. *Tree of Rivers: The Story of the Amazon.* London: Thames & Hudson, 2008.

Medina, Jose Toribio. *The Discovery of the Amazon: According to the Account of Friar Gaspar de Carvajal and Other Documents.* Translated by Bertram T. Lee. Edited by H. C. Heaton. New York: American Geographical Society, 1934.

McIntyre, Loren. *Amazonia.* San Francisco: Sierra Club Books, 1991.

Plotkin, Mark J. *Tales of a Shaman's Apprentice: An Ethnobotanist Searches for New Medicines in the Amazon Rain Forest.* New York: Viking Penguin, 1993.

Popescu, Petru. *Amazon Beaming.* New York: Viking Penguin, 1991.

Plotkin, Mark J. *The Amazon: What Everyone Needs to Know.* New York: Oxford University Press, 2020.

Salgado, Sebastião. *Amazonia*. Cologne, Germany: Taschen Books, 2021.

Spruce, Richard. *Notes of a Botanist on the Amazon and Andes*. Edited by Alfred Russel Wallace. Vols. 1 & 2. London: Macmillan, 2018. A facsimile print of the original 1908 edition.

And Why Not

Burroughs, William and Allen Ginsberg. *The Yage Letters*. San Francisco: City Lights Books, 1963.

TSODILO HILLS, BOTSWANA

Books by Sir Laurens van der Post

Van der Post, Sir Laurens. *The Lost World of the Kalahari*. London: The Hogarth Press, 1958.

Van der Post, Sir Laurens. *The Heart of the Hunter*. London: The Hogarth Press, 1961.

Van der Post, Sir Laurens. *A Story Like the Wind*. London: The Hogarth Press, 1972.

Van der Post, Sir Laurens. *A Far-Off Place*. London: The Hogarth Press, 1974.

Van der Post, Sir Laurens and Jane Taylor. *Testament to the Bushmen*. London: Viking Penguin, 1984.

Van der Post, Sir Laurens. *A Walk With a White Bushman*. London: Chatto & Windus Ltd., 1986.

Van der Post, Sir Laurens and David Coulson. *The Lost World of the Kalahari with the Great and the Little Memory*. New York: William Morrow & Co., 1988.

Van der Post, Sir Laurens. *The Voice of the Thunder*. New York: William Morrow & Co., 1993.

Book about Sir Laurens van der Post

Jones, J. D. F. *Teller of Many Tales: The Lives of Laurens van der Post*. New York: Carroll & Graf, 2002.

Other Books about the Bushmen

Gall, Sandy. *The Bushmen of Southern Africa: Slaughter of the Innocent.* London: Chatto & Windus, 2001.

Suzman, James. *Affluence Without Abundance: The Disappearing World of the Bushmen.* New York: Bloomsbury Publishing, 2017.

Wannenburgh, Alf. *The Bushmen.* Secaucus, NJ: Chartwell Books, 1979.

Books/DVDs by/about the Marshalls

Barbash, Ilisa. *Where the Roads End: Photography and Anthropology in the Kalahari.* Cambridge, MA: Peabody Museum Press, 2016.

Marshall, John, director. *A Kalahari Family 1951–2001.* Kalfam Productions, 2002. 6 hr. https://store.der.org/a-kalahari-family-p937.aspx.

Thomas, Elizabeth Marshall. *The Harmless People.* New York: Alfred A. Knopf, 1959.

Thomas, Elizabeth Marshall. *The Old Way.* New York: Farrar, Straus and Giroux, 2006.

Books about Tsodilo Hills

Campbell, Alec, Larry Robbins, and Michael Taylor, eds. *Tsodilo Hills: Copper Bracelet of the Kalahari.* Lansing, MI: Michigan State University Press, 2010.

PHOTO AND ILLUSTRATION CREDITS

KEY: **CHAPTER** *Caption* Contributor

PRINCETON, NEW JERSEY

Princeton University EQ Roy/Alamy

Halliburton at the Taj Mahal Richard Halliburton/Princeton University

Halliburton Jumps into the Well of Death Richard Halliburton/Princeton University

The Flying Carpet Rhodes College Digital Archives

Seven League Boots Rhodes College Digital Archives

The Sea Dragon Public Domain

WADI RUM, JORDAN

The Seven Pillars of Wisdom Ahmad Atwah/Alamy

Portrait of T. E. Lawrence by James McBey, 1918 NPL-DeA Picture Library/G. Nimatallah/Bridgeman Images

Subscriber's Edition Jonkers Rare Books

First Trade Edition Merrill Whitburn/Pride and Prejudice Books

Wadi Rum Yousef, Discovery Terhaal and KE/Adventure Travel

Tony Howard and Di Taylor with HM Queen Noor of Jordan Courtesy of Tony Howard

East Face of Jebel Rum Walter Neser, www.africanvultures.org

Di Taylor and Tony Howard Courtesy of Tony Howard

SAN ANTONIO DE ARECO, ARGENTINA

La Portegna Writing Room Hemis/Alamy

The Encyclopedia Britainica: Eleventh Edition Author Photo

Don Segundo Sombra, 1926 Edition Dust Wrapper Public Domain

Don Segundo with Ricardo Guiraldes Public Domain

It Takes Two Buenos Tours/Palacio Tango

Ricardo Güiraldes Public Domain

LUXOR, EGYPT

The Rosetta Stone   Hemis/Alamy
Portrait of Jean-François Champollion by Léon Cogniet, 1831
   Zuri Swimmer/Alamy
A Hieroglyph from the Temple of Horus   Mike P. Shepherd/Alamy
The Ramesseum   Diego Fiore/Alamy
The Temple of Luxor   Alfredo Garcia Saz/Alamy
The Luxor Obelisk in Place de la Concorde   Andia/Alamy
Here Comes the Sun   Alain Guilleux/Alamy

ILULISSAT, GREENLAND

The Red House   Edwardje/Dreamstime
Don't Ride Into the Sun   ImageBROKER/Alamy
Don't Jump, Don't Fall   Bruce Yuanyue Bi/Getty Images
Kiviaq—Yum   Seabird/Alamy
Knud Rasmussen   Public Domain

BADALING, CHINA

William Lindesay Running   Courtesy of William Lindesay
East of Mule-Horse Pass; William Geil Sitting   Courtesy of William Lindesay
East of Mule-Horse Pass; William Lindesay Running   Courtesy of William Lindesay
William Edgar Geil   Courtesy of William Lindesay
The Great Wall in Disrepair   Courtesy of William Lindesay
A Smiling HM Queen Elizabeth and HRH Prince Philip at the Great Wall
   PA Images/Alamy
U.S. President Barak Obama Greeted at the Great Wall   REUTERS/Alamy
The Lindsay Family at the Great Wall   Courtesy of William Lindesay
James and Thomas Running the Great Wall   Courtesy of William Lindesay

PHOTO AND ILLUSTRATION CREDITS | *415*

ZERMATT SWITZERLAND

The Broken Rope   Emanuel Ammon, Matterhorn Museum
The Matterhorn   Funkystock—Paul Williams/Alamy
Edward Whymper   The Print Collector/Alamy
Jean-Antoine Carrel   G L Archive/Alamy
Gustave Doré, Arrival at the Summit, 1865   Matthias Taugwalder/Keystone
Gustave Doré, The Fall, 1865   Matthias Taugwalder/Keystone

RIOBAMBA, ECAUDOR

The Whymper Refuge   Boriss Andean/www.summitpost.org
The Heart of the Andes by Frederic Edwin Church   Metropolitan Museum of Art
Covered in Ash, Etching by Edward Whymper   Public Domain
Marco Cruz   Courtesy of Ian Mount
The True Heart of the Andes   Courtesy of Jorge Juan Anhalzer

EL CHALTÉN, PATAGONIA

The Road Less Traveled   Roberto Benzi/Alamy
The "Dirt Bags" and Their Van   Patagonia Historical Archives
Left Hanging on Cerro Torre   Lincoln Else/Novus Select
Yvon Chouinard   Terry Straehley/Shutterstock
Doug Tompkins   MCT/Getty Images

ABIQUIU, NEW MEXICO

The Ghost Ranch Sign   B Hammond/Alamy
Children on Burros   McKinley/Pack Collection, Ghost Ranch Archives
Pedernal   Ann Moore/Alamy
The Cliffs Out Back   Liz Coughlan/Alamy
My Backyard, 1937, by Georgia O'Keeffe   © 2023 Georgia O'Keeffe Museum/Artists Rights Society (ARS), New York
The Trinity Detonation, July 16, 1945   Jack Aeby, Public Domain
The Fossil in the Subway   The American Natural History Museum
Arthur Newton Pack with Baby Antelope   McKinley/Pack Collection/Ghost Ranch Archives

PHOTO AND ILLUSTRATION CREDITS | *416*

TAKANAWA, JAPAN

Lord Asano   CPA Media PTE Ltd/Alamy
The Night Raid by Kuniyoshi   William Pearl/The Kuniyoshi Project
47 Ronin (2013)   Photo 12/Alamy
The Sengaku-Ji Temple Main Gate   Sengaku-Ji Temple
Oishi Kuranosuke   Cowardlion/Shutterstock
Tomb of Lord Asano   Public Domain
The Graves of the Forty-Seven Ronin   Travel/Alamy

VILLNÖSS, SOUTH TYROL

Villnöss/Val di Funes   Brian Jannsen/Alamy
Drei Zinnen   Robert Moiola/Sysaworld/Getty Images
Tre Cime di Laverado   Buena Vista Images/Getty Images
Reinhold Messner   Mauritius Images GmbH/Alamy
The Castle on a Hill   Image Professionals/Alamy

AL-AIN, UNITED ARAB EMIRATES

The Al Jahili Fort   F1Online Digitale Bildagentur GMBH/Alamy
Sir Wilfred Thesiger, 1949   Pitt Rivers Museum/Bridgeman Images
Sheikh Zayed bin Sultan al-Nahyan, 1949   Pitt Rivers Museum/Bridgeman Images

LHASA, TIBET

The Eiger, the Mönch, and the Jungfrau   Jon Arnold Images Ltd/Alamy
Heinrich Harrer with Ropes   Heinrich Harrer Museum
Heinrich Harrer with the Young Dalai Lama   Heinrich Harrer Museum
The Dalai Lama with the Old Heinrich Harrer   dba picture alliance archive/Alamy

BYGDØY PENINSULA, NORWAY

The Fram Ship Model   Michael Czytko, www.modelships.de
Fridtjof Nansen   Archivio GBB/Alamy
Bored on the Ship   Heritage Image Partnership Ltd/Alamy
Nansen Saved   Historia/Shutterstock

PHOTO AND ILLUSTRATION CREDITS | 417

Roald Amundsen   Everett Collection Historical/Alamy
Norway at the South Pole   Pictorial Press Ltd/Alamy
The Fram Museum   Mauricio Abreu/Alamy

ISLA NEGRA, CHILE

Bombing of the Presidential Palace   Associated Press Images
Young Pablo Neruda   Archivo Fundación Neruda
The Bells at Isla Negra   Hemis/Alamy
The Chuquicamata Open Pit Copper Mine   Avalon Construction Photography/Alamy
Neruda on Horseback, 1949   Jorge Bellet/Colección Archivo Fotográfico, Archivo Central Andrés Bello, Universidad de Chile
Salvador Allende and Pablo Neruda   Archivo Fundación Neruda

ST. PETERSBURG, RUSSIA

The Stray Dog Cabaret   Matteo Omied/Alamy
Portrait of Anna Akhmatova by Nathan Altman, 1914   Peter Barritt/Alamy
The Sheremetev Palace   Russ Images/Alamy
Kresty Prison   Maurice Savage/Alamy
Anna Akhmatova   Bridgeman Images
Robert Frost   American Stock Archive/Getty Images
The Stray Dog Logo   Mstislav Dobuzhinsky, Public Domain
The Ashtray   Anna Akhmatova Museum at Fountain House
Monument to Anna   Sergi Afanasev/Dreamstime.com

STAVROS BEACH, GREECE

Zorba's Dance from Zorba the Greek   Allstar Picture Library Limited/Alamy
Nikos Kazantzakis   The Nikos Kazantzakis Museum, Kazantzakis Archive
Georgios Zorbas   The Nikos Kazantzakis Museum, Kazantzakis Archive
Epitaph of Nikos Kazantzakis   Constantinos Pliakos/Alamy

PHOTO AND ILLUSTRATION CREDITS | 418

KALADHUNGI, INDIA

The Kumaon Foothills   Fernando Quevedo de Oliveira/Alamy
Big Pad, Small Pad   Oxford Books, England/Erin Greb
The Champawat Man Eater   Ravi Dayal Publisher/Erin Greb
The Rudraprayag Leopard   Ravi Dayal Publisher/Erin Greb
Jim Corbett at Camp   Constable, London
Shoot Nothing But Pictures   R. J. Prickett/Sangam Books, London

MARRAKESH

T'Hami El Glaoui   Historical Collection/Alamy
The Glaoui Cannon   geoffwiggins.com/Alamy
The Fantasia   Rudi Ernst/Shutterstock
The Magical D'Jemma el-Fna   Mlenny/Getty Images
Dar Moha   Courtesy of Dar Moha Restaurant
Fantasia Sur Fund Bleu, a Painting by Hassan El Glaoui   Courtesy of the Estate of Hassan El Glaoui and Brian Bexter

BANGKOK, THAILAND

Jim Thompson with Cocky   The James H. W. Thompson Foundation
Sitting Buddha   The James H. W. Thompson Foundation/Luca Internizzi Tettoni
The Jim Thompson House; Rear but Main Entrance   Joerg Hackemann/Alamy
Moonlight Cottage   Atlantide Phototravel/Getty Images
The Order of the White Elephant   Xiengyod/Wikimedia Commons

KATHMANDU, NEPAL

Rum Doodle Sign   Rum Doodle Restaurant
The Hillary Step in 1953   Royal Geographic Society/Getty Images
The Ascent of Rum Doodle   Max Parrish & Co.
Rum Doodle Restaurant   Rum Doodle Restaurant
Hillary on a Yeti Footprint   Betula103/Tripadvisor
Elizabeth Hawley   Tone Skarja and Gore-Ljudje
The Real Danger on Mount Everest   Subin Thakuri/14 Summits Expedition

PHOTO AND ILLUSTRATION CREDITS | 419

MANAUS, BRAZIL

Schultes in the Field   Richard Evans Schultes/Govinda Gallery
Peyote in Ground   Charlie Edward/Shutterstock
Magic Mushrooms   Alan Rockefeller/Wikimedia Commons
Morning Glory Flower   Roman Shyrin/Alamy
Morning Glory Seeds   Thitimon Royal/Alamy
Curare Leaves   Sally Wiegand/Alamy
Cooking Ayahuasca   Brian Van Tighem/Alamy
Boys with Snuff   Richard Evans Schultes/Govinda Gallery
Plants of the Gods   Hutchinson/AKG-Images/Werner Forman
Kai–ya–ree Dance   Richard Evans Schultes/Govinda Gallery

TSODILO HILLS, BOTSWANA

Bushman Family in Bush   Temistocle Lucarelli/Alamy
Sir Laurens van der Post   Robert Estall Photo Agency/Alamy
Flowers Appear from Nowhere   Arterra Picture Library/Alamy
The Tsodilo Hills   Courtesy of Desert and Delta Safaris
Eland on Rock   Juergen Ritterbach/Alamy

EPILOGUE

Road Sign at Zagora, in the Draa Valley, Morocco   Hemis/Alamy

A WORD ABOUT THE TYPE

This book incorporates type styles and sizes intended to enhance readability. The primary text is set in 12 point Verdigris MVB Pro Text Regular and the back matter in 10.5 point. MVB Verdigris is a Garalde text family inspired by works of 16th-century punchcutters Robert Granjon, Hendrik van den Keere, and Pierre Haultin. Created to deliver good typographic color as text, Mark van Bronkhorst's 21st-century design meets the needs of today's designer using today's paper and press.

A WORD ABOUT OUR MAPS

The maps featured in this book were designed by Erin Greb Cartography. They were created using Adobe Illustrator and Photoshop with Avenza MAPublisher and Geographic Imager.

Erin Greb custom-designs maps as required by the circumstances: reference maps for books and magazines, hiking and race maps for competions, and scholarly maps for university presses. In this book, she varied the style and colors of her maps to highlight the features discussed in the text. For inquiries, see www.eringrebcartography.com

A WORD ABOUT THE DESIGN

This book was designed by John Lotte, a fine art painter and commercial graphic designer specializing in book design. Being a former professional photographer, he was much at home balancing *Legend*'s text and imagery. Adobe InDesign and Adobe Photoshop were his primary tools used during its design production.